Love (lwty)

Reflections on a Mountain Lake

REFLECTIONS

ON A

MOUNTAIN LAKE

Teachings on Practical Buddhism

Venerable Tenzin Palmo

SNOW LION PUBLICATIONS
Ithaca, New York
Boulder, Colorado

Snow Lion Publications
P. O. Box 6483
Ithaca, New York 14851 USA
Tel: 607-273-8519
www. snowlionpub. com

ISBN 1-55939-175-8

Library of Congress Cataloging-in-Publication Data
Tenzin Palmo, 1943-
  Reflections on a mountain lake : teachings on practical
Buddhism / Ven. Tenzin Palmo.
     p. cm.
  ISBN 1-55939-175-8 (alk. paper)
  1. Tenzin Palmo, 1943- 2. Buddhist nuns—Biography. 3. Buddhism—
China—Tibet. 4. Spiritual biography—England. 5. Spiritual life—
Buddhism. I. Title.
  BQ992.E6 T46 2002
  294.3'44—dc21

                                        2002003142

Printed in Canada

∾ Contents

✍ Preface

THIS BOOK GREW out of a series of talks that I gave in the
United States in 1996/97 and in Australia in 1998, which
were recorded and later transcribed and edited for publication.

When I am invited to speak I often prefer that the hosts select a subject,
on which I then speak extemporaneously. I usually don't know precisely what
I am going to say or just where the talk is heading. This open-endedness
allows me to respond to the particular audience at hand, and also makes the
discussions more lively. However, as a result, these talks do not present an
exhaustive analysis of the subject under discussion, but merely what seemed
important at the time.

Inevitably there is also some overlap and duplication, which has been
edited out in some cases and allowed to remain in others where it seemed
that the point needed emphasis or that the repetition formed a part of the
whole explanation.

In the East and West, the nature of the audiences hearing Dharma teachings is very different. In the East, monks and nuns, who are the professionals
so to say, make up the bulk of hearers at any Dharma discourse. But in the
West the vast majority of the audience are lay people who often have a sincere interest in the Dharma but relatively little time for formal practice. In
each case the perspective of the discourse must accommodate the needs of the
listeners.

In this book I have tried to present things in a way which would be both
useful and relevant, not of merely academic interest or too remote to be
applied to our everyday situations. So I mostly use everyday language and try
to make the teachings accessible to any person of average intelligence. The
Lord Buddha himself used the common speech of his day to express techni-
cal meanings. For instance the word "skandha," translated as "aggregate" or

"psycho-physical component," literally means a "heap" of something. He also made use of everyday examples and stories to elucidate his meaning. So there is no need for the Dharma to seem obscure and difficult to penetrate.

This book would never have come into being if not for the devoted effort of many friends and helpers. The easiest part was mine, who merely had to chatter away before friendly audiences. Then came the tedious and demanding task of transcribing those endless hours of talk and putting it all into some sort of order and coherence. It took weeks and months of dedicated labor to complete that task and my gratitude and amazement are both immense. In particular I must thank Venerable Tenzin Wangmo for organizing the transcription of the Australian tapes, which was faithfully undertaken by Sonia Davies, Christina Peebles, Jennie Beswick and Wangmo (Whitethorn). The American tapes were transcribed with great diligence and devotion by Arya Aham (Francesca Jenkins). My sincere thanks are also due to the editors at Snow Lion, who went through the whole manuscript and made many valuable suggestions. Above all I owe a deep debt of gratitude to Pauline Westwood, who not only helped transcribe the tapes but also took on the onerous task of selection and editing. This book is due as much to their work as to my words. To all of the above and the others whose names have not been mentioned, I say thank you from my heart.

‿ I

A Western Yogini

I AM TOLD that I'm supposed to talk about my experiences in retreat. I think that's probably the last thing I would ever want to talk about! I don't know what you want to know, so I will begin by describing how I got to my retreat in the first place. Let's start at the beginning and see where we go. I was born in England and brought up in London during the war. My mother was a spiritualist and we had seances in our house every Wednesday evening, with tables flying around the room and that sort of thing. I am very grateful for this background because it meant that from an early age I believed in the continuity of consciousness after death. In fact, death was a frequent topic of conversation in our family, so I never felt any fear or reservations about it. I suppose I think about death every day in some way or other. An awareness of death gives great meaning to life.

As a child, I believed that we are all innately perfect, that our original nature was perfection, and that we are here to discover who we really are. I believed that we have to keep coming back again and again until we uncover our original perfect nature. The question for me was, "How do we become perfect?" I raised this question with many people who I thought might know, such as teachers and priests. I even asked the spirit-guides during a seance. Everybody seemed to reply along similar lines, saying, "Well, you have to be good," or "You have to be kind." But even though I was only a small child, I remember thinking, "Yes, of course, but that's not all there is to it." Naturally people needed to be good and kind. However, I knew people who were very good and very kind, but who were nonetheless not perfect. I knew that perfection lay beyond that. Being good and kind was the foundation, but there was something more we needed to do. I didn't know what. Throughout my adolescence, I searched for the answer to "How do we become perfect? What does perfection mean? What is it that I'm looking for?" I tried different religions. I remember discussing religion with various priests and vicars. My sister-in-law was Jewish, and I discussed God with her. When I was about thirteen, I attempted to read the Koran, but didn't get very far. The problem for me was that all these religions started with the notion of a soul and the soul's relationship with its creator. The path laid out was a path of devotion, of the soul seeking its creator outside itself. But this had no meaning for me. As far as I was concerned, God was a sort of superior Santa Claus.

When I was eighteen, I became interested in existentialism, and I read Sartre and Camus. I was working in a library at the time, and one day I happened to pick up a small book entitled *The Mind Unshaken*. I liked the title. It was written by an English journalist about his time in Thailand. It gave the very basics of Buddhism—the Four Noble Truths, the Noble Eightfold Path, the Three Characteristics of Existence, and that sort of thing. I still vividly remember what an outstanding revelation it was to learn that there was a perfect path already set out and that it embraced all the things I already believed in. To think that there could actually be a religion that taught this was truly amazing to me! All the other religions I had encountered posited a deity as a *sine qua non*. In contrast, Buddhism was a path which led inwards, rendering any notion of an external creator or God totally superfluous. When I was halfway through the book, I said to my mother, "I'm a Buddhist." And she said, "That's nice, dear. Finish reading the book and then you can tell me all about it." Six months later she became a Buddhist too.

So there I was, living in London. All the books I read kept saying that the essence of the practice was to be without desire. So I gave away my clothes. I stopped wearing makeup and broke up with my boyfriend. I started wearing a yellow costume, a sort of Greek tunic, which was the nearest approximation I had to what robes might be like, and I wore black stockings. I should mention that I hadn't met any other Buddhists at that time.

My mother was so patient. She didn't say a word. After about six months, I thought, "Maybe I should find some more Buddhists. I can't be the only one." So I looked in the telephone directory under "Buddhist" and came across the Buddhist Society. I went there one day and discovered that the Buddhists there were not wandering around in Greek tunics. Here were Buddhists who had been at it much longer than I, and they were actually wearing ordinary clothes! The women even wore makeup and high heels! Then I remarked to my mother what a pity it was that I had given all my clothes away. At that, she handed me the key to my wardrobe and said, "Go and look in there." I opened the door and there they all were!

At that time, I was strictly Theravadin, and I became quite closely associated with the Singhalese Vihara in London. I loved the clarity of the Theravada. In fact, I loved everything about it. Of course, the way Theravada is taught in the West has very little to do with what happens in Theravadin countries, where you see a completely different picture. In the West, there's little ritual or devotion. It's very logical and clear, with lots of emphasis on meditation. This appealed to me very much. The only thing I didn't like about it was the concept of the arhat. Somehow the arhats seemed kind of cold, and this worried me, because attaining arhatship was supposed to be the culmination of this path. I remember lying in bed and worrying about it, because I was on that path, and I wasn't sure whether I liked where it was leading me. I even asked myself whether I was on the right path after all.

Whenever I thought of the Buddha, I would cry tears of devotion. I loved the Buddha, and I wanted to be like him. I didn't want to be like those arhats. Then one day I read about bodhisattvas and thought, "Ah ha!" Here was what I wanted to be. This was the element of compassion missing from the notion of the arhat. I loved the idea that we were following the path not just for ourselves, but for the benefit of others. I thought, " That's what I want. I want to be a bodhisattva." This was in the early sixties, and in those days most Buddhists in London were Theravadin. Also prevalent at that time was a phenomenon which might be described as "Humphries' Zen." I am referring to Christmas Humphries, of course. He had developed his own form of Zen, which wasn't like anything else. When Zen masters visited his center in England, they were stunned into silence. Christmas Humphries would deliver a very long talk, then turn to the Zen master and ask, "Now, would you care to say something?" They usually replied, "I think you've said it all," and just kept quiet. These were the two kinds of Buddhism available at the time: Humphries' Zen and Theravada. At that time, Tibetan Buddhism was regarded as little more than degenerate shamanism, black magic, and weirdo sexual rituals —basically not Buddhism at all. Nobody wanted to be associated with it. It was referred to as Lamaism. Anyway, it looked very complicated and ritualistic, and I was not interested in all that.

It seemed to me like I was involved with this Buddhist milieu for ages, but in fact it could only have been about a year. It's just that there was so much going on inside me. Anyway, one day I was reading a general overview of Buddhism, and at the end of the book there was one small chapter on Tibetan Buddhism. It described how in Tibet there were four traditions: the Nyingmapa, the Sakyapa, the Kagyupa and the Gelugpa. As I read the word "Kagyupa," a voice inside me said, "You're a Kagyupa." And I said, "What's a Kagyupa?" And it said, "It doesn't matter. You're a Kagyupa." My heart sank, and I thought, "Oh no. Wouldn't you know it? Life was so simple and now look what's happened." So I went to see the only person around who knew anything about Tibetan Buddhism (not that she knew very much), and I said to her, "I think I'm a Kagyupa." So she said, "Oh, have you read Milarepa?" And I replied, "Who's Milarepa?" She handed me Evans-Wentz's biography of Milarepa. I went away, and I read it, and my mind went through a thousand somersaults. It was like nothing I'd ever read before. At the end of it all, I realized that I was indeed a Kagyupa.

It became obvious to me that I would need to find a teacher. I was reading many texts at the time, and I noticed that there was never any mention of nuns, only monks. I was actually getting a little depressed about this. Then one day I heard that there was a Kagyupa nunnery in India, at a place called Dalhousie. So I wrote to Freda Bedi, who was the organizer. She was an Englishwoman and an amazing person. She had married an Indian she'd met at Oxford University, lived in India for about thirty years, and had been part of the Indian Freedom Movement. Although she was English, she'd been imprisoned by the British. After India gained independence, she had worked for the Indian government. She was a good friend of Nehru and Mrs. Gandhi. She had been sent to help the Tibetan refugees and eventually had ended up in Dalhousie, starting both a school for young incarnate lamas and a nunnery. I wrote to her and asked if I could come there and work with her.

In the meantime, I had met a few lamas in England. I was working at the School of Oriental and African Studies, where they let me study Tibetan. Among the lamas I met was a young tulku named Chogyam Trungpa, who had arrived with Akong Rinpoche. They were both studying at Oxford. In those days, in 1962 to 1963, few people in England were interested in Tibetan Buddhism. So whenever we met Trungpa and asked him, "When can we see you again?" he would say, "Next weekend." One weekend he would come to us and the next weekend we would go to him. He had very few friends. One day he said, "You might find this difficult to believe, but in Tibet I was quite a high lama, and I never thought it would come to this, but please can I teach you meditation? I must have at least one disciple." So, I said, "Sure, why not?"

I was still intent on traveling to India, and he encouraged me in this. So in 1964, when I was twenty years old, I travelled by ship to India. It was a very pleasant trip. I went up to Dalhousie and was working for Freda Bedi in the Young Lamas Home School. That is where I first met Lama Zopa, one of the young tulkus who lived there. I lived at the nunnery and served as a secretary to Freda Bedi. One day we received a letter about Tibetan handmade paper which some community was producing. They wanted to know if we could find a market for it. The letter was signed, "Khamtrul Rinpoche." As soon as I read that name, faith spontaneously arose, as they say in the books. The next day I asked Freda Bedi who Khamtrul Rinpoche was. She replied, "He's a high Drukpa Kagyu lama. In fact, he's the lama we're waiting for."

I knew we had been waiting for some lama, for whom we had rented a small house. We were expecting him to come for the summer. I said, "He's a Kagyupa." She said, "Yes." And I said, "So I can take refuge with him." And she said, "Yes, yes, he's a wonderful lama. When he comes, you must ask him." This was at the beginning of May. We waited all through May. We waited all through June. On the last day of June, my twenty-first birthday, there was a lama giving a long-life initiation because it was full moon day. The telephone rang and Freda Bedi answered it. When she put down the phone, she said, "Your best birthday present has just arrived down at the bus station." I was terrified. My Lama had come at last! I ran back to the nunnery and changed into a long Tibetan dress and got a *khata*, a long white offering scarf. Then I ran back to the house we had rented to tell them Rinpoche was coming and to get it prepared. By the time I got back to the school, he was already there. I remember how I kind of crawled into the room. I was too terrified to look at him. I had no idea what he was like; I'd never even seen a photograph. Was he old? Was he young? Was he fat? Was he thin? I had no idea. All I saw was the bottom of his robe and his brown shoes. I prostrated to these brown shoes and then sat down.

Freda Bedi was saying, "This is so and so and she's a member of the Buddhist Society." Then I said to her, "Tell him I want to take refuge." So she said, "Oh yes, and she would like to take refuge with you." Rinpoche said, "Of course," in this voice which seemed to be saying, "Of course she wants to take refuge, what else could she want to do?" When I heard him say "of course" in that voice, I looked up and saw him for the first time. As I looked at him, it seemed as though two things were happening simultaneously. There was a sense of recognition, like meeting an old friend you haven't seen for a long time. At the same time it was as if the very deepest thing inside me had suddenly taken an external form.

There it was. Freda Bedi was very kind. She would send me to Rinpoche every day so I could act as his secretary while he was there. One day I told him, "I would like to be a nun." Again he replied, "Of course." But he told me he would not ordain me there. "I want to take you back to my monastery," he explained. About three weeks later, we went back to his monastery, and I took my first ordination. I also went to visit His Holiness Sakya Trizin, and then I traveled to Thailand. When I returned about six months later, Khamtrul Rinpoche and his monks had moved to Dalhousie.

Rinpoche was the head of a community of about eighty monks and between three and four hundred lay people. He was organizing them into a craft community. He himself was a wonderful artist, painter, and poet, and the whole community was very talented. They had wonderful thangka painters, they made beautiful carpets and they produced the most incredible wood carvings. The community is still renowned for its artistic talent. When they moved to Dalhousie, I accompanied my Lama as his secretary. I also taught English to the young monks. Looking back, it was a very blessed time because I was with my Lama and all the other tulkus and yogis every day. At the same time, it was probably the most painful time of my life, because I was the only nun and usually the only Westerner around this monastery of eighty monks. I was extremely lonely. I couldn't live with them, I couldn't eat with them, I couldn't do rituals with them, I couldn't study with them. I wasn't a lay person, but I wasn't a monk, either, and there was no place for a nun in that society.

It would have been much easier if I had been a man, because I could have lived with Rinpoche and there would have been no problem. But because I was a female, they didn't quite know what to do with me. Once Rinpoche said to me, "Previously I was always able to keep you close by me. But in this lifetime, you took form as a female so I'm doing the best I can, but I cannot keep you close forever because it's very difficult." He certainly did the best that he could. After another six years, the community moved to its present location in Tashi Jong, which is in the Kangra Valley about three hours from Dharamsala. About three months after this move, Khamtrul Rinpoche said to me, "Now it's time for you to go away to practice." I suggested going to Nepal, but Rinpoche said, "Nepal is not so good. You should go to Lahoul."

Lahoul is a Himalayan valley located at an altitude of about 11,000 to 12,000 feet. The Himalayas form a long ridge across the north of India. On one side of the mountains lies Tibet and on the other side, India. Lahoul is one of the many little valleys in the Himalayas which are geographically Indian, but whose culture and religion are Tibetan. It lies between Manali and Ladakh, and for about eight months of the year it's cut off from the rest of India by snow. On both sides of the valley there are very high passes which become snow-bound for eight months at a time. In those days, there were no telephones nor any other means of long-distance communication. For the most part, there was no electricity either. Sometimes there would be no mail for weeks at a time. It is considered to be like Siberia by all the Indians stationed there, who loathe it because of its extreme isolation. But it was perfect for someone who just wanted to do a retreat.

When I first arrived, I stayed at a small Kagyupa monastery. There was a temple beside the mountain and above that there were separate houses. They were flat-roofed, made of stone, and finished with mud inside and out, like Tibetan houses. As is the custom in Lahoul, the monastery was shared by monks and nuns, which was nice. Of course, the monks were up front doing the rituals while the nuns were in the kitchen doing the cooking. I joined the monks. I made sure that I was out front doing the rituals too, because I hadn't come to Lahoul to learn how to cook! I had a little house in the monastery precincts. It was very pleasant there. It was a small community and everyone was friendly. The Lahoulis are very sociable people, so that whenever there is a task like spinning to be done, they get together and work as a community. They move from one person's house to another's in turn, and each house provides food and everybody works. This is very nice, but it was also a big distraction for someone wanting to do retreat. When I first arrived, one of the nuns said to me, "Well dear, of course you will need twenty plates and twenty cups." I replied, "Twenty plates and twenty cups, what for?" She explained, "In the winter, we like to get together and have parties, and there are twenty of us." So I said, "In the winter I'm going into retreat. And even if I do hold a party, you can all bring your own cups and plates." When the winter came, I went into retreat, but I was the only one who did.

It's very cold there, but it's quite pleasant when the sun shines. After each snowfall, everybody has to clear the snow from the rooftops, which are made of flattened earth. When the rooftops are dry, they all sit up on their roofs in the sun and carry on shouted conversations from one rooftop to another. There I was, in the middle of this, doing my mantras. The location wasn't really conducive to retreats. One day, a young monk moved into the room above me, and that was like having a wild yak living upstairs. So I decided it was time to move out and find somewhere quiet. I went up above the monastery to look for some land with the idea of building a small retreat house. Lahoul is called Karsha Khandro Ling in Tibetan, which means Lahoul, Land of the Dakinis. The sacred mountain of Vajrayogini and Chakrasamvara is located here. Many lamas have confirmed to me that there are still dakinis living there. Nowadays we don't see them so much, but they are definitely there.

It's a very sacred place, and I truly felt that the dakinis were close to me. So when I went up above the temple to look for somewhere to stay, I said to the dakinis, "Now, if you find me a place for retreat, I promise I will sincerely try to practice." Then I felt this tremendous sense of "Yes, we heard you, it's going to be done." I was extremely happy about the project then. I came down the hill believing that everything would fall into place. The next morning, I went to see one of the nuns and told her that I was thinking of building a small retreat house above the temple." She said, "How can you build a house? To build a house you need money, and you don't have any. Why don't you live in a cave?" I replied, "As you know, there are very few caves in Lahoul. Where there are caves, there's no water. Where there is water, there are too many people." "Yes, that's true," she replied, "We always used to say that, but just last night I remembered an old nun mentioning there was a cave up on the hill. There's a meadow in front, there are trees and a spring nearby. I've never actually seen this place, but this old nun found it." So I said, "Okay, let's go and look for it."

We had to bring this old nun with us, and she was about eighty! But fortunately for us, she was as agile as a mountain goat. Up the hill we went, the head lama, some other monks, some of the nuns, this old nun and I. And as we were going along, they kept telling me, "No, no, no, you can't stay here. This is too far away. We have to be able to see the smoke from your chimney." The idea was that if they didn't see smoke from my chimney for a few days, they would know that I was sick. However, I was not convinced by this line of argument because once when I had in fact been very sick in the monastery for several days, nobody came to see me. On the other hand, there was another occasion when I was perfectly healthy and making my fire as usual every day and yet two people came around and said, "We haven't seen your fire for some days, are you okay?" So I knew this system of theirs was certainly not infallible!

Eventually we came upon the cave, about an hour away from the monastery. It wasn't actually a cave, to be honest. It was more like an overhang. Several years previously, some villagers had dug it out so that one could stand up in it, and they had flattened the land in front and reinforced it with stones. Then they had built a stone wall in front and stayed there during the summer months with their flocks. All the stones were still there. It was basically ready to move into. I said, "This is it. I'm going to stay here." Everybody protested, "No, no, no, you can't stay here. It's too high. Nobody ever lives at this altitude. You will die of the cold." I argued, "Caves are warmer than houses, so I won't die of cold." They still kept insisting, saying, "You can't live here, it's too isolated, people will come and rob you." I reminded them that there were no thieves in Lahoul.

They had to agree with me. And in fact the whole time I was there nobody ever broke in, even when I left the door open. People came by, but they never took anything. Then they told me, "Men from the army camp will come up and rape you." So I said, "By the time they get up here, they'll be too exhausted for that, so I'll just invite them to sit down and have a cup of tea. I'm not going to worry about that one!" Then they said, or at least I thought they said, "There will be snakes." The Tibetan word for snake is *drul*. I thought they had said, "There will be *drul*," and so I said, "I don't mind snakes, I like them," which is true. Everybody looked terribly impressed when I said this. But later on I thought, wait a minute, there aren't any snakes in Lahoul. Then I realized that they hadn't said *drul*, they'd said *trul*, which means ghosts. So they thought I had told them that I didn't mind ghosts and that I actually liked ghosts! They were so impressed by this that they unanimously announced, "Well then, you can stay."

Shortly afterwards, a couple of monks and some masons from the village below came up and dismantled the wall, built some windows and doors, and divided the cave in half so I could have one little part for a storeroom and the other part to live in. And then they built it all back up again, and the nuns and I mudded it up inside and outside. They made the whole thing, including my meditation box and the shrine. The total cost was two hundred rupees, and as I lived there for twelve years, it was a pretty good value!

It snowed in the winter, so for six months of the year nobody could come around. There was this tremendous stretch of time during which I knew I wasn't going to be interrupted. On a strict retreat, of course, we are not supposed to see anybody who is not also doing the retreat. But because I was so isolated, I could go out during the day even on strict retreat, whereas at the monastery I could only avoid running into people if I went out at midnight. This had been very difficult at times: for example, when the snow was deep and I had to make my way carrying a lantern in one hand and a tin of water in the other. In the cave I didn't have any of those problems. In the winter I got water by melting snow. I could sit outside and not be afraid that anyone was going to come and see me. The mind becomes much more spacious when you can look out and see the trees, the distant mountains, and the vastness of the sky.

There was a beautiful little spring about a quarter of a mile away. In the summer, I made a garden in front of the cave and planted it with potatoes and turnips. Turnips were very good because I could use the green part as well as the bulb. I chopped them up and dried them for the winter, because there was this long, long stretch during which nothing grew. Once it snowed, that was it. If I'd forgotten matches, too bad. I had to spend the short summers getting ready for these long, long winters.

Many animals used to come roaming around the cave. The morning after a snowfall I would see all these hoof-prints and paw-prints everywhere. Once I even saw the paw-print of a snow leopard. I didn't see the leopard itself, but I found a very distinctive paw-print, which I drew, and later showed to a couple of zoologists. They confirmed that it was definitely a snow leopard, because only a snow leopard has that particular kind of print. It had left its paw-print on my windowsill, evidently while taking a look inside my cave. There were wolves, too. I love wolves. Once when I was sitting outside, a pack of five wolves came trotting up. They just stood and looked at me, very peacefully, and I looked back at them. They stayed for several minutes, just looking quietly, then the leader turned and they trotted off after him. Sometimes they would sit above my cave and howl for hours on end.

I usually spent the long winters in retreat. I was generally not on retreat during the summer. I spent the short summer months getting ready for the winter. Then in the autumn, I would go down to Tashi Jong to see my Lama, tell him what I had been doing, and get instructions or further direction. During my last three years there, I did a three-year retreat, and then of course, I didn't leave the cave at all. I had a Lahouli brother who brought up supplies for me. One year he didn't bring up any supplies for six months. That was quite an interesting experience!

I was very happy up there. Sometimes I would ask myself, "If you could be anywhere in the world, where would you be?" I always chose the cave. And I would ask myself, "If you could do anything in the world, what would you want to be doing right now?" And the answer was, I would be doing my practice in this cave. So it was a good time for me. Looking back, I am deeply grateful for the opportunity to practice there, because Lahoul is such a wonderful place. First of all, it is blessed by the dakinis, and secondly, the people there are very honest. They're not violent. Even when they get drunk, they just get maudlin. They cry and say, "Oh, how I've wasted my life. If only I'd been a monk and studied the Dharma." They're not at all violent, unlike the Khampas. They don't get out their knives and start stabbing people. In fact, in the old days when the Mongols used to come marauding, the people would bury all their treasures and run off. Later when the Mongols had left, they would come out of hiding, dig everything up and resume their lives. They're very peaceful people who preferred not to stand and fight. The whole time I was there, I never had any problems from the local people, which is quite something for a woman living in such isolation. Everyone knew I was there. If any men came by, it was because old Abi had lost a yak. "Have you seen a yak?" Or, "We lost three sheep. Have you seen any sheep?" And that was it. In the rest of India, and even in the West, one couldn't live alone in that kind of solitude and feel so confident and safe.

This experience of solitude was very rewarding because I had to learn to deal with whatever happened, be it internal or external, on my own. When you live in such isolation, you can't get on the phone and call a technician or have a chat with your best friend. You can't turn on the television to divert yourself. In the winter, you can't even go for a walk. Whatever happens, you just have to sit there and deal with it! This period helped me develop inner resourcefulness and confidence. I learned that I didn't need to keep running to somebody else to solve my problems. That was very useful for me because I'd always thought that I wasn't very practical or capable, and quickly turned to others for help and advice.

Through those years of having to deal with everything myself, I not only learned how to mud walls, chop wood, and generally do practical things, but also how to deal with the mind. I learned how it works. There was an infinite amount of time without external distractions just to see how the mind functions, how thoughts and emotions arise, how we identify with them, how to dis-identify with them and to resolve all the thoughts and emotions back into spaciousness. I was very fortunate to have the opportunity to do this. I look back upon that time as one of the greatest learning periods of my life.

At the end of my three-year retreat, I had been in India for twenty-four years and I felt it was time to reconnect with the West. I needed to appreciate Western culture again and reestablish what I suppose could be termed my "Western roots." But I had no idea where to go. Some people said, "Come to America." Others suggested Australia. Some said, "Come back to England." Nowhere seemed right. I asked myself, "Well, where do you want to go?" And there was no answer. There wasn't anywhere in particular I wanted to go. But I sensed that it was time to move on. Then some friends, an American couple I'd known in India who had been traveling around Europe, wrote to me and said, "We've found the perfect place. Come to Italy—to Assisi." And I thought, "That's it. Assisi." Italy seemed a logical step after India. It's very like India—the bureaucracy, the postal system, the general nothing-quite-works environment. I immediately felt very much at home there.

Assisi is a wonderful place. It's the birthplace and home of Saint Francis and it has a very spiritual atmosphere. There are several groups associated with India in the hills surrounding Assisi. There are about three ashrams and a school of Indian music. All our friends there were engaged in some kind of spiritual journey, whether it was Hindu, Buddhist or Christian. Of course, Assisi is the home of the Franciscans, which is a delightful order. Despite all the commercialism and the hordes of tourists swarming about, it has a very special and powerful spiritual quality, much as Bodhgaya does. Many people have had profound spiritual experiences there, even some who just came as tourists. It's that sort of place.

I stayed there and did a variety of things. I went back to Asia a few times. Then in 1992, the lamas of my monastery asked me to start a nunnery. Khamtrul Rinpoche had passed away in 1980, but before that, he had said on several occasions, "I want you to start a nunnery." Back then there was no way I could even begin such a project. However, this time, when the tulkus of Tashi Jong said, "We really want a nunnery here, please start it," I thought, "Yes, now is the time." That's basically what I've been doing ever since. The nunnery will reintroduce a very special yogic tradition passed on through Milarepa's disciple Rechungpa. The tradition itself is very vast and very profound, but there is one part especially for women. In Tibet they had female practitioners known as *togdenma*. These were yoginis, special nuns who lived in caves up in the mountains and focused on this practice. Unfortunately, they seem to have disappeared since the Chinese takeover. Now there are about two lamas left who still hold this transmission. After we set up the nunnery, we will select suitable nuns from those who come to study, and they will be given the opportunity to receive and learn this practice. If we don't do something soon, it will be too late. The practice has to be passed from person to person, like a flame. Once the flame goes out, that's it, you can't transmit it. It's what is known as an "oral transmission." If these two elderly lamas pass away without transmitting the practice, it will be lost forever. Along with the nunnery, there will also be an international retreat center for women so that women from all over the world can come and meditate under conducive circumstances. Men will also be welcome to stay at the guest house. In the future, I hope the nuns themselves will teach. I've been traveling to various parts of the world for the past couple of years in order to raise international support for the project.

✍ QUESTIONS

Q: Did you end up liking the ghosts?
TP: Yes, because I asked my Lama about all these problems the villagers had warned me about, like army soldiers raping me and people robbing me and ghosts, and he said, "I don't know about the other things, but I am certain there will be no evil spirits." So when anything peculiar happened, I thought, "That's okay. There are no evil spirits here, so it doesn't matter." My mind didn't fabricate any fears, because I had this confidence that whatever appeared would be benign.

Q: It sounds like you were blessed with confidence and clarity. I'm very interested in a nervous disorder called *lung*, which some people get in retreat, especially as it manifests as doubt and panic. I wonder if you have any advice about that?

TP: When I was about to do my three-year retreat, I went to a Tibetan doctor in Dharamsala, and said, "I'm going to do a long retreat. I think I'm healthy, but please check my pulses in case there's anything latent there." So he took my pulses and said, "No, you're fine. You're a little bit weak," which I knew, "but otherwise you're fine. However, almost all Westerners get *lung* when they go into retreat, so I'll give you some *lung* medicine." So I took this medicine along with me, but I never needed to use it. People get *lung* because they try too hard. They set themselves impossible goals, modeling themselves on the ideal practitioner, and push themselves beyond their limitations. Tibetan practice encourages this because it gives you vast numbers of repetitions to accomplish—hundreds of thousands, or millions—and when you come out of any kind of retreat, the first question you're asked is, "How many mantras did you do?" Not, "How well did you do them?" Or, "What experience did you have," but, "How many?" There is this idea that one needs to do more and more, and everything needs to be absolutely perfect. This creates a lot of tension which often leads to *lung*.

We need to learn how to relax, to make the mind spacious while keeping it clear. In this way, we can practice within a sense of openness, not within a tight knot of tension. If you are tense to begin with, the more practice you do, the tighter you become. It's a vicious cycle. Once you get *lung*, you become extremely tense and uptight. Because you're tense and uptight, you get *lung*. It's important therefore to start a little loosely and not do too much, as with physical exercise, otherwise you just hurt yourself. Gradually do more as you get into it, until you're going fully for it, but still with this very relaxed mind. Then, at the end, wind down so that when you come out it's not a shock to your system. It's very important to keep the mind relaxed, even while it is alert. A relaxed mind doesn't mean a sleepy mind. It means a mind which is open and spacious, rather than gritting its teeth, as it were. I think it's a pity that people going into retreat are not always told how to keep the mind in this open space. Longchen Rabjam talks a lot about this. He explains about not letting the mind go wherever it wants, but keeping it within boundaries while in a relaxed state. Of course, once you develop *lung* it is too late for all this. The only thing you can do is find a sunny beach somewhere and lie on it.

Retreat should be a pleasure, not an ordeal. It should be a delight, because if the mind is delighted with what it's doing, it engages and becomes one with the practice. If the mind is pushed too much, it becomes rigid and rejects the practice, leading to conflict. It's this conflict which produces *lung*. We need to understand our own limits and have compassion for ourselves. Then we need to learn how to use the mind as an ally, so it does the practice with joy. It's very important, therefore, not to push ourselves beyond our capacity. In our sessions we should stop before we become tired, because if we stop while the mind is still enjoying the experience, the mind remembers, "That was fun." It will be enthusiastic again next time. On the other hand, if we push to the point where we're exhausted and the mind says, "Enough," it remembers that. The mind remembers that it got bored and tired, and puts up resistance next time we sit. If we have the support of the mind, and the mind really enjoys what it's doing, then there's no way we will get *lung*. We only get *lung* when there's conflict.

Q: What happened when your food didn't get delivered for six months?
TP: I got very thin. I rationed myself. I was already eating basically once a day, and I started to eat smaller and smaller portions. Milarepa said somewhere that he always prayed that he would die alone in a cave, and from my heart I made the same prayer. Once we had a huge blizzard that raged for seven days and seven nights and the whole cave was in complete blackness. When I opened the windows, there was just a sheet of ice out there. When I opened the door, there was a sheet of ice covering it, and I was in a tiny space unable to get out. I thought, "This is it." So I got my little *dudtsi* pills, which you're supposed to take at the time of death. I got them ready for the last breath I would take. I was sure the air was already getting much thinner and I was taking deeper and deeper breaths. I prayed to my Lama from my heart. I really understood at that moment that the only thing that mattered was the Lama. Oh, did I have devotion!

Looking back on that time today, I'm amazed. I wasn't claustrophobic. I was perfectly calm about it. I was perfectly resigned. It was okay. I don't know how it would have been had I actually gone through the death, but in the meantime, I was okay. Then I heard Rinpoche's voice inside me say, "Shovel out." Fortunately, the door opened inwards, otherwise I couldn't have done that much. At first I used a shovel. I had to bring the snow inside because there was nowhere else for it to go. Then I used a saucepan lid. I dug a tunnel. Then I was just crawling on my hands and knees, and I looked behind me and it was all black, and I looked in front of me and it was all black, but I saw this tiny hole, and eventually I got out and I looked up and the blizzard was still raging. Then I crawled back inside again and the tunnel filled up. I did that three times. It took an hour or two to tunnel out.

The third time I got out and looked around. There were no trees. There was nothing to see. It was all just white. My prayer flags, which were very high up, had disappeared. No cave. Nothing. Then all these helicopters flew over and I thought, "Oh, maybe someone's organizing to see beautiful Lahoul in the snow." Later I learned that several villages had been totally destroyed, and two hundred people had died. The helicopters were flying out the wounded and bringing in supplies. But at the time I had no idea. Lahouli houses have very thick walls and are three stories high. They often have ten to thirteen huge rooms. Each house is a fortress. Nevertheless, many were leveled by ava-lanches. I spent weeks clearing away the snow and got snow blind, but I sur-vived to tell the tale.

Q: What did you find was your most powerful meditation or reflection to keep you inspired?
TP: I don't really know, it's hard to say. I didn't need to be inspired to stay in retreat; I stayed in retreat because it seemed like the most wonderful thing to do. But I remember once when the spring snow melted and the cave became completely flooded. It was May, and the ground was no longer frozen, and it was snowing and snowing, which meant the snow penetrated through the roof because there was no longer any ice to hold it out. It was just dripping down and everything in the cave was soaking wet. I also had a cold or some-thing. I remember feeling extremely unwell. I was thinking, "Yes, they were right in what they told me about living in caves. Who wants to live in this horrible wet?" It was cold and miserable and still snowing. Then suddenly I thought, "Are you still looking for happiness in *samsara*? We're always hop-ing that everything will be pleasant and fearing that it won't be. Didn't Bud-dha say something about *duhkha*?" And suddenly I realized, "It doesn't matter. It really doesn't matter. *Samsara* is *duhkha*. There's no problem. Why expect happiness? If happiness is there, happiness is there. If happiness isn't there, what do you expect? It really doesn't matter." When I felt that in my heart, this whole weight of hope and fear just dropped away. In that moment, all thought evaporated and it just didn't matter any more. It was an enormous relief. I felt so grateful to the Buddha because I had realized that it's so true:

samsara is *duhkha*. And so what? What do we expect? Why do we make such a big fuss when we suffer? It doesn't matter. We go on.

This time was an incredible blessing to me. To be in a situation in which I had an infinite amount of time and space to practice, in which I had a practice to do, in which the people around were so sympathetic and helpful, where my health was fine, and where any problems were irrelevant. All that is what kept me going. It was a great joy. I felt that I was also fulfilling my Lama's wishes, upholding the lineage, and so on. And I thought at that time that it was exactly what I was meant to be doing and that it was also how eventually I would benefit other beings.

Later, when I left retreat, I went to see the Dalai Lama. One of the things I wanted to ask him was whether I should help to start a nunnery in the West or go back into retreat. I was sure he was going to say, "Oh, after eighteen years of doing practice, of course you should start a nunnery. Where's your bodhichitta? Go out and help others." It seemed almost irrelevant to ask him this question, but I decided I would anyway. I did and he replied, "Well, of course, to start a nunnery is very good, and you should do that. But don't give it too much of your time. One or two years is enough. Then go back into retreat because for you it is most important to serve beings by being in retreat." That was what I thought too, and that is what sustained me, along with the knowledge that I was indeed fulfilling my Lama's intention.

Q: Why did you leave retreat at that time?
TP: I had already decided beforehand that after the three-year retreat was finished I would leave. I knew that. What actually happened was that I was supposed to finish the retreat the following March, but during the autumn of the year before, I heard noise and then knocking at my door. This was extremely alarming because I had a wall all around me and there were gates and notices in three languages which read, "In retreat, don't enter." The first noise I had heard was somebody scrambling over the gate. I hadn't seen anybody for a year except for my Lahouli brother who brought up the supplies. I opened the door and there was a policeman standing there. He handed me a notice. I opened it and saw that it was signed by the Superintendent of Police. It read, "I've been looking through the records. I see you've been in the country illegally for the past three years. Come down within twenty-four hours or we will have to take action against you." That was the end of my retreat! According

to the books, you're supposed to spend a week or two gradually getting your-self accustomed to coming out. I had to leave the next day to go down to Key-long to see this Superintendent and explain. He said, "I'm very sorry but. . . ."

It's a long story. The other Superintendent had promised to keep renewing my visa, which he had done in the past, but apparently he was no longer able to do so. When this new Superintendent came, he looked to see whether there were any foreigners here, because he'd just come from Simla where there were so many. The only foreigner there was me. Then he looked at the paperwork and decided it was illegal, and sent the policeman to try to get me down. He said, "I'm very sorry, but you've been in the country illegally. I real-ize it's not your fault, but I have to give you a 'Quit India' notice. You have to leave in ten days." I replied, "But that's impossible, I've been here twenty-four years, I can't just leave in ten days. Anyway, I've just come out of retreat, thanks to you." Then he told me that he was going on vacation for a month. He told me that he would delay giving the order until he returned. "In the meantime," he said, "you can go and get your things and say goodbye to your teachers, but after that you have to leave." So he went off and I returned to my cave. Then the other Superintendent came back. He sent a message up to me saying, "I can give you a whole year at one time." So he gave me another year. I stayed there and after that I came down. So that's how I left retreat, rather precipitously.

Q: Was there a set number of hours that you meditated each day?
TP: Yes, usually. I got up at three and started the first session, until about six. Then I had some tea and *tsampa*. Then I started again around eight, did another three hours until eleven and had lunch. Then after lunch, I used to paint, you know, Buddhas and bodhisattvas, that kind of thing. I was also the local scribe. My Tibetan handwriting and spelling was much better than that of the monks, so they would give me texts to copy. I also had a number of Tibetan books to read. Then I had another cup of tea. After that, I started the third session of the day, then at six, I had more tea. Then I did the evening session. I had a meditation box in which I practiced and slept.

Q: You slept sitting up?
TP: For some time I slept sitting up. I liked sitting up. It's very good for the awareness. I didn't sleep for very long, but very deeply, and then the moment

I woke up, I just straightened my back. But it was not much good for my body, especially for my back. I've always had back trouble, and so eventually I would just curl up in the box and sleep that way.

Q: Do you ever wonder if or when there might be a female reincarnation?
TP: There are female reincarnations.

Q: Of lamas?
TP: Not many, but there are a few. For example, there's Khandro Rinpoche. She's said to be the reincarnation of Yeshe Tsogyal, Guru Rinpoche's consort. However, any woman with special qualities might be regarded as Yeshe Tsogyal—otherwise why would a female have such qualities? She's also more directly an incarnation of the Fifteenth Karmapa's consort, who was the meditation teacher of Tsurphu Monastery in Tibet. She's the daughter of Mindroling Rinpoche, who's a very high Nyingma Lama, and she's wonderful.

Q: I'm wondering what your mother thought about all this?
TP: My mother came to India and lived with me for about ten months. She loved India. She adored the Indians, she adored the Tibetans, she took refuge with Khamtrul Rinpoche and she was devoted to Tara. Eventually she had to go back to England because she couldn't take the food. She was a wonderful mother. When I told her I was going to India she said, "Oh yes, when are you leaving?" She was incredibly supportive. She never used emotional blackmail to get me back. From time to time after I'd gone away, about every ten years, she would say, "Wouldn't you like to come back, just for a holiday?" And so every ten years I would go back for a month. She was wonderful. She supported me for some years to the best of her abilities. She would send me a little money every month until she stopped working and couldn't do it any more. She died about ten years ago, when I was in retreat. My father died when I was two, so he's not in the picture.

Q: Did you find it difficult to adjust when you went to Italy after spending so long in retreat?
TP: I have the kind of mind that wherever I am, that's where I am. And so when I landed in Italy, that was where I was. I hardly ever think of Lahoul these days. It's only now that I'm talking to you that I think about it. Now that

I'm in America, I'm not thinking about Europe, unless people ask about Assisi, then I start thinking about Assisi. But normally I don't think about Assisi at all. In my mind, wherever I am is where I am. Therefore if I'm by myself, that's fine. If I'm with people, that's fine too. It's what's happening.

Q: You said that you had so much time to develop expansiveness of mind. I'm wondering what your insights were about the purpose of the mind.

TP: The purpose of the mind is to be aware. If we didn't have a mind, we wouldn't be aware, would we? What makes us who we are is that we know we are conscious. In meditation, we try to understand the mind and to become ever more conscious, ever more aware, ever more awake. Our minds are usually half asleep, and even though it seems as though we're always thinking a lot and we're very vital and present, in fact we are almost somnolent and robotic in our reactions. The whole point of meditation is to learn how to wake up, to develop greater clarity, to be more aware and more absolutely in the moment. It is to be conscious in the moment without all our usual projections, opinions, ideas and mental chatter going on. At a fundamental level, we are awareness. It's really all about learning to connect with that awareness and how to develop it and be with it.

Q: You mentioned pills you take before you die. What are they, and what are they supposed to do?

TP: They are pills made of various substances, herbs, precious stones, various relics and other precious items. For example, the black color of the famous black pills of the Karmapa is ascribed to the fact that they contain some of Marpa's plow. All sorts of things go into the pills. After making them, the lamas perform puja over them, sometimes for months. They do a lot of ritual and prayers to instill energies into these pills, so they're supposed to be highly magnetized. They will certainly bless your mindstream. You take them if you're depressed or sick, and especially at the time of death. Unfortunately, the really special ones are wrapped in silk, very tightly, so that if you're dying, trying to open them could be quite difficult. What is more, they're very hard. How exactly you're supposed to manage that at the time of death, I've never quite worked out. Anyway, they are blessed substances for helping the mindstream, especially in emergencies such as death. I had several varieties with me in the cave.

∽ 2

Motivation and Practice

I MUST SAY I feel somewhat intimidated to be speaking at a Zen center, especially with a Roshi sitting right beside me! When I came here, I had no idea what I was going to speak about because I'm sure that most of you, certainly those of you who are studying under the Roshi, have no need to hear anything I have to say. But last night it came to me that what I wanted to talk about this morning was motivation—to get back to the deep roots of why we are here and why we are practicing.

In the Mahayana tradition, there are considered to be three basic motivations for practicing Dharma. The first one of these is the realization that something in our life isn't quite the way we want it. There is always a fly in the ointment. Even people who have beautiful homes, loving relationships, children who fit in with their plans, a job they really love, in short everything seems perfect, still feel that there's something lacking in their lives. Most people have more tangible difficulties, and there are a lot of inner problems from early childhood or past lives which affect our ability to adapt to our circumstances. Whatever our situation, we just don't feel comfortable. So we look for a way to make life easier, to give it some meaning, to make it more bearable. Some of us come to the Dharma with the hope that practicing its methods will somehow release the tension and make us feel better. We are looking for more inner calm and a bit more understanding. Basically, we are hoping that it will make samsara more comfortable. Like successful psychotherapy, it will enable us to adapt to our everyday life and relationships.

Some people come to the Dharma with the hope that it will make their lives more interesting and give them exciting experiences. This hope soon fades. Last night, we were discussing the effect that psychedelic drugs had in introducing people to the Buddhist path, especially in the 1960s and 1970s. Of course, the drug culture did open up people's minds to the fact that there is another reality. But as has also been pointed out, the problem with people who have had too much to do with psychedelic drugs is that they become conditioned to look for exciting experiences. Something always has to be happening. It's another kind of hedonistic attachment. It's considered a spiritual outlook by some people, but it's not really spiritual at all. If something exciting doesn't happen after a few days of sitting in zazen, these people are likely to give it all up as a waste of time.

The first level of genuine Dharma motivation comes through appreciating that there is suffering in the world and that merely creating pleasant external circumstances won't alleviate our inner hunger. This is considered to be the narrowest level of motivation that we can bring to our Dharma practice. After a while, we reach the point where we realize that no matter how peaceful we may be or how happy we may feel, our lives are very insecure. We never know what will happen. Today we are healthy, tomorrow we may be sick. Today the people we love and care about are with us, tomorrow they could be gone. Today we have nice secure jobs and nice houses. Tomorrow we might lose our jobs, then we can't pay the mortgage, and we're out on the streets. We come to realize that our situation is somewhat akin to living inside a large prison.

Once I had a dream about this. I dreamt that I was in this enormous prison with many, many different levels and many different apartments. Some of them were like penthouse suites: very luxurious quarters full of people enjoying themselves. There were other levels like dungeons where people were being tortured. But whether one was up high and living in luxury or down below and being tortured, it was still prison, and one never knew where one was going to be put next, because there was no real freedom. Now we're up, now we're down. We don't know. In this dream, I went around thinking, "We've got to get out of this prison. We must leave." I went to many people and said, "Look, this is terrible. We're all completely trapped here. We must get out." And some people said, "Well, it's true, it's prison. But it's quite nice, it's quite comfortable, it's all right here." And other people said, "Well, yes, we'd like to get out, but it's really very difficult. People don't ever get out." Although I spoke to many people, it was very difficult to find anyone motivated to leave. Eventually we come to realize that no matter where we go, no matter what situation we are in, we are always insecure. We never know what will happen, not just in this lifetime, but in future lifetimes. This lifetime is so short. What about all those future lifetimes? Where are we going?

Then we develop the second motivation, which is to get out of samsara once and for all, to really make the effort to go beyond samsara into nirvana. From this point of view, nirvana is the final refuge. We don't have to come back, ever. We can stay in whatever state nirvana is. It's beyond thought, so by definition we can't think about it. But we can aspire to it, and we can realize it. Nirvana is something one can realize in this lifetime. Therefore, the second motivation which many people in the Buddhist world definitely have is to make a big effort to get out of samsara altogether. And this is a valid aspiration.

But then we come to the third motivation which faces the question of who is getting out. The fact is that we are not, as it may appear to us, autonomous globules. We cannot take one globule out and leave the others behind, because in fact we are all intensely, deeply interconnected. We are all part of a huge web. It's impossible to remove just one strand from a web without affecting the entire structure. The traditional example is that we are all caught in a huge, vast swamp. It is a thick, muddy, polluted swamp, and we're all drowning in it. We all want to get out onto firm, dry land. So we make enormous efforts and pull ourselves out. And there we are, a bit muddy, but nonetheless okay. Then what are we going to do? Are we going to turn around and say, "Sorry folks. I'm really sorry you're all drowning there in the swamp, but I'm out, so just keep going and maybe eventually you can get out, too," and then turn our back on them and leave? Could a mother or father leave their children drowning in a swamp and say, "Well, sorry kids but I got out"? Could you leave your parents, your husband, your wife, your brothers, your sisters, your dear friends behind and save only yourself? If you were in a burning house, would you run out and leave your children, parents, and everyone else inside? Some people race back in just to rescue their dog. Once we appreciate that all beings have been our children, our dear mothers and fathers, our friends, our husbands and wives in infinite lifetimes, there's no question of leaving them behind. This is the traditional way of seeing things. We are standing on the shore only because being there puts us in a position to pull others out. As long as we are still in the swamp, even though we long to help, we cannot. If we try to help others out, we will just sink deeper into the mire with them. If we want to benefit others effectively, we must first be standing on firm ground.

What is the meaning of bodhichitta? What is the significance of the Bodhisattva Vow? If we limit ourselves to saying, "I vow to save all sentient beings," that's very nice, but when and where and how? The point is that we have to ask ourselves, "Why are we practicing?" Are we practicing so that we can be happy, or free, or are we practicing so that we can benefit others? This is not just an academic debate, because it is our true motivation for being on the spiritual path, rather than what we chant, that will color everything that happens to us. It's like adding different colored dyes to water. It's going to become red or blue or green, depending on the color of the dye we add. In the same way, our true reasons for practicing will color the results of our practice.

It's not much use for us just to say, "Well, of course, I'm on the Mahayana path, so I'm a bodhisattva, and therefore I'm aiming to save all beings." We must examine our motivation for everything we do. Are we doing it for ourselves, or are we doing it for others? This is an essential point, because when we vow to save countless sentient beings, we must understand what this means. When the heart really comprehends this, something in the mind turns around and our attitude is completely transformed. And to the small extent that we worldlings are capable of, there is a deep inner change of direction. It's not something we can speak about, but we definitely know when it's there.

I don't think this true motivation is always there. In the beginning, as incipient bodhisattvas, we are not always truly altruistic. If we claimed to be, it would just be self-deception. But sometimes, even if only for a very short time, we understand what we're talking about. That is why bodhichitta is so infinitely great and so highly praised in the Mahayana sutras. It transforms even the smallest virtuous action into something of vast proportions, because we are not doing it any more for ourselves or just for the object, but for the whole world. Then even the most minute thing has infinite ramifications, not just in this lifetime, but throughout the vast stretch of future lifetimes. This is the birth of genuine spiritual altruism.

It is very easy to talk about benefiting all sentient beings throughout time and space, although in fact this is a unique aspiration. You see, in most religious traditions, including the most ascetic disciplines, even the most altruistic attitudes are cultivated in order to gain some kind of a reward later on, be it a place in heaven, paradise, nirvana, or a better rebirth. Even the greatest saints of certain religions are still aiming for heaven. They may live the most difficult and self-abnegating lives, but it's all because they think that this lifetime is relatively short. They live in anticipation of eternity in heaven, in glory. Now we're turning that concept right around and saying, "Forget the glory, forget heaven, forget paradise, forget nirvana, we don't have time for that. There are too many beings out there suffering endlessly in samsara. There is no end to their suffering." We can see just by looking around us that there is no end to the sufferings of samsara.

The United States is regarded as a model country for the rest of the world, and everyone is supposed to be aspiring to this lifestyle. But look how many problems everyone has! Look how much suffering there is in this "best of all possible worlds"! We definitely have to make ourselves capable of helping other beings. That is the only reward worth having. Nothing else matters. That is why in Buddhism when we do an especially virtuous deed, we dedicate the merit. We give everything away, all our realizations, all our happiness, all our virtue. We dedicate all the good things in our lives to others. When this attitude starts to grow in the heart, little sprouts of understanding begin to appear and transform everything.

In the Tibetan tradition there's a Dharma protector called Mahakala, whom some of you might know of. Once when it was time for me to do this practice, I thought to myself, "Oh no, I'm very tired, I won't do this." Then the thought came into my mind, "Who are you doing this practice for? You're not doing this for yourself. You're doing it as a substitute for all the beings in the world who don't know how to do it. So what if you feel tired?" It's not a matter of how we feel. We have a responsibility to do things not because we want to or because they will benefit us, but because many other people don't at this point know how to do these things. We must do them on their behalf. When we sit zazen, we're not just sitting for ourselves, we're sitting for all beings. All beings are sitting here with us. When this idea really penetrates our minds, it makes everything seem very light, even though it may sound like a heavy idea. At first we may think, "I am supposed to have responsibility for all sentient beings, yet I can't even take responsibility for myself." But then we realize that apart from the fact that all beings are interconnected, we are also interconnected with all the Buddhas and bodhisattvas. We are not alone in doing this. We are supported by all the Buddhas and bodhisattvas who are likewise here only to benefit other beings.

Do you understand this? We are not autonomous beings. We're not sepa-rate little bubbles. We are all interconnected. We are responsible for each other. In addition, we are all closely connected with the Buddhas and bodhi-sattvas. They're not creatures up in the sky somewhere, or some kind of ori-ental fantasy. The Buddhas and bodhisattvas are right here and now, right in front of us, right with us. If we open ourselves to their inspiration, they will support us. They are here and now because they are none other than the essential nature of the mind. And they are here to help us and support us because they are also working ceaselessly to benefit all sentient beings. Once we plug into all that energy, we no longer feel alone.

Sometimes when people sit on their cushions to meditate, they feel iso-lated. But they're not isolated. We all share this same air. We share this ground. We share food, water, everything. We are all sharing, and we are all interconnected, not just with ordinary sentient beings, but also with many, many layers of higher, evolved beings. They are all here to support us. So our motivation is not just for this hard little ego sitting here. It's very vast, very expansive, going through endless aeons of time. We have vowed to be with sentient beings for endless aeons, not just this lifetime, the next lifetime, and the one after that, but endlessly, infinitely. Not as "I." I mean, I, Tenzin Palmo, am not going to come back in the next life. Something else will be here, but this stream of consciousness and this energy force will be part of it.

The other important aspect of motivation is that we should be conscious of it in everyday life. We should be conscious of the body, we should be con-scious of what we do, how we speak, and what we think. We should always be aware of the underlying root of each action. In Buddhism, we talk a lot about awareness. We talk a lot about being mindful. One of the beautiful things about Zen practice is its emphasis on integrating mindfulness into everyday tasks. But it's not enough merely to be mindful. After all, one could be very mindful while robbing a bank! That is why we also need to be aware of our underlying motivation.

The Buddhadharma identifies three roots of evil and three roots of good. The three evil roots are greed, aversion, and the underlying cause of greed and aversion, our basic ignorance. Any action of body, speech, and mind per-formed under the influence of any of these emotions is unskillful. It doesn't matter if it looks nice on the surface or if it's not doing any harm. If the under-lying intention is tainted with ignorance, aversion, anger, hatred, or greed and desire—and that encompasses a lot of what we do and think and say—then the action is basically unwholesome. On the other hand, any action motivated by the opposite of these three, such as non-ignorance, non-aversion, and non-greed, meaning discernment, love, kindness, generosity, and a sense of inner renunciation or detachment, will be wholesome. Not only will the results of these actions be good in the future, but performing them will also help purify our mind. They help transform the mind because they are in touch with our Buddha-nature. That's why they're so important. They're not arbitrary. It's not that 2,500 years ago the Buddha suddenly decided that aversion was a bad thing for Magadha, but maybe nowadays it's okay. These are eternal truths.

During the break just now, I was reading a book of essays by a feminist Buddhist author. There seem to be a lot of them around nowadays. I just opened it up arbitrarily, I wasn't reading through it consecutively. But what struck me most about it was the anger underlying the writing. In fact, one of the articles was a defense of anger. It maintained that women have a right to be angry, that they should be angry, and that it is incorrect to say that their anger is wrong. The article claimed that anger is a very clear and forceful emotion which can drive people to do great things and overcome many evils. What the author was really saying is that it is wrong to say that anger is a negative emotion, and to try to transform it into love would be counter-productive, especially for women. In this way of thinking, men shouldn't get angry because they are angry enough already, right? They're nasty, violent, horrible creatures. Only women have the right to be angry.

It struck me that if we act out of the root of anger, we will only experience more anger in return. The Buddha himself said, "Hatred doesn't cease by hatred. Hatred can only cease by love or by non-hatred." This is because if you're putting out anger, no matter how justified the cause, you will stir up the huge reservoir of anger in your antagonist, whoever it may be. So however justified it may seem at the time, all you'll get in return is more opposition. It's obvious. All anger, no matter how justified, how righteous, how holy it is, comes from the same source, which is antipathy, aversion, or hatred. Whether it expresses itself in violence or nonviolence, it's still anger, and so however "justified," it will never bring about circumstances leading to peace, love, and reconciliation. How can it?

Many feminists are angry with men, whom they see as the big, bad, wicked oppressors. But if you go to the East where women are kept in a submissive state, you will see that when a woman gets married and goes to live with her husband's family, it is her mother-in-law and sisters-in-law she has to fear, not the men. So who are we going to blame for this? When I was living in Lahoul, the nuns there were in a very subordinate position indeed. But they were not just being kept down by the monks. The ones who really kept them down were other nuns. Who should be the focus of our anger? If we're angry with men and also with women, we're going to be angry with everybody, and then what? Who is the culprit? It's endless. We can always find some "justification" for our anger. The problem is not the object out there, although, of course, we should try to deal with that. The real problem is the anger which lurks within us, just waiting for an excuse to express itself. And since we're Buddhists, we want to find some nice justifiable focus for our anger so we can feel self-righteous and self-satisfied about expressing it! Of course there will always be something to act as an excuse. It's just samsara out there. But the real problem is our negativity, and this is what we have to deal with. The Buddha dealt with many wars, feuding tribes, and conflicts. He reconciled them and gave advice people could accept. But he did this from a totally wise and loving space. What I'm trying to say is that a negative emotion is always a negative emotion, no matter what justification we give to it. It is the emotion within ourselves that we need to examine.

Many people ask how to get rid of anger, because it is an uncomfortable feeling. We don't like feeling angry. We don't like feeling hatred. But nobody has ever asked me, "How can I deal with my desire and my greed?" Yet greed and desire, along with ignorance, keep us trapped in samsara. But greed and desire are not really regarded as negative emotions in the West. After all, where would our consumer society be if we didn't have desire? On the whole, desire is regarded as a positive thing, especially if you can satisfy it. Desire is seen as a motivating force. It propels people to go out and buy more and more, and that keeps the economy churning. This is the idea behind all this.

In a Pali sutra the Buddha said that the karmic effects of hatred are eight times heavier than those of greed, but hatred is relatively easy to get rid of. Greed is less heavy karmically in that it may not directly cause harm to others, but it is extremely difficult to uproot because nobody sees greed as a problem. Within reasonable boundaries, we like being a little greedy. It's nice. We want nice clothes, nice food, a nice place to live. Our senses are stimulated.

We have the idea that if we were not attached to all these things, we would somehow become cold, dried out and uninteresting people. So we are not highly motivated to relinquish our desire.

Khandro Rinpoche, a Tibetan Lama, once said that if you say certain words to Western audiences, they press everybody's buttons. She likes to say them and watch the reactions. One of these words is "surrender." Another is "renunciation." Everybody cringes when she says, "We need to renounce." And everybody says, "What do we need to renounce? What do I have to give up?" And yet renunciation is one of the main stages on the path. Renunciation doesn't necessarily mean giving up your home and family and going forth into homelessness like the Buddha did. Leaving home is not the only form of renunciation. I think in many ways, mental renunciation is much harder. It is not easy to give up cherished (though unhelpful) thought patterns and to be in the moment instead of getting caught up in our memories, anticipations, fantasies, and clever speculations. All of that is very difficult to renounce. Even if people appear to be living in great simplicity, and not many people are, they often still have a luxuriously furnished inner life. I speak from experience here. It is hard to cling to nothing at all. It is particularly hard to stop clinging to our image of who "I" am, to just let it all drop. We need to learn gradually how to do that. This is what zazen is all about. You sit nakedly. Your body is not moving. Your voice is not expressing. And the mind itself is letting go and just being present. Hopefully we are not elaborating on our fantasies. Hopefully we are sitting in a state of nakedness and absolute simplicity.

That is the ultimate renunciation. We could be sitting thinking of the lovely things we did on our honeymoon or on a holiday, or we might be speculating on something that's going to happen next week or what we're having for lunch. We could be just sitting. Nobody will ever know. We're sitting here now, all looking like a bunch of little arhats. As long as the body and the speech are under control, nobody knows what the mind is doing, right? But to renounce the games of the mind and just sit in a state of openness and clarity is the greatest renunciation. The mind is extremely greedy. It's not just greedy for external pleasures, it's also greedy for mental comforts, which are much more difficult to renounce. But if we can manage to do that, we naturally enter a state of openness, simplicity, and clarity, and this leads to the birth of understanding. This is because we have finally dealt with the root of all negativity, which is our ignorance.

This type of existential ignorance cannot be removed only through learning. Of course, studying and thinking and trying to understand are good things, and they are particularly necessary for people like us from the West who don't have a background in Buddhist thought. Of course we need to read and understand what the Buddha was saying, because otherwise we will interpret it according to our own concepts, and change the teachings around to make them fit comfortably with our mental predispositions. It's very important for us to read, study, and understand, "What did the Buddha actually say? What was the Buddha's intention?" But that alone won't remove our unknowing, because our unknowing is not an intellectual thing. It's not on the level of our mind. It percolates through to our minds, of course, so our thought patterns are also ignorant. But the underlying cause is extremely deep, as you all know. Therefore reading, thinking, and discussing can help deal with the surface ignorance, but will not affect our underlying unknowing. This is why you are all sitting here. It's because you know that the only way to reach that very deep root of ignorance is through contacting the essential nature of the mind, through discovering who we really are. In other words, by uncovering our Buddha-nature.

Yesterday when I arrived, Roshi was talking about that huge oak tree out there, and he said he had been told that the roots go down as far as the trunk we see on top. I thought then, "This is really a metaphor for ignorance." We have this much on top. If we can cut down the tree at its root, there will be no more tree of ignorance. We Westerners study very hard. We seem to know a lot. Superficially, it looks as though the tree has disappeared. All that ignorance is gone. We can give all sorts of lectures, and we can get Ph.D.'s in Buddhist philosophy. But if that's all we do, the underlying roots will remain untouched. And from a Buddhist point of view, they will spring up again into a new tree, maybe with even more foliage because it's been pruned. What we really need is to get right down and pull up those incredibly deep roots of ignorance. The only way to do that is to have a decisive realization of the nature of the mind. To have this experience once is not enough. It's only the beginning. My Lama always told me that once you realize the nature of the mind, that's the beginning of the path. Then you can start to meditate. Nowadays some people get some realization of their true nature and think they're enlightened. They start writing books and setting up Dharma centers and so on, but that's really just the beginning.

Until we are in contact with our true omniscient mind continually, moment to moment, without ceasing, twenty-four hours a day, we are not fully enlightened. That's why there are many bodhisattva levels. Our task is to deal with our ignorance. But in the meantime, moment to moment in our everyday life, it is very important for us not only to be aware, but to exercise discernment. We must know how to discern the true intention behind everything we do, say and think. When we recognize unwholesome things coming into the mind, we let them go. We recognize them, we accept them, we don't deny them. We don't get into conflict about them. We see them, we recognize them, and we let them go. We encourage and rejoice in wholesome things. In this way, step by step, we purify the mind.

‿ 3
Ethics and the Three Trainings

TODAY WE ARE GOING to discuss the role of ethical conduct in transforming our everyday lives into spiritual practice. Many of you probably realize that in Buddhist countries throughout Asia the main task of studying and practicing has traditionally been carried out by monks and nuns. They are considered to be the professionals. They have the time to practice, and furthermore, lack the distraction of family and other worldly commitments. So it is expected that people who are really serious about practicing will opt for the monastic life. The principal role of lay people is to support the monks. In return, the monks should exemplify the spiritual life well lived. They are also traditionally the teachers. The schools are run by monks, and children go to monasteries to study. The monks are also the traditional herbal doctors, marriage counselors, psychologists and so on. Monasteries play a very central role in people's lives, and as I mentioned, the primary task of the lay people is to support them.

However, in the West, where Buddhism began to put down roots after 2,500 years, there was a shift in the patterns of practice. For the first time in the history of Buddhism, monks and nuns were no longer the majority of practicing Buddhists. In the West, the majority of aspiring Buddhists wish to actively participate in the religion, but lack sufficient time to undertake the full range of traditional practices. They are people with families, careers and social lives who are nonetheless devoted to the teachings and wish to follow the spiritual path. This is a big challenge. Sometimes traditional teachers from Asia do not sufficiently appreciate this point, and so they make a distinction between what they regard as "spiritual practice" on the one hand, and "everyday life" on the other. According to this traditional approach, specific

Dharma practices such as meditation, ritual, attending centers, and making offerings are considered to be spiritual activities, while the rest of life, such as being at home with the family, going to work, and social interaction are regarded as mere worldly activities. I once heard a very venerable lama, when asked by one of his Western disciples, "I have a family, children, and a job, so I don't have much time for spiritual practice, what should I do?" replied, "Never mind, when your children are grown up you can take early retirement, and then you can start to practice."

Lamas have said to me, "Oh, you are so lucky, Anila. I have so much work I don't have time to practice." This idea that only formal sitting, doing prostrations, going to the temple, listening to Dharma teachings, and reading religious books constitute practice, and the rest of the day is so much ballast, can cause us to feel very frustrated with our lives. We may end up resenting our families and our work, always dreaming of a time when we will be free to do "actual practice." We might spend the best part of our lives resenting those very circumstances which could provide us with the most profound means of progressing on the spiritual path. We must ask ourselves now, assuming most of us are not going to go off to do twelve-year retreats, "Does Dharma practice have any relevance to my life?" Because if there is no possibility of real practice outside of full monastic commitment, what use is Dharma to us in the West?

There are changes happening now, not in the practices themselves nor in the basic underlying philosophy, but in the emphasis. There is ample precedent to be found in Zen Buddhism, which teaches that everything we do, provided it is done with total awareness, is spiritual activity. On the other hand, if we perform an action distractedly, with only half our attention, it becomes just another worldly activity. It doesn't matter what it is. One could be a great master meditating upon a high throne, but unless one is present and conscious in the moment, it is meaningless to sit there. On the other hand, one might be sweeping leaves, chopping vegetables or cleaning toilets, and provided one maintains complete attention, all these activities become spiritual practices. That's why in films about Zen monasteries everything is done with such remarkable inner poise, with an air of being completely present in the moment.

Therein lies the key for those of us who have busy lives. We can convert actions we normally regard as routine, dull, and spiritually meaningless into

Dharma practice, and transform our entire lives in the process. This is what I would like to discuss today. However, first I would like to talk a little about another aspect of using our everyday lives as spiritual practice. I inwardly wince at the word "spiritual," but I don't know what other word we have. Maybe I'll just call it "practice" and you will understand. I will use "practice" in this context to mean something which helps us to transform ourselves inwardly.

There are two separate aspects to bringing about this transformation, although they do converge. One is to create inner space. This is an inner centeredness, inner silence, inner clarity, which enables us to begin seeing things more as they really are and not how we normally interpret them. The other aspect is learning to open up our hearts. In this talk I will be dealing more with the latter aspect. At the most basic level, this is about non-harming. It is about living in the world in a way which harms neither ourselves nor others, so that whoever comes into our orbit knows there is nothing to fear from us.

I should mention that the entire Buddhist path is based on three principles, called the three trainings. The first is training in ethics, or moral conduct, the second is training in meditation, and the third is training in wisdom. Nowadays everybody seems to be very interested in meditation. But to take meditation out of its context is like building the walls of a house without first laying the foundations: the walls may be very nice, but without a sturdy foundation, they are likely to collapse. I will explain these three aspects very briefly, so that you get a more complete idea of what the training is about.

Buddhist ethics are about putting harmlessness into practice. One of the main methods of training in ethics is to follow a code of precepts. There are five basic Buddhist precepts—not taking life, not stealing, not engaging in sexual misconduct, not telling untruths and not indulging in intoxicants. These are not commandments, they are simply tools to help us develop conduct which is non-harmful. We will discuss ethics in more detail a little later on when we look at the Six Perfections.

In order to develop meditation, we need to behave in ways which make the mind more peaceful, more simple, and more open. After all, meditation is not just about attaining inner peace. It is also concerned with opening up the heart. How can we talk about opening up the heart while we are indulging in any kind of conduct which harms others? These two kinds of action are in conflict. That's why the Buddha advised us to first understand how to live in this world as lightly as possible, without harming beings. Only then can the mind become settled.

We are each living in our own soap opera. We do not see things as they really are. We see only our own interpretations. This is because our minds are always so busy. When we try to look into the mind itself, we cannot see anything below our surface consciousness. But when the mind calms down, it becomes clear. This mental clarity enables us to see things as they really are, instead of projecting our commentary onto everything. When we look within, we can now see increasingly subtle levels of the psyche. This kind of meditation is called *shamatha*, which means "calm abiding meditation," or "tranquilizing meditation." It is the first stage of meditation, and it is used to quiet the mind. But there is more to meditation after achieving shamatha. At this stage, although the mind has become quiet and peaceful, much of the rubbish is still there, lying below the surface. We can see it clearly now, but it certainly has not gone away.

In order to deal with this deep layer of rubbish, we need to practice *vipashyana*, or insight meditation. This type of meditation involves activating a large question mark. In the Tibetan school especially, we question the whole concept of thought and emotion and we ask, "Who is the thinker?" Descartes said, "I think, therefore I am." From a Buddhist perspective, all we can say is, "I think, therefore there are thoughts." The fact that there are thoughts does not necessarily imply there is a thinker. We say, "I think, I feel, I want or I don't want." But who is this "I" appearing like a spider in the middle of a web? We ask, "What is a thought?" We don't know, yet we are thinking continually. But how often do we turn the focus of our attention onto the actual thought or onto the mind itself and ask,"What is a thought? What does it feel like? Where does it come from? How long does it stay? Where does it go?"

We can ask the same kinds of questions about our emotions. We may say, "I'm angry." But what is anger? Where is it? How does it feel? Who is angry? Who is this "I" we posit in relation to everything? In a way, you could say vipashyana meditation is like peeling away layers from an onion. We question until we begin to ask ourselves, "Where is this essential 'I'? What is it?" The moment we understand this, we understand everything. Once we pass beyond our ordinary conditioned level of thinking to deeper and subtler layers, we reach a state known as "the unconditioned."

Our normal mode of thinking is based on dualism. It is based on "I" and what "I" am thinking or doing. Practicing vipashyana brings us into direct contact with non-dual awareness. For example, if we were to look up at the sky on a cloudy day, we would normally associate ourselves with the obscuring clouds of our thoughts and emotions—whether they be white, black, or shades in between. We rarely associate ourselves with the vast blue sky of naked awareness. The sky is infinite. Where does it begin? Where does it end? It is because we identify with the clouds rather than the sky that we suffer. As we go deeper and deeper into questions such as, "Who are we, what is an emotion, what is a thought," we give rise to what is called wisdom.

Wisdom has nothing to do with intellectual knowledge. Intellectual knowledge can be very helpful. It can clarify things. But there is an enormous difference between "knowing about" and "knowing." Knowing has the sense of direct experience. We could read many books on sugar, for example. We could learn its chemical components, how it's made, how it's produced, the different kinds of sugars, how long sugar has been used by the human race, the kind of sugars we have in the body, how carbohydrates convert into sugar. We could become "experts" on sugar. But until we taste sugar, we do not know sugar. We only know about it.

Wisdom occurs when we become what we experience. It is the nature of direct realization to transform. Once this happens, we will never be the same again. It doesn't mean that we are totally enlightened. Some people imagine that they are going to sit and meditate for a while and then, in the space of one minute, they're suddenly going to get this big breakthrough full of bright lights, trumpets, angels, and flowers falling. It's not like that. Actually, when we meditate we do experience little breakthroughs, like tiny flashes of the unconditioned mind. But that's just the beginning of the process. It's certainly not the end!

Wisdom is a huge subject. It is all about understanding the underlying spacious and empty quality of the person and of all experienced phenomena. It is the direct result of our inward search. It is not something we can learn from books. It has to be directly experienced. To attain this quality of deep insight, we must have a mind which is both quiet and malleable. Achieveing such a state of mind requires that we first develop the ability to regulate our body and speech so as to cause no conflict. In this way, all of the three trainings rely on and support each other, like a triangle in which each side is needed to support the other two. You can't take one part away and expect the triangle to remain.

The three trainings are to help us develop the Six Perfections, or *paramitas*, which are transcendental qualities needed for making progress towards enlightenment. There are actually many qualities involved, but six are included in the traditional framework These are giving, or generosity; ethics, or moral conduct; patience, or tolerance; enthusiastic effort; meditation; and wisdom. You will notice that meditation is just one of the six qualities. What about giving, ethics, and patience? Perfecting these first three qualities, which are essential for attaining the full spiritual path, requires a social context. Living in isolation, one might put out crumbs for the birds to develop the quality of giving, one might have patience with the howling of the wind or the fact that it is still snowing day after day, but beyond that, what? We really need other people around if we are to develop the first three perfections. How can we learn to give if we have no one to give to? Giving is placed first because it is something that we can all do right now. We don't have to be ethically perfect, we don't have to be great meditators, we don't have to develop great patience and avoid anger in all circumstances. We can be extremely flawed, extremely problematic people, but still be generous. Giving opens up the heart, which is another reason why it is placed first.

While I was in England, I had some friends who were English Sufis. Their sheik was in Morocco. These friends had a son who was about three years old. One day they had given him a box of sweets and suggested he offer one to me. His immediate reaction was, "No, they're mine!" His father said, "Yes, of course they are yours. That's why you can share them with others." The little boy thought about that, then he smiled. He opened up the box and not only gave one to me, but offered them to everybody in the room, with a big smile. That was right. They were his, therefore he could offer them to others!

Do we think about our possessions that way? How lucky we are to possess this so we can share it with others! That is the first lesson, the first opening up of our hearts to acknowledge those around us. Not just giving away things we don't want anyway—although that could be a start—but also giving things because we really like them. This is a beautiful way to relate to people, and we can do this any time. People understand about generosity in the East. They believe that everything that comes about happens due to causes and conditions, so if they want to be prosperous, they have to create the causes for future prosperity. The cause of prosperity is generosity. Knowing this, they are very happy to give and very grateful to the recipient for enabling them to accumulate this good karma. Not only does it help them to open up their hearts, but it also plants seeds for their future prosperity. For this reason, when a person gives something, the recipient doesn't say "thank you," because it is the giver who should give thanks for the opportunity to manifest generosity.

We can begin by giving in small ways. If we meet some friends, we can buy them coffee. If we have two of something nice, we can give one to someone else. I know a swami who lives in India. Apparently he is quite well known. People are always giving him gifts, including nice things from abroad, which are highly coveted in India. What struck me about him is that his first thought upon receiving anything is always, "Who can I give this to? Who would be an appropriate recipient?" He never retains anything for himself, but he is always happy!

The second quality which we can easily incorporate into our everyday lives is ethics. The basics of Buddhist ethics are the five precepts. The wording used for undertaking these precepts says, "I undertake the rule of training to . . ." In other words, they are not commandments. The Buddha did not say, "Thou shall not. . ." He just said, "This is a rule of training to develop conduct which harms neither oneself nor others."

The first of these five precepts is not to take life. That means not to kill intentionally. This includes not taking the life of any being, not just humans, but also animals, fish, insects and any creature possessing consciousness. Each being regards its own life as its most precious possession, just as we regard our life as our most precious possession. There is a story about a king who reigned at the time of the Buddha. One day he was standing on a balcony with his chief queen. He asked her, "In all the world, whom do you love the most?" She was thoughtful for a while, then answered, "You know, I think in all the world, I love myself the most, what about you?" The king thought about that for a while, then said, "Hmm, actually that's true. When it comes down to it, in all the world, I love myself the most." Then he went to the Buddha and related this discussion to him. "What do you think?" he asked. The Buddha answered, "That's true. Each being is the most dear to itself. And because of that, we should neither harm, nor cause harm." As I mentioned earlier, the entire system of Buddhist ethics is based on the principle of non-harming. This covers not harming ourselves as well as not harming others. It is about living in such a way that every being who comes into our presence knows we are no threat to its well-being and that it is completely safe with us.

The second precept is not to take that which is not given, in other words, not stealing. This precept is taken very seriously in Buddhist countries. For example, when monks and nuns go to someone's home, they are not supposed to even pick something up to admire it, lest their action be interpreted as a wish to take it. We are supposed to actually hand things to them. Even if we invite them to lunch, we are supposed to hand them each thing, so that there is no question they are taking something which was not offered. In some Buddhist countries, monks and nuns follow this very scrupulously indeed. This is another aspect of harmlessness. People must know that they can trust us, that we won't take anything from them, because we don't like people taking things from us. This also applies to returning things that we borrow. We must return them promptly, in as good a condition as when we borrowed them. We must respect other people's property, just as we want others to respect ours.

The third precept concerns avoiding sexual misconduct. This means not engaging in any kind of sexual behavior which could cause harm to oneself or to another. That involves taking responsibility for our actions. We must not simply seek immediate gratification, but consider the long-term results and implications of our actions. It's not really a matter of whom we sleep with or what kind of sex we have. The question we must always ask ourselves is, "Is anyone being harmed by this behavior? Could anyone be harmed by this behavior?" Adultery is therefore always regarded as harmful because it hurts people and leads to jealousy, deception, and lack of trust.

The fourth precept is against telling untruths. Keeping this precept ensures that people can trust what we tell them. They know that we are telling them what we believe to be true. At the same time, our speech should be helpful. It should not only be truthful, but also kind. Some people pride themselves on having very truthful speech, but that truthful speech can actually be quite mean. It's interesting to notice that when people pride themselves on telling the truth, they usually mean truths which are hurtful to others! I remember an occasion that took place when I was young, just after the war. At that time everything in England was rationed, including food and clothing. We had clothes coupons and we would eagerly save them up to buy something new, which was a big treat. My mother had bought a cream-colored coat. She put it on to show me. She was very pleased because she hardly ever got new clothes. She asked, "What do you think?" I said, "It makes you look fat." What I said was true. It did make her appear fat. But the look of hurt and disappointment on her face was heartbreaking. She took the coat off and put it in her wardrobe. She never wore it or even looked at it again. I could have said, "Yes that's a nice color," or, "The cloth is nice," or "That's an interesting design." These statements would have been just as true. When we tell the truth, we also have to remember it should not just be truth; it should be helpful and kind. We must remember that our aim is not to harm others, and that includes considering their feelings.

The fifth precept is against taking intoxicants. This one is not very popular in the West. Many people say, "Oh, it really just means not getting roaring drunk." Actually the precept doesn't say that you should not get drunk. It says that you should not indulge in intoxicants. Why not? Well, first of all, Buddhism is a path of increasing awareness and clarity of mind. It is all about increasing our mastery over the mind, not weakening it. Indulging in intoxicants is counterproductive because it clouds the mind. Not only that, it opens the door to all our negative qualities. When people are drunk, their best qualities do not emerge. People rarely get drunk and then go and join Mother Theresa. More often, they get drunk and beat up their wives!

There's a Tibetan story which illustrates this. There was once a monk who was living in a mountain cave and meditating. His benefactor down below would bring up food from time to time. His daughter would carry up the supplies, and over time, she became completely smitten with this monk. Eventually, she suggested to the monk that he sleep with her. He said, "I couldn't possibly do that. I'm a celibate monk. What are you talking about? No way." She was greatly disappointed as she returned down the mountain. The next time she went, she took a goat up with her. Then she said to the monk, "If you won't sleep with me, at least slaughter this goat so we can enjoy a feast together." "Are you out of your mind?" he replied. "I'm a Buddhist monk. I don't kill. Just go away." So back down the mountain she went, musing to herself, "That Buddhist monk is very difficult to trick."

The next time, she returned with a big jug of Tibetan beer, which is known as *chang*. She said, "Okay, this is my ultimatum. Either you make love to me or we eat the goat. Otherwise, at least share this chang with me. If you don't do any of these things, I will despair and kill myself." The monk pondered, "What to do? I can't be the cause of this poor girl losing her life. The least harmful of these things would be to drink the chang." So he said, "Okay, we'll drink the chang." And they did. Of course, the monk got completely drunk.

Then he made love to the girl. In celebration of that, they slaughtered the goat and had a big party!

Alcohol in itself is not a problem. The problem is that it opens the floodgates to all our negative actions, so we should be very careful about using it. Drunken drivers kill people not because they are evil, but because they have lost possession of their faculties. I correspond with a prisoner in America who is serving a twenty-six-year sentence for a drunken driving incident in which he killed a mother and her daughter. Not only did his drunken driving take the lives of those two people, but in a way, it took his life too. Twenty-six years is a long time to be imprisoned!

Buddhist ethics are based on the conduct of a completely realized being. A completely realized being would naturally not take life, steal, indulge in sexual misconduct, tell lies, or take intoxicants. By living in a harmless way, we are bringing our actions into conformity with those of a fully awakened being. I think you can see that these precepts are not just culturally conditioned. It is not accurate to say that they were relevant 2,500 years ago in northern India, but lack relevance in the modern world. In fact, they are just as relevant—if not more relevant—in today's society, based as it is on greed and violence. Adhering to these ethics is like building the foundation of a house—it's not exciting work. Nobody ever described the job of laying foundations as thrilling. But it can nonetheless be very rewarding. If you build solid foundations, you can then build up sturdy walls easily and quickly. On the other hand, if the foundations are weak, the walls will be unstable, however attractive they may appear. If we make our conduct pure, helpful, and non-harming, our minds will become serene. We will have less conflict. We will have nothing to reproach ourselves with. From this firm base, we can begin to practice meditation. I am not saying that our conduct has to be absolutely impeccable before we can begin to meditate. But if we persist willfully in behavior such as hunting animals, beating up our wives or children, shoplifting on the weekend, delighting in malicious scandals, or conducting illicit love affairs, our minds will be too agitated to meditate properly. In fact, it would be counterproductive for us even to try.

It is very important for us to try to lead a life which does not harm our own bodies and minds, because we are responsible for them. We should be mindful of how we nourish them, just as we take care to fuel our cars with high quality gasoline and good oil. We don't pour kerosene or other harmful substances into the engine because we know it will cause damage. We are careful to look after our cars, but we take less care with our bodies. We put all sorts of harmful things into the body. We need to take more responsibility for ourselves, our minds, and our place in society. Buddhists spend a lot of time sitting and meditating on loving-kindness and compassion and sending out loving-kindness and compassion to all beings. But if we do not have compassion towards ourselves, how can we expect to send it out to others?

It's relatively easy to sit on our cushion and think, "May all sentient beings be well and happy," and send out thoughts of loving-kindness to all those little sentient beings out there on the horizon somewhere! Then somebody comes in and tells us there is a telephone call and we answer crossly, "Go away. I'm doing my loving-kindness meditation." The best place for us to begin our Dharma practice is with our family. We have the strongest karmic connections with family members; therefore, we have a great responsibility for developing our relationships with them. If we cannot develop loving-kindness towards our family, why even talk about other beings? If we really want to open up our heart, it has to be to those directly connected to us, such as our partners, children, parents, and siblings. This is always a difficult task, because we need to overcome deeply entrenched behavioral patterns.

I think this can be especially challenging with couples. Sometimes I think it would be a good idea to have a tape recorder or even a video camera to record how couples relate to each other, so they could see and hear themselves interacting later on. He says this, she says that, every time, and each time the responses are so unskillful. They get locked into a pattern. They cause pain to themselves and to those around them, including their children, and they can't get out. Putting loving-kindness into practice really helps loosen the tight patterns we have developed over many years. It's sometimes a very good idea just to close our eyes, then open them and look at the person in front of us—especially if it's someone we know very well, like our partner, our child or our parents—and really try to see them as if for the first time. This may help us to appreciate their good qualities, which will then aid us in developing loving-kindness for them.

The third of the Six Perfections requiring the presence of other people is patience. Patience is the antidote to anger. From a Dharma perspective, patience is considered extremely important. The Buddha praised it as the greatest austerity. We must develop this wonderful, wide, expansive quality.

It has nothing to do with suppressing or repressing or anything like that; rather, it's about developing an open heart. In order to develop this, we need to have contact with people who annoy us. You see, when people are being loving and kind towards us, saying the things we want to hear and doing all the things we want them to do, it may feel great but we don't learn anything. It's very easy to love people who are lovable. The real test comes with people who are being absolutely obnoxious!

I'll tell you a story. Have any of you ever heard of Saint Thérèse of Lisieux? She is sometimes called the "Little Flower." For those of you who haven't, she was a girl from a middle-class French family living in Normandy. She became a Carmelite nun at the age of fifteen and died of tuberculosis at the end of the nineteenth century when she was only twenty-four. She is now the patron saint of France, along with Joan of Arc. She lived in a small enclosed Carmelite nunnery with about thirty other women. Four of her sisters were also nuns in the same nunnery. Her eldest sister was the Mother Superior.

You have to try to imagine life in a contemplative order. You see only the other people in the group. You haven't chosen them. It's not like you choose all your best friends to come into the order. You go in there and then find out what you've got. You are going to sit next to the one who came before you and the one who came after you for your entire life. You have no choice. You eat with them, sleep with them, pray with them and spend your recreation time with them. It is as if all of us here in this room were suddenly told, "This is it, folks! You are never going to see anyone else for the rest of your lives. You didn't choose each other, but here you all are." Imagine!

Now there was one nun whom Thérèse absolutely could not abide. She didn't like anything about this woman—the way she looked, the way she walked, the way she talked or the way she smelled. Thérèse was quite fastidious. The nuns used to have silent contemplation in the morning in a big stone chapel, where all the sounds reverberated. This nun used to sit in front of Thérèse and make strange clicking noises. The noises weren't rhythmic, so she never knew when the next click was going to happen. She was supposed to be contemplating, but instead she would be drenched in cold sweat, just waiting for the next click to come. She knew that she would be around her for the rest of her life and that the woman was never going to change. Eventually, she realized that it was no use trying to escape by slipping down a corridor whenever she saw the woman approaching. Obviously something about her was pleasing to God, because he had called on her to become a bride of Christ.

Thérèse decided there must be something beautiful about this nun which she was unable to see. She realized that, as this woman was not going to change, the only thing that could change would be Thérèse herself. So, instead of nursing her aversion or avoiding the woman, she began to go out of her way to meet her and to be as charming to her as if she were her closest friend. She began to make her little presents, and to anticipate the woman's needs. She always gave her her very nicest smile, right from her heart. She did everything she possibly could to treat this woman as though she were her most beloved friend. One day the woman said to her, "I really don't know why you love me so much." Thérèse thought, "If you only knew!"

Through acting in this way, Thérèse became genuinely fond of this woman. She was no longer a problem to her, but nothing about the woman had actually changed. I am sure she still sat there clicking away, oblivious. Yet everything had changed. The problem had been surmounted, and for Thérèse there was a great deal of inner growth. She didn't perform any great miracles. She didn't have any great visions. She did something very simple, which we are all capable of doing—she changed her attitude. We cannot transform the world, but we can transform our mind. And when we transform our mind, lo and behold, the entire world is transformed!

Shantideva, the seventh-century Indian scholar, wrote that the earth is full of pebbles, sharp rocks and thistles. So how can we avoid stubbing our toes? Are we going to carpet the whole earth? No one is rich enough to carpet the entire earth wall to wall. But if we take a piece of leather and apply it to the bottom of our soles as sandals or shoes, we can walk everywhere. We don't need to change the whole world and all the people in it to our specifications. There are billions of people out there but only one "me." How can I expect them all to do exactly what I want? But we don't need that. All we need do is change our attitude. We can consider the persons who annoy us and cause us the greatest problems as our greatest friends. They are the ones who help us to learn and to transform.

Once when I was in South India, I went to see an astrologer and told him, "I have two choices. Either I can go back into retreat or I can start a nunnery. What should I do?" He looked at me and said, "If you go back into retreat, it will be very peaceful, very harmonious, very successful, and everything will be fine. If you start a nunnery, there will be lots of conflicts, lots of problems, lots of difficulties, but both are good, so you decide." I thought, "Back into retreat, quick!" Then I met a Catholic priest and mentioned it to him. He said, "It's obvious. You start the nunnery. What is the use of always seeking tranquility and avoiding challenges?" He said we are like rough pieces of wood. Trying to smooth our ragged edges down with velvet and silk won't work. We need sandpaper. The people who annoy us are our sandpaper. They are going to make us smooth. If we regard those who are extremely irritating as our greatest helpers on the path, we can learn a lot. They cease to be our problems and instead become our challenges.

A tenth-century Bengali pandita named Palden Atisha reintroduced Buddhism into Tibet. He had a servant who was really awful. He was abusive to Atisha, disobedient, and generally a big problem. The Tibetans asked Atisha what he was doing with such an awful guy who was so completely obnoxious. They said, "Send him back. We'll take care of you." Atisha replied, "What are you talking about? He is my greatest teacher of patience. He is the most precious person around me!" Patience does not mean suppression, and it doesn't mean bottling up our anger or turning it in on ourselves in the form of self-blame. It means having a mind which sees everything that happens as the result of causes and conditions we have set in motion at some time in this or past lives. Who knows what our relationship has been with someone who is causing us difficulties now? Who knows what we may have done to him in another life! If we respond to such people with retaliation, we are just locking ourselves into that same cycle. We are going to have to keep replaying this part of the movie again and again in this and future lifetimes. The only way to break out of the cycle is by changing our attitude.

When the Communists took over Tibet, they imprisoned many monks, nuns, and lamas. These people had done nothing wrong. They were merely there at the time. Some were imprisoned in Chinese labor camps for twenty or thirty years and are only now being released. A while back, I met a monk who had been imprisoned for twenty-five years. He had been tortured and treated badly, and his body was pretty much a wreck. But his mind! When you looked into his eyes, far from seeing bitterness, brokenness, or hatred in them, you could see that they were glowing. He looked as though he had just spent twenty-five years in retreat! All he talked about was his gratitude to the Chinese. They had really helped him develop overwhelming love and compassion towards those who caused him harm. He said, "Without them I would have just continued mouthing platitudes." But because of his imprisonment, he had had to draw on his inner strength. In such circumstances, you either go under or you surmount. When he emerged from prison, he felt nothing but love and understanding towards his captors.

Once I read a book by Jack London. I can't remember the title. It was called something about the stars. It was a story about a college professor who had murdered his wife and was in San Quentin prison. The prison guards did not like this guy at all. He was too intelligent. So they did everything they could to harass him. One of the things they did was to bind people in very rigid canvas sacking and pull it tight so that they could hardly move or breathe, and their whole body would feel crushed. If anyone stayed in this for more than forty-eight hours, they died. They would continually put the professor in this for twenty-four or thirty hours at a time. While he was wrapped up like this, because the pain was unendurable, he began to have out-of-body experiences. Eventually he began to go through past lives. Then he saw his interrelationships in past lives with the people who were tormenting him. At the end of the book he was about to be hanged, but he felt nothing but love and understanding towards his tormentors. He really understood why they were doing what they were doing. He felt their inner unhappiness, confusion, and anger which were creating the scenario.

In our own modest way, we too must develop the ability to transform negative occurrences and take them on the path. We learn much more from our pain than from our pleasures. This doesn't mean we have to go out and look for pain—far from it. But when pain comes to us, in whatever form, instead of resenting it and creating more pain, we can see it as a great opportunity to grow—to get out of our normal thinking patterns, such as, "He doesn't like me, so I'm not going to like him." We can begin to transcend all that and use this method to open up the heart. The Buddha once said, "If somebody gives you a gift and you don't accept it, to whom does the gift belong?" The disciples answered, "It belongs to the person who gave it." Then the Buddha said, "Well, I do not accept your verbal abuse. So it's yours." We don't have to accept it. We can make our minds like a vast open space. If you throw mud into open space, it doesn't sully the space. It only sullies the hand of the person who threw it. This is why it is so important to develop patience and learn how to transform negative events and negative people into a positive spiritual response.

QUESTIONS

Q: What happens if you take on these precepts and other people lie to you and you believe them?

TP: Well, you don't have to be gullible. When the mind becomes clearer, we begin to see things as they really are, and to see people as they really are. As we begin to see people as they really are and not the way they represent themselves, we develop great compassion for them, but that doesn't mean we have to be idiots. Compassion is not sentimental, it's razor sharp. I am not talking about idiot compassion. Genuine compassion is aligned with clear vision. We can see the situation and spontaneously know the appropriate response. Because we are so muddled, we usually don't know the appropriate response. Therefore, while we are trying so hard to be happy, we just create more and more confusion and distress for ourselves and everyone around us. That's not our intention. Our intention is to be happy, and maybe to make other people happy too. But we don't do it because we are so confused. The better we understand ourselves, the better we can understand others. Then we can respond to situations in an appropriate manner without causing harm. The basic principles of Buddhism are used worldwide by people who are not Buddhist, because they are applicable to everybody. You don't have to be a card-carrying Buddhist to understand them. The Dalai Lama himself always says, "We are not trying to convert people to Buddhism, we are trying to help people to be happier, kinder, and more peaceful."

The Buddha said, "One thing only I teach: suffering and the end of suffering." He had looked around and seen that people wanted so much to be happy and yet, because of their confusion, they were continually creating more and more misery for themselves and others. He showed them the way to transform all this. It's as if we are all tied up in knots, pulling in all directions trying to untangle ourselves. But because we don't know how to disentangle ourselves, we just pull blindly at the knots and make them tighter.

How many people are genuinely happy? I don't mean happy because they've just met the man or woman of their dreams, or because they've got a new car, or a new house, or the job they've always wanted. I'm talking about being inwardly happy. I'm talking about having a wellspring of inner joy and peace bubbling up in their hearts continually, no matter what happens. How many people do you know like that? There are some, but not many.

Q: You said that Buddhism is non-theistic. How do you reconcile that with your attitude towards the Buddha?

TP: The Buddha was not a god. He was an Indian prince who attained perfect enlightenment through his own efforts. He broke through all the boundaries of ignorance and unknowing; his mind expanded in all directions and he saw clearly. He woke up. The reality is that we are all sleeping in a sea of ignorance and we also need to wake up. When we bow down to the Buddha, it is out of enormous gratitude to him for his example and for the fact that he spent forty-five years wandering around northern India teaching so many different kinds of people and showing so many different paths to achieving this breakthrough. He is not a god. He never created anything. He is not manipulating our lives. He is not judging us. He is an example of our human potential.

Q: If all religions have similar codes of ethics, why is Buddhism so special?

TP: All religions tell us not to harm others and to be good. They all tell us to love others. They all tell us to treat others as we would have them treat us. One of the things that is special about Buddhism is that it doesn't just tell us to love our neighbor as ourselves, it tells us how to do it. It gives us techniques for developing loving-kindness and compassion.

Q: Doesn't Buddhism also teach about karma?

TP: Yes. You see, the basis of Buddhist ethics is that everything we do with our body, speech, and mind has results. Mind does not just mean intellect, it also includes the heart because the foundation of the mind comes from the heart chakra, not from the intellect. The intellect is the brain of the computer, not the energy driving it. We are constantly planting seeds. Any actions motivated by ignorance (meaning confusion and delusion), by greed or grasping, anger or aversion, will have negative results. It doesn't matter how we justify them to ourselves. Our justifications are not the point. The point is the true underlying motivation. Actions motivated by clear understanding, love, or generosity will have positive results.

We are constantly writing our own script. The results of all our actions will come to pass, either immediately or later on, in this life or in future lives. Therefore what is happening to us now is mostly the result of things we have done in the past, either during this lifetime or past lifetimes. It is how we respond to what is happening now that creates the future. We have total responsibility for everything in our lives. We can't blame anyone else. We are responsible for what's happening right now and for how we deal with it. Things happen to us and we respond to them. Whether we respond in a skillful manner and learn from them or not is up to us. Buddhist ethics are about taking responsibility. We need to realize that in each moment we are molding our future. There's no one outside of us pulling the strings. There is no one to judge us. On one level, we judge ourselves from moment to moment, in the sense that whatever we do will produce results. If we plant good seeds, we'll get a good harvest. If we plant poisonous seeds, our harvest will be poisonous, too.

Q: Are you saying that after we die, we keep coming back again and again?
TP: Absolutely, yes. You see, the notion of rebirth gives us an incredibly vast picture. We don't have to wonder, "Why is this happening to me?" based on some tiny partial perspective of what is going on. Many things in life are inexplicable. Why are some people so good and yet horrible things seem to happen to them? Why are other people are absolutely obnoxious and yet they seem to have a wonderful life? If we were able to see the entire tapestry, a very different picture would emerge. This gives us a great sense of spaciousness.

The fact is that in the course of our myriad lifetimes, we have all done everything a human being can do, both good and evil, many times over. Sometimes we read about people doing appalling, inexplicably evil things and we might be tempted to think, "I could never do that!" Actually we have done such things many times in the past, so how can we judge anyone? However, the important thing is not what we have done in the past, but what we are doing in this moment. Are we present? What is our mind doing? Is it in a skillful space or an unskillful space?

Q: Is there a female Buddha?
TP: Well, Buddha-nature is neither male nor female. And of course we have all been females and males countless times. Whatever sex we happen to have in this life is almost arbitrary. Sometimes we are male and sometimes we are female, but the nature of the mind is neither male nor female. However, in the Mahayana school of Buddhism there are some—not many, but some—

very high bodhisattvas who might be considered "female Buddhas." For example, there is Prajnaparamita who is the Perfection of Wisdom. She is known as the Mother of all the Buddhas. There is also Tara, who is a very popular figure amongst Tibetans. She has many aspects, but she is like a mother because she is always reaching down to help, a bit like the Virgin Mary. She doesn't judge. You don't have to be a good person before she helps you. Like a mother, whether the child is good or naughty, she's there just because she is a mother. She's always there as a protector and a helper for all beings.

There are a whole group of female energy beings known as dakinis who are dedicated to removing obstacles and creating auspicious connections for practitioners. They are often invoked. The queen of the dakinis, Vajrayogini, is also considered to be like a Buddha. There are many practices centered on her. So yes, there are female Buddhas. They also represent the energy required for breaking through to higher spiritual levels.

Q: How important was your cave to your path?
TP: Well personally, I think a cave is just a cave, but the opportunity of spending so many years in solitary practice was very important to my particular path. For me to be practicing alone in that way was extremely helpful. My teachers recommended it to me. Solitary retreats are not helpful for everyone, of course. It depends on the person's psychological make-up. Some people space out, or become afraid, or overly introverted and unable to relate to others. But it was very helpful for me, and I'm grateful for having had the chance to do it. When I said goodbye to the cave, I thanked it for having supported me so much. But a cave is not a necessary part of everybody's spiritual path.

Q: I would like to know more about the question you asked the Dalai Lama in the video called *In the Spirit of Free Inquiry*. Could you relate that for us?
TP: It wasn't actually a question. This was during a conference in Dharamsala of Western Buddhist teachers from America, Europe and Australia. There were Zen teachers, Theravadin teachers, and Tibetan-style teachers. We all came together, about twenty-five of us. Every day we were with His Holiness for about four hours, which was wonderful. Different people were selected to make presentations on various themes. On the last day the theme was monasticism. I was asked to make a presentation about the problems and difficulties

for Western monks and nuns. I spoke out about the difficulties monastics experience in the West, where there is neither financial nor psychological support for them. That's what made him weep. And then he said, "Well we must do what we can to help." He was very supportive.

4
The Six Realms

MANY OF YOU, I'm sure, have seen thangkas of the "Wheel of Life." For those of you who haven't, they depict a big wheel held in the jaws of Yama, the Lord of Death. On the outer rim are the twelve links of interdependent origination. Inside that are the six realms of existence, and at the hub are three animals—a cock, a pig and a snake, each biting the tail of the one in front. They make up the inner circle. The cock represents greed, the snake anger, and the pig ignorance. According to Buddhist psychology, it is these three negative emotions which keep the wheel of samsara turning. It's our underlying ignorance about how things really are which projects greed and anger. In other words, the "I want" and the "I don't want" which govern the way we live. We spend our lives trying to get what pleases us and to avoid the things we don't like. These are the motivating forces which keep us chained to the wheel.

At the very bottom of the picture, you will see the depiction of the hell realms. Of course, nowadays many people don't believe in hell realms. Ironically, they still believe in heaven but consider the hell realms to be pure fantasy! I have my own views about this. As I was brought up a spiritualist, I feel at ease with a belief in other realms of being outside of this concrete material realm. But anyway, even in Buddhism, the hell realms are not necessarily considered to be physical places. In the *Bodhicharyavatara*, Shantideva says, "Who made the red-hot iron floors? Who made the demons tormenting the beings? All this is a projection of the perverted mind." Even if we don't believe in the physical reality of the hell realms, we can definitely believe that a mind filled with anger, which loves harming others and takes pleasure in cruelty, could easily project a paranoid environment for itself. The Buddhist belief is that after we pass on to other realms and lose the physical support which keeps us grounded here, the content of our inner mind is projected outward and becomes our entire reality. We already project quite a bit on this plane, but the extent of our projection increases once we lose our physical base. So if the mind is already filled with anger and sadistic pleasure in others' pain, that state of mind will be projected outwards and the person involved in it will respond in a paranoid way. We can get some understanding of hell realms right here and now. We all know people who are physically located in hell realms, such as those living in war zones. There are also people suffering from incurable and painful sicknesses, people in prisons, and people in asylums for the mentally ill who are tormented by their own paranoid fantasies. We know people living with partners who are extremely abusive and children living with abusive parents. These are the hell realms we all know about right here.

One of the big problems with hell realms is that the suffering is so intense that we become completely engulfed by it, rendering us incapable of action. For this reason, it is very difficult to break free. That's why so many women who live with abusive husbands can't break away. They're completely trapped in the relationship. There is a story of the Lord Buddha in one of his past lives. In this life, for some reason, although he was already a bodhisattva, he was reborn in hell and had to drag a very heavy chariot backwards and forwards. There was another person beside him, and they were yoked together. They had to carry this heavy chariot back and forth over red-hot pavement. There were guards on either side whipping them if they flagged. At one point, the Bodhisattva's companion collapsed. They were both very tired and weak because this goes on practically for eternity. Anyway, the Bodhisattva said, "You rest a while. I will carry this all by myself," because he felt so sorry for his friend. He said to the guards, "Let him rest a bit. I will carry it alone." The guards replied, "You can't do that. You're all the heirs to your own karma," and they hit him with a big iron-spiked ball. At that moment he died and was reborn in heaven.

This instant death and rebirth occurred because in that very painful, paranoid situation, it is almost impossible to generate a thought for the welfare of others, and yet the Bodhisattva managed to do so. For this reason he died and was immediately reborn in heaven. Hell is self-perpetuating and this is why it is so difficult to get out of it and why it is traditionally considered, although not eternal, to last for so long. Hell-beings are entrapped by their own paranoia. We can see this in our everyday lives. We can see this in people who are caught in deep depressions or in schizophrenia or paranoia.

The next is the realm of the *preta*, the hungry ghosts, or unsatisfied spirits. These are traditionally shown as beings roaming the surface of the earth, invisible to ordinary humans. They are usually shown with huge empty stomachs and very thin necks. It is said that even if they manage to get a morsel of food, it can hardly pass down this hair-thin neck. Even if the food manages to pass through the neck, the stomach is like a mountain. So a morsel of food is of little benefit to them. Others may be able to drink or eat, but the water they drink turns into pus or fire, and their food turns into disgusting, indigestible substances. In other words, they are always being tortured by their intense hunger and their longing for food and water. This is considered to be the result of stinginess. The Buddha said that if people only knew the results of giving, they would give continually. Even more so if they understood the results of not giving! We can also see hungry ghosts in our everyday lives. There are people who, no matter how much they have, inwardly always feel poor. They are perpetually looking to see what others have. Not only are they always wanting more and more, but they find it very difficult to give anything away unless they happen not to want it. It's very easy to give away something we don't want, like last year's fashions. It's much more difficult to give away something we like and value.

When I was very young, there was a man living opposite our house. The windows in his room were completely black because he hadn't cleaned them for probably about thirty or forty years. He shuffled around in rags. His room was absolutely bare, filthy, and very dark. He was a gentle person, but he was angry with his relatives. He hated them. He said he didn't want his relatives to have the pleasure of seeing him enjoy anything. It was a very convoluted way of thinking. When he died, they found stacks and stacks of shirts and suits still in their plastic wrappings and thousands of pound notes. These were concealed inside chairs, under the bed, under the floorboards, everywhere. Of course the moment he died, his family descended and took it all away. One could imagine that because of his inability to enjoy his own wealth or to share it with others, he might stay around the room as a kind of ghost haunting the place.

Sharing is very important. It is the opposite of a hungry ghost mentality. It's

noticeable in Buddhist countries that the people who give the most to char-
ities, who give the most offerings to the monks and nuns on alms rounds in
the morning and so on, are the poor people, or the emerging middle class. The
people who do not give are the more established middle class and the wealthy,
unless they give as a big show, inviting everybody along to rejoice in their
merit. We should be very careful to avoid miserliness. We need to learn to
open up the heart and be able to give wherever we see a need. This includes
even little things. Not just material things, but smiles, a nice word, time to
listen, sometimes just being there for others. This is giving, having a generous heart and not always thinking, "What can I get out of it? What's in it for
me? If I give that, then I won't have it for myself."

The third realm is the animal realm. According to Buddhist theory, this
realm is characterized by basic stupidity. I think this is a little unfair to animals. I don't think animals are as stupid as all that, but they do lack a certain
quality of self-knowing. They can't stand back and look at situations objec-
tively. They always become very subjectively involved in whatever they're
doing. Their biggest concern is getting something to eat. Have you ever
noticed how much time animals spend just eating and looking for food? They
also spend a lot of time sleeping and trying to keep themselves warm and
comfortable. Their other great preoccupation is procreation. This is not so different from many human lives, if you think about it.

Unless we develop the mind, we are not much better than animals ourselves. There are people who are totally concerned with their instincts, their
pleasures, and making themselves comfortable. There are so many people
who don't even try to develop the mind, who don't try to think, discrimi-
nate, or analyze. They go along with the crowd, creating pleasant situations
and avoiding painful ones, just like animals. Many of us are pretty much like
that. How to be comfortable? How to keep ourselves warm but not too warm;
cool, but not too cool? Comfortably fed. Nicely clothed. Everything comfortable. We are basically animals unless we develop that part of ourselves
which is distinctly human, by which I mean the mind. Animals think too, but
they are not capable of creative thinking. The potential to use the mind cre-
atively is the main thing distinguishing humans from beings in the animal
realm.

The next segment on the wheel is humans, but we'll come to those last.
The one after that is the realm of what are called the *ashuras*. These are demi-

gods. The demi-god realm and the god realms are iconographically depicted one above the other from the grossest to the most sublime. Just below the grossest of the god realms is the realm of the ashuras. They're also very beautiful, like the gods. Many of the female ashuras are captured by the gods. I haven't noticed male ashuras being captured by female goddesses, but anyway, the ladies are taken up from time to time. The main problem for the ashuras is the wish-fulfilling tree. The roots and the trunk of this tree are in the realm of the ashuras, so the tree gets all its nourishment from the ashura soil. However, the branches, and therefore the fruit of the tree, are in the realm of the gods. Consequently the ashuras are devoured by jealousy. They cannot appreciate all the good things they already have, and they do have good things because they are demi-gods. They could lead perfectly happy lives. But they do not permit themselves happiness because they are consumed by this competition against the gods to try to regain the fruit of this tree which they believe is rightfully theirs. And so they're always at war—the titans against the gods.

We can see this very easily in our own realm in the psychological patterns of people who already have more than enough. Because there's always someone who has more, they can't ever appreciate what they have. They're always consumed with envy for those who have more than they do, who have higher promotions or bigger houses or bigger cars, a larger income, or whatever. We can also see this happening in big business. I think many businessmen will be reborn as ashuras because they are always organizing takeovers and all kinds of deals. This is the mentality that is never satisfied. All of us slip into this ashura mentality sometimes. Whatever we have is just not enough. If we had what somebody else has, we would be happy. But even if we get it, of course it's not enough, because somebody else has even more—a newer model or a bigger one, or something like that. This kind of mindset torments many people, yet today it is considered a good thing, because it is the basis of our consumer society. We have to keep consuming. The only way to keep us consuming is to generate all these artificial needs, and the way to generate artificial needs is to point out that other people have these things and look how happy they are! All the advertisements assure us that if we had a bigger car or better clothes or a better brand of whiskey, we would be sublimely happy. Of course there's a part of us that knows this is not true. But another part of us is under such pressure to believe the myth that we tend to go along with it anyway. Our whole society is very much based on this ashura mentality of competition for material goods.

Recently I was staying in Singapore. In some ways, Singapore is sort of a god realm, but it's also very much an ashura realm because the whole society is based on competition. It's a very small island off the Malaysian peninsula, and it does not have any land to cultivate. It doesn't have any resources of its own. It's basically a small city-state. So it relies totally on trade and commerce, and this creates a sense of instability, because it knows that if for some reason business went elsewhere, its economy would collapse. No matter how successful they are economically, you will always hear people saying, "Yes, but Taiwan is doing better," or, "Malaysia is catching up with us." One day, I was driving with a Chinese friend who had a white Mercedes. We parked it, and when we came back there were eight white Mercedes all in a row. Everybody has white Mercedes because without one you're nothing. Unless, of course, you have an olive-green Rover, which is the second choice. Everybody seems to have three jobs. Meanwhile, children are committing suicide because they can't stand the pressure. This is very much the ashura mentality of competition, insecurity, fear, and resentment. The Singaporeans themselves are very nice people, but nowadays the whole structure of their society is geared towards this extremely stressful way of living. Yet at the time I was there, the government found themselves at the end of the fiscal year with a surplus of millions and millions of dollars, which they didn't know what to do with. What a problem! "What should we do with all these millions of dollars," they cried. And still they said, "That's very good, but we must not rest on our laurels. We must do even better next year because Taiwan is catching up."

At the top is the realm of the *devas*. This word is sometimes translated as "god," but *deva* literally means "a shining one," a being of light. It is related in the sutras that in the middle of the night, devas would often come and light up the grove where the Buddha was sitting and ask him questions. In Buddhist cosmology there are twenty-six different heavens. So no one can say that Buddhism is pessimistic. We have many more happy realms than miserable realms, actually! The heavenly realms begin with the grossest. The descriptions are written from the male point of view, so there are beautiful young gods with lots of lovely pink-footed nymphs serving them—every man's fantasy! Everything you wish for just appears spontaneously. The branches and fruits of the wish-fulfilling tree are located in the lower realm of the gods.

This is a bit like the Californian life-style, I always think. Beautiful homes, beautiful cars, beautiful children, hopefully beautiful bodies, everybody doing yoga or tai chi, everybody on healthful diets, everybody thinking positive thoughts.

Above this there are many levels, each more rarefied and more refined than the one below. Finally, we come to the realms that are the result of advanced meditational abilities. They correspond to various meditational levels. In those realms the gods are androgynous, neither male nor female. After this there are the formless realms, which correspond to the formless attainments like infinite space, infinite consciousness, neither perception nor nonperception, and so on. But however rarefied these states become, they are still within the realm of birth and death. However long we stay there, the karma which created the causes for rebirth there will eventually be exhausted, and we will have to descend again.

From the Buddhist viewpoint, the heavenly realms are not considered such good places to be reborn. Life is so pleasurable there that we have very little motivation to make spiritual progress. Instead, we just use up our good karma, which means that eventually we're left with only the bad. We saw that in the lower realms, there's too much misery for beings to think about spiritual progress, but in the higher realms, there's too much happiness. Both realms present equal impediments to spiritual growth.

California is like the deva realm. Many Tibetans who come here from India are convinced of this. But of course any realm which is wholly focused on youth, beauty, joy, and light is very fragile because life isn't all youth, beauty, joy, and light. Those who deny the shadow are in a very insecure and precarious position. To be exclusively in a deva realm and not recognize its precarious nature is a form of gross self-delusion. I remember a very nice lady from California who was a yoga teacher and a masseuse. When I first met her she was in her fifties, but she looked very youthful because she ate all the right things and did all the right kinds of exercise. She came to Nepal and was always talking about joy, love, and light. One lama used to call her the Bliss Cloud. Then she got sick. Everybody gets sick in Nepal. That brought her down from her cloud. Then she began to develop genuine compassion. It is hard to develop true compassion when you are continually blocking out all suffering from your own life.

From a Buddhist point of view, the best rebirth we can possibly have within samsara itself is the human realm, because we have this unique combination of joy and sorrow. We are able to see things much more clearly, and we have the motivation to go beyond all of it. What is more, in the human realm we have choice. We can choose how we will act, how we will speak, and how we will think. We are in training. Because of actions we have performed with body, speech, and mind in this and in past lives, we do not have much control over most of the circumstances which occur in this lifetime. But we can control our response to those circumstances, and in that lies our freedom. We can respond with negative roots or with positive roots. If someone shouts at us, we can shout back or we can try to deal with the situation more skillfully. If someone is angry with us, we have a choice. We can be angry in return or we can try to bring some understanding and patience into the situation. If we respond positively, we will attract more positive occurrences into our life. If we always respond negatively, we will create more and more negativity. According to whether we respond skillfully or unskillfully, we create our own future from one moment to the next. It's up to us. We are not computers. We are not completely programmed.

The main purpose of meditation is to create self-knowing and awareness so we can break through our patterning and respond with more openness, clarity, and understanding. Meditation is not just to make us feel peaceful; that's just the basis for further progress. Meditation is about arousing self-knowledge. Once we know ourselves, we can understand others. When we understand others, we can put an end to suffering. We can respond to everything with great skill. We can respond to others with respect and compassion. In this lies the importance of the human realm. This is our great opportunity. If we waste it, it might be a long time before we get it back again. It's here and now. It's not just in sitting, it's in everyday life, in everybody we meet, in every circumstance. It is up to us whether we act with awareness or with delusion. It is up to us whether we create further suffering for ourselves and for others or whether we gradually release this and create positive circumstances. That's what the Buddhist path is about—helping us to make the best of the opportunity that is our human life, not just when we're sitting on our meditation seats or visiting Dharma centers, but the whole of our human life, with all our relationships, our work, our social life, everything. All of it is within the province of Dharma practice. We really must not waste this chance.

5
Women and the Path

BEFORE WE BEGIN to look at the position of women in Buddhism, I think it is important for us to understand something about the social conditions prevailing 2,500 years ago in Magadha, central India, when the Buddha was alive. Unless we examine the context, we might fall into the trap of unfairly judging his decisions about women from the perspective of late twentieth-century California. In the time of the Buddha, Indian women were defined in relation to their menfolk. A woman was a daughter, a wife, or a mother, especially a mother of a son. Her relationships with her menfolk were what gave her standing in the community. Even in present day India, if a woman does not fulfill any of these female roles, she's regarded as a nobody. This is why women in India are often desperate to marry and have a son. This is the legacy of the early Hindu code known as the Law of Manu.

According to this point of view, a woman may attain *moksha,* or liberation, only through devotion to her husband. She is like a moon which can only be illuminated by the light of the sun. Like the moon, she possesses no radiance of her own. Therefore it is essential for a woman to marry. Without that she has no hope. In addition to this, women are socially very dependent on their menfolk. They will not even get onto a bus alone; they will always travel either with another female or a male relative. If they travel alone, they are likely to be harassed by men, because any woman traveling on her own is regarded as a loose woman. This is one of the problems faced even by Western women traveling within India. If the situation is still like that today, imagine how it would have been at the time of the Buddha! It is not surprising, then, that when the Buddha was asked by his stepmother, Mahaprajapati, to start an order of nuns, he was very hesitant to do so, and in fact said, "No." She requested this of him three times, and three times he replied, "No, don't even ask it." She was very upset by his refusal. When Ananda, who was the Buddha's attendant and also his cousin, asked her why she was weeping, she explained she was sad because the Buddha would not allow her and this large crowd of women to go forth into the homeless life.

Ananda took pity on the women. He went to see the Buddha and asked him to reconsider giving them ordination. Again the Buddha refused. Then Ananda asked, "Are women capable of leading the holy life and attaining liberation?" The Buddha replied, "Yes, yes, of course they are." Then Ananda asked, "So why are you creating an obstacle for them?" Then the Buddha said, "Okay, so be it," and he created the order of nuns. This is the only recorded occasion when the Buddha actually changed his mind like that. All of us nuns throughout the centuries have been very grateful to Ananda, because without his intervention, we wouldn't be here to tell the tale!

During the time of the Buddha there were very great female practitioners. Many of them attained the fruits of the path and were praised by the Buddha. They were praised for their wisdom, their learning and their skill in teaching. Over and over again in the early sutras the Buddha commended his female followers and disciples, and there is no doubt that many women at that time left their families and went into the homeless life. This was an extremely unusual thing for Indian women to do. Even today in modern Hinduism, while there are many thousands of sanyasins, mendicants, and sadhus, there are almost no female renunciates, because it is still considered that a woman's place is to serve the family.

It is important for us to realize how revolutionary it was for the Buddha to start this order of nuns. Many women rushed to join it. There are lots of stories about this in the early sutras. However, although there was at that time a female order complementary to the male order, there is no mention of an *arahati*, or a female *arhat*, attending the council of five hundred arhats, or perfected saints, held after the Mahaparinirvana of the Buddha. The members of this council were called upon to recite everything they could remember of what the Buddha had said and thereby to establish the canon. But there were no females in it, and one might ask why not? Obviously the Buddha must have given teachings to the females which he hadn't given to the males, but we have no record of what these were.

There appears to have been institutionalized bias against women right from the earliest times. I don't think anybody sat down and thought, "Oh, let us be biased." It's just that it was part of the prevailing social scene. As the years passed, everything was recited and recorded from the male point of view. I am sure this was not intentional, it was just how it happened. Because most of the texts and the commentaries were written from the male point of view—that is, by monks—women increasingly began to be seen as dangerous and threatening. For example, when the Buddha talked about desire, he gave a meditation on the thirty-two parts of the body. You start with the hair on the top of the head and then go all the way down to the soles of the feet, imagining what you would find underneath if you took the skin off each part; the kidneys, the heart, the guts, the blood, the lymph and all that sort of thing. The practitioner dissects his body in order to cut through the enormous attachment to physical form and see it as it really is. Of course, in losing attachment to our own bodies, we also lose attachment to the bodies of others. But nonetheless, the meditation that the Buddha taught was primarily directed towards oneself. It was designed to cut off attachment to one's own physical form and to achieve a measure of detachment from it; to break through any preoccupation the meditator might have about the attractiveness of his own body.

However, when we look at what was being taught later, in the writings of Nagarjuna in the first century, or Shantideva in the seventh, we see that this same meditation is directed outwards, towards the bodies of women. It is the woman one sees as a bag of guts, lungs, kidneys, and blood. It is the woman who is impure and disgusting. There is no mention of the impurity of the monk who is meditating. This change occurred because this tradition of meditation was carried on by much less enlightened minds than that of the Buddha. So instead of just using the visualization as a meditation to break through attachment to the physical, it was used as a way of keeping the monks celibate. It was no longer simply a means of seeing things as they really are, but instead, as a means of cultivating aversion towards women. Instead of monks saying to themselves, "Women are impure and so am I and so are all the other monks around me," it developed into "Women are impure." As a consequence, women began to be viewed as a danger to monks, and this developed into a kind of monastic misogynism. Obviously, if women had written these texts, there would have been a very different perspective. But women did not write the texts. Even if they had been able to write some works from the female point of view, these still would have been imbued with the flavor and ideas of the texts and teachings designed for males.

As a result of this pronounced bias, an imbalance developed in the teachings. I think that at a certain point, this imbalance was recognized. With the rise of the Mahayana, two things began to happen. One was that the main protagonist in several important Mahayana texts was a woman who proceeded to scold the monks for their very partial views and ask them where in the innate reality of our Buddha-nature lies the male and where the female. She would then go on to explain that the male and female dichotomy exists only at the relative level. At the absolute level, who is male and who is female? When we sit and meditate, where is the male, where is the female? There are texts in which these female protagonists sometimes even transformed themselves into males and back again. One of Buddha's chief disciples, Shariputra, renowned for his wisdom and regarded as the epitome of a perfect monk, was once transformed into a female. Then the female protagonist asked, "Who is Shariputra?" Then she changed him back again. In this way, these female protagonists attempted to break through gender stereotypes. They also did this by emphasizing the fact that female qualities, regardless of whether they are attached to a male body or a female body, are associated with a kind of intuition, a higher awareness known in Buddhist teachings as wisdom. Even in the earliest Mahayana texts, transcendental wisdom is portrayed as a female known as Prajnaparamita. As she is the Perfection of Wisdom, she is the mother of all the Buddhas. Therefore, in the early Mahayana sutras of Prajnaparamita, she is depicted as a beautiful matriarchal figure. Many scholars wrote prayers to Prajnaparamita, who was also known as the Bodhisattva of Wisdom. She was dearly loved. Much poetry was composed on the subject of her elusiveness. You could never find her, no matter how hard you sought her, because perfect wisdom is beyond the mind. By its very definition, it can be attained only where there is no thought. Writers played with this image in their praises of her like lovers seeking their elusive lady. In this way, an appreciation of the female was incorporated into the Mahayana philosophy. However, all the great commentaries and shastras were still being written by men. I can't think of any written by a woman.

At some stage, a new movement known as *tantra* appeared in India. Nobody is quite sure where it came from or exactly when it originated. This was a very interesting movement. I think part of its appeal arose from the fact that the goal of the Mahayana was to attain perfect Buddhahood, and, following the example of the Buddha, this takes three and a half incalculable aeons. Now an aeon is an immensely long period for attaining Buddhahood. I'm sure that at a certain point some people asked themselves, "Why bother? What can it matter what I do in this lifetime if I have an infinity of time and space before I can hope for accomplishment?" This thought can really dampen a person's enthusiasm. This new movement, on the other hand, promised Buddhahood within one lifetime. As a result, many people perked up and started practicing seriously again. It seems that some of the main instigators were women. The biographies of early Tibetan masters who went to India during the eleventh, twelfth, and thirteenth centuries often contained accounts of meetings with groups of women practitioners who always had a female leader. In these accounts, the Tibetan masters would beg and plead to be allowed to join the women in their rituals. Eventually, with great condescension, the women would relent and allow them to come in. Invariably the Tibetans remarked that this experience had been the highlight of their practice. Gyalwa Gotsangpa, the twelfth-century master, said, "Twenty years of living in a cave and eating stones was fulfilled all at once by being with these women."

We don't know who these women were because all the biographies were written from the male practitioner's point of view. Who were their teachers? What did they practice? Many advanced masters went to these women to seek teachings, and we don't know why. Their stories were never written down. But references to them appear again and again in the texts. And in the various texts it is recorded that these lamas traveled to different places, so they could not all have met the same group of women. What is more, these meetings cover a span of one hundred years. Who were these women? This is a question which often came to my mind as I read those texts. We do know that there was a significant movement which included women in India at that time. In those days, most Buddhist activity was centered in huge monastic colleges such as Nalanda, Vikramashila, and Taxila. They were enormous centers, the Oxford and Cambridge of their day. Thousands of students poured in from all over to study in these places. Many of the early tantric masters such as Naropa and Atisha were originally professors at these huge monastic universities.

Naropa was one of the principal professors at Nalanda University. At one time when he was studying his books, an old woman appeared and asked him,

"Do you know what you are reading? Do you understand the words of what you are reading?" And he replied, "Yes, of course I understand the words." Then she smiled and asked him, "Do you understand the meaning of what you are reading?" And he replied, "Yes, of course I understand the meaning." Upon hearing this she burst into tears, and he asked, "What's the problem?" She said, "When you said you understood the words, that's okay as far as it goes. When you said you understood the meaning, you don't have a clue what the meaning is." And he asked, "Well, who does understand the meaning?" And she replied, "My brother, Tilopa."

At that point, Naropa abandoned everything. He was a Kashmiri Brahmin and a very respectable professor. You can imagine the type. Yet he turned his back on it all and wandered throughout India in search of Tilopa until at last he came to Bengal. Eventually, of course, he found Tilopa, who was an old, black, wizened beggar sitting on the banks of the river, throwing live fish into a red hot pan and eating them. That was his guru! Much has been written about Naropa's discipleship under Tilopa. But what is significant for our discussion is the fact that there were so many great scholars seeking genuine experience at that time. They had to go forth from their cloistered environments and look for teachers who could give them the meditative methods to discover for themselves what they had been studying about. That is how the tantra began.

In those early days, tantra was kept very secret. You found your teacher and then you had to endure unimaginable trials before you were accepted. Later on still, tantra was carried to Tibet, where it eventually became the state religion. This it was never intended to be. It was outside the mainstream. There's no doubt that many of the early tantric masters were women. Some of the movement's early texts were in fact written by women, and those texts have survived up to the present day. One of the most interesting of these female teachers was known as Machik Drupa'i Gyalmo in Tibetan and Siddharani in Sanskrit. According to the texts, she lived for five hundred years, which really just means that she lived for a long time. She was a teacher of Rechungpa, one of the chief disciples of Milarepa. It is said that when he was in India, Rechungpa was told that he would die within one week. He went into total panic and asked, "How can I stop this?" Somebody advised him to go and see this woman, who had a very special practice for the Buddha of Long Life. So Rechungpa went to see her, and she asked him, "Can you stay awake for one week?" And he said, "Yes, I can do that." So she initiated him and gave him the practice. Then she asked him, "How long do you want to live?" And he replied, "I want to live to be the same age as my teacher Milarepa." So she said, "Well, he will live to be eighty-one, so you will also live to be eighty-one," which he did. Then she told him her story, which was fascinating. She's one of the few who actually has a story written about her, giving an account about whom she practiced with, what practices she did and so on. It's in the biography of Rechungpa.

However, the identities of many of the women who started lineages have been lost. We just don't know who they are. For example, even the great Mahasiddha Saraha lived for about fourteen years with someone known as "the arrowsmith's daughter." She was his guru. He was a very respectable Brahmin, but he abandoned everything to go and stay with this low-caste girl, becoming a social outcast as a consequence. She continually gave him "pointing out" instruction and guidance, and was his main guru. Although she was with him for fourteen years of his life, we still do not know her name! She was just referred to as "the arrowsmith's daughter." But who was she? Who was her teacher? Where did she come from? Everything is written from the side of Saraha, so she's like a mere prop in his biography. It's like this with almost all of these biographies. Rechungpa also met a group of women led by one Vajravarahi of Bengal. He took initiations from her, but again we don't know who she was.

In a place called Jvalamukhi in North India, Gotsangpa was walking past a temple one evening when he saw many very beautifully dressed young girls going inside. There were female guardians stopping any males from entering. His friend tried to get in, but the guardians beat him up. Then, while they were busy beating up his friend, Gotsangpa took the opportunity and rushed through the door. He doesn't tell us what happened once he was inside, but he does say it was the greatest experience of his life. Once again, we're left to conjecture. Who were the women? What were they doing in there?

Buddhism was imported into Tibet during the period of the final flowering of Indian Buddhism. Therefore Tibet, unlike many other countries which encountered Buddhist teachings much earlier, received the whole panorama of Buddhist thought right up until the twelfth century. This is why Tibetan Buddhism is so very rich and profound today. Not only did it receive all the philosophy through all the ages of Buddhism, it also received tantra. Now, while the tantra was in India it had remained quite marginal, in a way. It was not openly taught. If you wanted to practice, you had to leave the mainstream and find yourself a teacher. But when it was introduced into Tibet, first by Padmasambhava in the seventh century, and then later reintroduced in the eleventh and twelfth centuries, it became the state religion. However, tantra was always intended to be a secret practice for those who were qualified and willing to devote themselves entirely to it. But once it got into Tibet, everybody was initiated. There wasn't anybody who hadn't received at least initiations for Chenrezig, the Bodhisattva of Compassion, and Tara, the Mother of Compassion. Even little babies received long life initiations. There was scarcely anybody in Tibet who was not practicing tantra at one level or another.

Another departure from the Indian situation was that tantra was introduced to Tibet together with monasticism. This may be seen clearly in the Kagyupa lineage, whose first teacher in Tibet was Marpa, a householder yogi and a translator. His main lineage came through from Milarepa, who was a yogi living up in a cave, and not a monk. Then Milarepa passed it to Gampopa, who was a monk. After having practiced very hard, Gampopa went off and started a monastery. From then on, the Kagyupa lineage carried on in this way, as the Dharma has traditionally been preserved and transmitted through monastic communities. The monks were the professionals. They were the people with the time and the expertise. Of course, when such a hitherto secret practice was transplanted into a monastic environment, it was greatly transformed. One aspect of this transformation was that the role of the female, always the very essence of tantric practice, was sublimated or in some way changed.

In the original Tantras, the male represented skillful means or compassion while the female represented wisdom or insight. The union of these two would result in Buddhahood. So at the beginning, the female had a very exalted position. Even from the early Mahayana days, woman had always been seen as wisdom. She was Prajnaparamita. And as more than one lama has remarked to me, wisdom and compassion are seen as complementary, but everybody knows that wisdom is actually superior to compassion. On one level, then, women did very well because they represented the peak of Buddhist endeavor. However, because the tantric tradition was passed down in a monastic environment, problems arose, and although philosophically women were regarded as equal or even superior to men, in practice they were pretty much ignored.

If one talks about the inequality of women in Tibet, lamas will always say, "Oh, but what about Yeshe Tsogyal? What about Machik Labdron? What about this one or that one?" But you can count these women on your fingers. There's Yeshe Tsogyal, there's Machik Labdron. Already I've run out of names. Who else was there? There must have been somebody else. I'm being very honest here. The men are as numerous as the stars in the sky. But how many women did we have? What is more, even today, any woman who shows exceptional qualities is regarded as an incarnation of Yeshe Tsogyal, the consort of Padmasambhava of the seventh century. If any woman shows special qualities, she must be Yeshe Tsogyal, otherwise why would she have special qualities?

On the other side of this, the ordinary Tibetan word for a woman or a wife is *kye men*, which means "low born." So much for tantra's influence on Tibet! Nonetheless, it must be noted that in Tibet, as in Burma and other Buddhist countries, women are very strong. There were no harems or anything like that in Buddhist society. Women were not kept in purdah. If any of you have met Tibetan women, I'm sure you will agree that they are very outspoken. They often run businesses and travel around by themselves. They're very forthright with men, even complete strangers. In Burma also, the women are absolutely at ease in society and with the opposite sex. Now Tibet and Burma both lie between two countries which had such completely different examples, that is India and China, where the women, especially the higher class women, were kept largely removed from society. One has to think that this difference in the role of women in society can only have been due to the influence of Buddhism, because why else would it be so? Although the balance came out against the female in Tibet, it was not as bad as it was in most other countries, and women were very much out front, as they say. Nearly all the shops in Dharamsala, where the Dalai Lama lives, are run by women, whereas if you go to an ordinary Indian market, especially in a place which is predominantly Muslim, you don't even see any women.

Many of the men in Tibet became monks, but only a very small percentage of women became nuns. I find it puzzling, in a way, that a third of the male population in Tibet became monks, yet it was the custom to practice polyandry, which means that one woman marries several husbands. Usually she marries the elder brother first, and then she takes on the younger brothers as well. This means there must have been an enormous surplus of women without husbands. And yet there were very few nuns. But anyway, because it was in many ways a matriarchal system, with one woman and several husbands, the women were very strong.

There were many wonderful female practitioners in Tibet. There were great yoginis. One can only admire them; they were intrepid. They went to remote places, to caves up in the mountains, and they practiced and practiced. They were wonderful. But of course one never hears about them, because nobody wrote their biographies. Nobody considered it important to write the biography of some woman. It is not evident from the texts that there were many, but we know that there were. Even today, when lamas are giving teachings you will notice that a large percentage of the audience is always made up of women. Many lamas have said that women make superior practitioners because they are able to dive into meditation much more easily than males. This is because many males are afraid of dropping the intellect, especially monks who have been studying for a long time. To suddenly just let that go and be naked in the meditational experience is frightening for them, whereas women seem to be able to manage it naturally.

There were certainly many great female practitioners in Tibet. But because they lacked a background of philosophical training, they could not aspire to write books, gather disciples, go on Dharma tours, and give talks. When we read the histories, we will notice that nuns are distinguished by their absence. But this doesn't mean they weren't there. Even today if you travel to Tibet and go beyond the tourist trail into the regions where there are caves, you will find almost eighty percent of those living up there and practicing are women. When many Tibetans left Tibet in 1959 and came to India and Nepal, they were traumatized at finding themselves in such a different environment. Their first priority was to preserve their traditions. The lay people wanted spiritual centers for their communities, and because the lamas were male, they founded monasteries. A community without a monastery was regarded as having no heart. So in subsequent years they built several hundred monasteries and trained a whole generation of new monks. But in all this, of course, women were neglected.

When I first went to India in 1964, there was just one nunnery, which ironically had been started by an English woman. One Karma Kagyupa nunnery, and that was it. For twenty years it was probably the only Buddhist nunnery in India. Hundreds of monasteries were being built by the Tibetans, but nothing for nuns. And then, in the eighties, people began thinking about nuns. Often it was not the lamas, but Western nuns or other women who began to get the nuns organized. Before that point, any girl who became a nun usually ended up as a servant to some family, looking after somebody's children or working in the kitchen. It was a very difficult situation. When I was in Lahoul, I lived in a monastery which had both monks and nuns, and that was very nice. They all lived in their own little houses up the hill, but nonetheless, while the monks were in front doing the rituals, the nuns were in the kitchen cooking. And there were whole ranges of teachings to which the nuns were not admitted because "we do not teach this to women." Hearing this said again and again lacerated my heart.

"We do not teach this to women." No other reason was given. A friend of mine who was very intelligent, very enthusiastic, and a lovely person, was one of the nuns in that community. Her family had wanted her to marry, but she had kept putting it off. Finally they set the day. Then, on the day before her wedding was scheduled, she cut off all her hair. So then what could her family do? They had no option but to allow her to become a nun. She went and stayed with a wonderful lama, a family lama, who was teaching in these border regions. But even after all that, coming from a wealthy family and having given it all up, she ended up out in the kitchen making the meals while all the monks were out front getting Dharma teachings! Even though she traveled around with this lama and his family very devotedly for many years, she was always taking care of the children or doing the cooking. She was never given teachings. One often sees this kind of discrimination in the East, which no lama would dare to practice in the West where most of the people running the Dharma centers are women. You will never hear lamas in the West saying, "We do not give this teaching to women."

These days there is great movement afoot in certain quarters to try to redress the imbalance somewhat. We realize we cannot wait for the lamas to do it, although we have their goodwill. But as the head of my order remarked to me the other day, "Well, after all Ani-la, you know nuns are the bottom of the basket." So the only thing to do is for the nuns to organize themselves. They can't wait any longer. This is why I have been traveling around the world trying to raise funds for our nunnery. The lamas in my monastery at Tashi Jong have always been very supportive of our project and are doing everything they can to help us.

In my Lama's monastery in Tibet we had a very precious and unique lineage for women which was passed down from Milarepa to Rechungpa called the Oral Tradition of Rechungpa. It's a very large body of teachings, but one section is specifically about female yoga. There used to be a number of yoginis, or female practitioners of this lineage, in Tibet before the Chinese invasion, but it was all destroyed after the Communist takeover. Now we are trying to reestablish this lineage in India while there are still two or three lamas around who hold the transmission. You see, for a lineage to be passed on, it has to be a living lineage. It's an oral tradition as well. Although there are a few texts available, you still need to have the oral transmission and instructions. So we have started a nunnery where nuns can be trained initially in basic philosophy and ritual, and in particular, meditation. Those who prove suitable will then be selected for training in this yogini lineage. Along with this, we will also start an international Buddhist retreat center for women. Women from all over the world can come and practice, and we hope that in due time the nuns themselves will become teachers.

However, the situation for women is much better than it has been in the past. In 1995, at Dharamsala, sixty nuns debated publicly before His Holiness the Dalai Lama and many other great professors of philosophy. There were also lay people in attendance. The Tibetan tradition involves studying philosophy through dialectics, which is why debate is such an important part of the philosophical training. This was an historic occasion, because it was the first time in Tibetan history that nuns had debated publicly, and it was an enormous boost to their morale. It's probably hard for you to fathom how much this meant to them. It had a great effect not only on the public image of nuns, but on their own self-image. This is because they have internalized this sense of being unworthy. People ignore them because they don't believe them to be worthy of notice. Obviously, if you're always being told, "We don't teach you this, you're not important enough to have a nunnery, you're not important enough for support," naturally you're going to begin to believe that you are indeed unworthy. However, now that the nuns are starting to learn that they are just as capable as anyone else, they have developed enormous enthusiasm to practice, study, and accomplish. There is no reason why women cannot attain the highest goal. They have done so throughout history. In recent times, several very good nunneries have been established in India and Nepal, where nuns are studying the philosophical texts for the first time.

Today the West is making a significant contribution to the way the Dharma is presented. Every time the Buddhadharma travels to a new country, that country gives it something of itself. That is why each Buddhist country has its own unique national expression, so superficially it looks like Buddhism is quite different in different countries. But when you look below the surface, you see that the same heart is beating in them all. The Dharma is the Dharma, and it has a unique taste. So now the Dharma is coming to the West, and it will develop in a way which is suited to Western temperament, culture and needs. There are many perspectives which will be offered from a Western point of view, and one of them, undoubtedly, will be an appreciation of the feminine. There is no doubt that this is already happening. The omens are all quite positive. There is nothing that women cannot accomplish and have not accomplished in the past. It's up to us to support them and bring the two sides of the Buddhist community together as much as possible. It is time to appreciate the whole picture, instead of seeing only the lopsided view which has prevailed for some time.

QUESTIONS

Q: What is the meaning of the word *togdenma?*
TP: The words *togden* and *togdenma* are Tibetan terms for the kind of yogis and yoginis we were speaking about. In my Lama's monastery we have at the present time a group of togden. They follow the tradition of Milarepa and wear matted dreadlocks and white skirts, but they are monks. Back in Tibet they lived in caves, and they have their own unique way of practice. And back in Tibet, as we were saying, there were also female practitioners of this lineage, called togdenma. As far as I know, their practice was more or less the same, but there were also these unique lineages which emphasized the female aspect. I assume it has to do with the inner heat meditations and the yogic energies, written from a female point of view. Most of the texts are written from a male perspective and deal with the transmutation of the male energies. But togdenma all lived in remote locations and dedicated their lives to these yogic practices.

Q: Why are nuns held back to this day?

TP: I don't know, because it certainly isn't just the males' fault. I give as an example Lahoul, where I lived. Now it was the nuns, definitely second-class citizens in some ways, although very influential in others, who were discouraging other nuns from going on and learning more. Likewise, when a girl in India marries, leaves her home, and joins her husband's home, the people she has to fear are not only her husband or father-in-law, but her mother-in-law and sisters-in-law. They are the ones who are going to squash her and keep her in her place. So women's subjugation is not by any means just the fault of the males out there. Women have helped to create their own bondage and have also suppressed other women. If there is a girl who is very bright and trying to go forward, it's often other women who will pull her back. In the East you see this all the time, and I'm sure in the West it is also true. I mean you take someone like Hillary Clinton, who is very prominent figure, and who you would think is a feminist dream, yet the people who pull her down most are other women. Who was most vocal against the suffragettes in the last century? The answer is Queen Victoria. It's an interesting phenomenon.

Q: Could you explain in more detail the differences between the practices of the nun and the yogini?

TP: Well, the main practices for a monk or nun in a Tibetan monastery, for example, would be study and ritual. In the Tibetan cycle, as in a Benedictine monastery or nunnery, a great deal of attention is given to ritual, to performing the communal rituals together. In Tibetan monasteries, they meet at least twice every day, and large parts of what Catholics would call the liturgical year are given up to day-to-night rituals lasting maybe a week or ten days. These are set out throughout the year. The performance of ritual is very important in Tibetan Buddhism as it is practiced by Tibetans. On the other hand, the main focus for yogis and yoginis is in meditation and especially on the inner yogas, the manipulation of the energies, the opening of the psychic channels and things like this. And although sometimes monks and nuns might go off and do a lengthy retreat to practice these sorts of things, the yogis and the yoginis are the specialists. They're the professionals. They dedicate their whole lives to this, and they are not so much concerned with the happenings in the monasteries. That's the main difference.

Q: Why is the Buddha always male?

TP: Well, something inside me says, "Does it matter whether the Buddha was male or female?" He was an enlightened being, and his mind was beyond male and female. Obviously, throughout the times, there have been incredible females whose mind was also one with the Buddha, and of course in the tantric tradition there are many female figures, such as Tara and Vajrayogini. Vajrayogini, for example, is considered to be the mother of all the Buddhas. She is the symbol of this female energy. And in many ways the Buddha was sort of androgynous. Many great lamas have both male and female qualities. They are both a mother and a father.

In fact, the word "lama" means "high mother." "Ma" is feminine. It's not "la-pa." And as you know, the enlightened mind is neither male nor female. Once I asked my Lama, Khamtrul Rinpoche, "Why do you think there are not more female incarnations? Why don't you get reborn as a woman sometimes?" He said, "My sister had more signs at the time of her birth than I did, and when she was arriving everybody said, "Wow, this must be some really special being coming." But as soon as she was born, they said, "Oh we made a mistake!" You see, if she had been male, they immediately would have tried to find out who this child was, and he would have been given a very special kind of upbringing. Because she was only female, she was not given a chance. She had to marry and so on. This was the problem, that even if you came back as a female it would be very difficult to receive the kind of training and opportunities you could get as a male. I think things will start to change now. But that doesn't mean that her mind was not wonderful and that in her own way she could not have benefited many beings." One can benefit beings in many ways, not just by sitting up on a high throne. I'm sure that many bodhisattvas did take female form and benefited many beings, but not necessarily within the structured form of Tibetan Buddhism. I don't think it matters whether the Buddha is male or female. He transcends both in my mind. But if it helps you to think about female Buddhas, that's fine.

Q: Would you please tell us the story about the woman who gave His Holiness the Dalai Lama the hypothetical account of a female Buddhist hierarchy?

TP: In 1992, there was a meeting in Dharamsala called the Western Buddhist Teachers' Conference, which lasted for ten days. Four days were spent

with the Dalai Lama. Each day we had to give presentations on certain topics. One day, a woman named Sylvia Wetzel stood up in front of the Dalai
Lama and a whole group of Tibetan lamas. She said, "Now, your Holiness and
Venerable Sirs, I want you to do this visualization. Imagine that you are a
male and you are going into a temple. On the altar is the female Buddha,
Tara. Around the walls are thangkas of the sixteen female arahati, the female
saints, and then a large thangka of the lineage Lamas, from the Buddha to the
present day. Of course, all of these are female. In front of all the nuns, seated
upon the throne, is Her Holiness the Dalai Lama, who always comes back in
a female body, because that is superior, but who nonetheless has compassion
for all sentient beings. Now you, as a mere male, have to sit at the back behind
the rows of nuns, but don't worry about that, because we still have compassion for you, and if you try very hard and pray very deeply, you too can be
reborn as a female." She continued in that vein. At first the Dalai Lama and
all the monks went "Huh?" but gradually, as she was elaborating on this whole
picture, they began to see the point. And then they roared with laughter, but
also looked quite embarrassed. It was perfect because it did indeed show that
that's the way the monks think.

When I was the only nun in a monastery with eighty monks, the feeling
was, "Well, we like you anyway. And it's not really your fault that you—well,
it is sort of your fault that you got reborn as a female this time, but never
mind. Practice hard. Next time you can come back as a male and join our
monastery." And I don't think it ever occurred to them that I might not want
to come back and join their monastery. But, it's okay. It doesn't really matter.
I mean the Dharma is there, and we practice. And we should be grateful we
have a human birth. Male or female is really irrelevant.

Q: I would like to ask about child-rearing as a practice. When my daughter
was born, I felt that I couldn't practice as I was planning to. People kept saying, "Your child is your practice," which I certainly believed was true. However I couldn't find a meditation instructor who would instruct me in formal
practice. What would your advice have been?

TP: Well I have never raised a child, so I am talking off the top of my head
here, but it seems to me that so many practices are integrated into taking
care of a child. First of all, being present in the moment, being with the child,
really experiencing the child. Then, there's all these things like generosity,

giving, not just giving things, which is probably the least of it, but giving your time, giving your attention and practicing patience. There's effort and dedication because you can't leave a child. When children are annoying or when you want to do something else, you can't just put them outside the door like a cat, and forget about them. You've got them the whole time. They are always with you. Even when they are not present, you're thinking about them. Then, of course there's all this love, compassion, and caring for another being more than yourself. And at the same time, without attachment, learning how to have that open spaciousness in which the child can develop as a being in its own right, without your clinging to him or her. There are many, many things you can practice with a child.

Q: I hear many stories about famous teachers, and they all happen to be male. It makes me feel very disheartened and sad. And since I came into the Dharma in 1986, this feeling has been with me all the time. I know that I should go past that, because there is much I could learn in the Dharma, but it's still there. When I go into the shrine rooms, do prostrations and look at the lineage tree, it just comes up, and I ask myself why I was born a woman.
TP: Maybe because we need to have many great female practitioners. So you should get on with your practice and then you can really benefit the female lineage. If we want to have women teachers in the West, we need women practitioners. So it's up to you, ladies, to practice and pass on the fruits of your practice to others. There's no other way. Nothing is preventing you from realizing the Dharma. And having realized the Dharma, you can give it to others. There's no short cut. Now there are so many fine female teachers in America. And there will be more and more in the future, because when they have three or seven or twelve-year retreats, many of the retreatants are females. So when they come out of retreat, you should create an environment for them and ask them to come and teach. Actually, this is a very good time for women.

∽ 6

Shamatha, or Calm Abiding

As we outlined briefly in an earlier talk, there are two streams of meditation practice within Buddhism. Their Sanskrit names are shamatha and vipashyana. Shamatha means "to calm the mind," whereas vipashyana means "to look into the mind." Shamatha is usually translated into English as "calm abiding" and vipashyana as "insight." It means seeing clearly. There is a traditional example used to illustrate the differences between these two approaches to meditation. Imagine a lake surrounded by hills and snow-capped mountains. It is a clear mountain lake which reflects the surrounding mountains so accurately that it can be difficult to tell which image is the mountains and which just the reflection of the mountains on the lake's surface. But when this lake becomes agitated by the elements, various things happen. First of all, the surface of the lake breaks up so that it no longer reflects the mountains accurately. The image is still there, but it is distorted. In addition, because there are many waves and the surface is choppy, it is difficult for us to see into the lake to any depth. Not only is the surface of the water choppy, but the mud at the bottom of the lake is also stirred up. This pollutes the water, making it muddy and opaque. This state is very much like our ordinary everyday mind, which is continually being agitated by the winds of the six senses.

The six senses are sight, hearing, smell, taste, touch, and consciousness. In Buddhism, consciousness is regarded as the sixth sense. Our minds are constantly churned up by our thoughts and our emotions, by what we see, hear, taste, and touch. Because of this, they do not accurately reflect what is happening outside. In other words, when something happens outside, we immediately interpret it in accordance with our biases and prejudices. We do not see things as they really are, but rather as we interpret them. This happens so automatically that we are not conscious of what is going on. If you talk to a number of people who have experienced the same event, each one will describe it differently.

The individual nature of our experience is caused by our pre-existing views and prejudices. We distort whatever information we receive by means of our sense organs, just as the surface of the lake is distorted by the elements. If we try to look into our mind when it is so agitated, we won't see much. All we see is the surface chatter. However, if you were to take this mountain lake and allow the winds to calm down, the surface of the lake would eventually become still, like the surface of a mirror. It would then reflect its surroundings accurately. When we look into a clear and peaceful mountain lake, we can see right down to the depths. We can see the fish, the water plants and the rocks at the bottom. We can see all those shining pebbles on the lake floor. These lakes are so clear, they look as though they are only a few inches deep, but if you throw in a pebble, it goes way down. Likewise, when our minds are no longer disturbed by the winds of the six senses, the mind calms down and becomes clear.

When the mind is silent, we receive accurate information from the six senses. We see things as they really are, without distortion. In other words, the way they are before we jump in with all our judgments, biases, and mental chatter. We see things clearly and nakedly. By the same token, when we look below the surface, into the mind itself, we can see to very profound levels. The difference between shamatha and vipashyana hinges on this point. When the waters of the lake are calm, the mud sinks to the bottom, but it is still there. The weeds are still there. Any agitation will stir it up to the surface and the water will get dirty again. Likewise, when we practice only calm abiding meditation and go into deep levels of mental absorption, the mind becomes extremely clear. It becomes highly concentrated or one-pointed and very powerful. But the basic mental defilements are still there, although they have become quiescent. They remain dormant, like mud at the bottom of the lake.

After practicing shamatha and reaching deep levels of absorption, we will appear radiant from the outside. But we haven't addressed those underlying negative emotions yet. In fact, because the mind is now so much more focused and powerful, when those negative emotions are stirred up they will rise to the surface in a much more virulent form. If we read early Indian epics such as the

Mahabharata or the *Ramayana*, we will come across stories of *rishis*, or hermits, who have been meditating for centuries, sometimes for thousands of years. Their minds have become extremely controlled and powerful. They can remain in very deep states of meditation for centuries at a time. However, if somebody interrupts their meditation and rouses them from this state, their immediate reaction is anger, even fury. Because their minds are so powerful, they may even emit fire from their third eye to ignite the offending intruder. There are stories which tell of occasions when the gods felt threatened by these rishis who were developing such incredible mental power that they feared being overthrown by them. In order to defuse the power of a rishi, the gods sent along some exquisitely beautiful celestial nymph to tempt him. The rishi would open his eyes, see the irresistible nymph, and jump on her. Within a very short time, all his accumulated power would be consumed. It was like removing the lid from a pressure cooker.

The message for us is that even if we spend centuries in deep samadhi, unless we apply wisdom, we might end up worse than when we started. The Buddha realized this early on. After he left his palace, he went looking for a teacher. He found one. Then, when he had learned all he could, he left this teacher and moved on to another. Each of these teachers taught very advanced forms of samadhi or mental absorption, known as the "formless realms." During these meditations the mind passes through infinite levels of consciousness until it breaks through to a state of neither perception nor non-perception, finally reaching a level at which there is nothing whatsoever. Both his teachers taught that this state was liberation. The Buddha practiced these methods and quickly attained these levels. But he realized this was not really liberation. We have to come back down. This state is a very high, subtle level of the mind which will result in rebirth in extremely high levels of consciousness, but it nevertheless falls short of liberation.

After abandoning these practices and these teachers, the Buddha adopted asceticism for a number of years. But that also failed. Then he asked himself, "Where is this liberation? In what does liberation lie?" He remembered as a child watching his father, the king, ritually plowing a field during the spring festival. He had been sitting under a crab apple tree, and had quietly entered the first level of absorption. From this state he had turned his attention onto the mind itself. As he sat under the bodhi tree years later, he realized that was the way to liberation. He had rediscovered an ancient path which had been hidden from view, and he had come back to uncover it again. This was the path of vipashyana, the path of insight, which I will talk about later on. The important thing to understand is that shamatha is the preparation and support for developing vipashyana.

What is shamatha? A high Lama once remarked to me that if we have a strong shamatha practice, the whole of the Dharma is in the palm of our hands. If we do not develop shamatha, no practice will ever be really effective. This makes sense. Anything we do with a distracted mind will lack power; it simply won't work. When we are studying anything, we have to apply our minds. If we are writing a letter, working on a computer, or whatever, we have to give our minds totally to what we are doing. At a basic level, this is what shamatha is all about: doing whatever we do with the whole of the mind—not with part of the mind thinking about something else, but totally. If we give our mind fully to whatever we are doing, it becomes effective very quickly. But if we give only half our minds to it, no matter how hard we work on it, we just generate inner conflict.

It's very important for us to motivate ourselves before we start to practice. Otherwise, when the initial flush of enthusiasm wears off, the mind starts to become bored and easily distracted. For this reason, when people start shamatha practice, they are advised to do very short sessions. We have to be skillful and work with our minds, not against them. There are two ways to approach this. One is to sit for one hour or maybe even three hours and just stay with it. Regardless of what arises, we don't get up and run out of the room screaming. We just sit there and go through it. The other way is to say to ourselves, "Let's be kind to our mind. Let's work with the mind." After all, we have to make the mind want to concentrate. If we are reading a book we find excruciatingly boring, it will be very difficult to remember what it's about. There will be this inner conflict—a desperation in the mind to do anything rather than read this material, and so it's very difficult for us. There is "me," and then there's this book which I'm forcing myself to read. But if we are reading something which really fascinates us, we are not even conscious that we are reading because it's a joy. We put the book down when necessary with great regret and can hardly wait to pick it up again. We can achieve something similar with our practice. Some people tell me that because they have very active minds which have been intellectually trained, it's boring for them to meditate. This is a problem many of us share.

The way to get the mind interested is, as I said, to keep the meditation periods very short when we first begin. The reason for this is that the mind can retain interest in almost anything for a short time. If we over-extend, however, it begins to get restless. It does this even if it is interested, because it is not used to remaining focused on one point for an extended period. Then, when we try to meditate again, there will be inner resistance because the mind remembers it got bored last time. Whereas if we stop before we get bored, while we're still enjoying it, the mind remembers that it had fun before, and wants to do it again. Therefore it is often advised, at least in the Tibetan tradition, that our shamatha sessions be short but frequent. Short means whatever we feel comfortable with. Less than ten minutes would not be of much use. I think twenty minutes is about right. It takes about ten minutes just to get the mind to quiet down. If we stop the session as soon as the mind becomes quiet, it's too soon. However, if we keep on too long, the mind reaches its peak and attention starts to dissipate. If we stop it at that point, we've gone too long. It's really best to stop the meditation just as the mind reaches its peak and just before it begins to dip down. When you find the mind getting weary, you can stop for a few minutes, look around, then start again.

A one-pointed mind may be likened to a broad beam of light which is narrowed into sharp focus until it becomes like a laser beam. That laser beam, when it finally turns inward, can cut through many layers of the mind. If the light is diffused, it can only light up the surface without penetrating deep within. We are really trying to develop qualities which are already present and innate within our minds. We all have the ability to concentrate. We all have the aptitude for tranquility. We all have some experience of how this can work. If we are doing something which really interests us, we do not have to make much effort to concentrate. Look at people watching a football match, or a good movie. They don't have to be told to concentrate. The key is to develop that faculty of mind which we all possess and to use it when we want to, in the direction we want. Meditation is about training the mind. When we embark on a course of physical training, our muscles ache and it's hard work. But if we persevere by doing a little bit every day, eventually our muscles start to grow strong. We find ourselves doing things which a short while ago we would not have believed possible. Nobody ever sat down and immediately started to meditate, not even the Buddha. Everybody encounters problems when they first sit. We all start out facing a wild, undisciplined mind.

Some people complain that their minds become disturbed when they meditate. There is so much mental chatter and so many memories and so forth. They think that this problem is unique to them. But in reality, everybody has this problem. Every single body and every single mind. Those who succeed are not necessarily spiritual geniuses, but they are the ones with patience and perseverance. These are the two main qualities required to make progress in meditation. Since the day we were born, and probably for many lifetimes before that, there have been very rare moments when we have tried to tame our minds. We are not generally encouraged to do so.

Our minds have been saturated by information coming from the senses and by all manner of intellectual stimulation for so long. When we sit down and try to still the mind, relinquish all thoughts, and stay on one point, this is just not going to happen right away. It doesn't happen through just wishing. Very often beginners find that the mind is even noisier than usual. We tend to think it is worse than ever. This is because we are not normally conscious of all the chattering that goes on. So when we sit down and try to deal with it, we meet resistance. Everybody has the same problem. They have it now, they had it at the time of the Buddha, they had it five thousand years before that and ten thousand years before that. If we don't have one set of problems, we have another. That's why we need enormous patience. But if we are patient and just keep going, it eventually pays off.

How do we start? There are many methods for achieving this one-pointed mind. All of them work. The Buddha himself taught many different techniques, depending on the personality of the practitioner. It really doesn't matter; anything which enables your mind to become one-pointed and more concentrated is useful. I will go through two or three methods to give you an idea. The most commonly used traditional Buddhist practice, which can be found in all schools of Buddhism, be it Theravada, Zen, Tibetan, Chinese, or whatever, is the awareness of the in-going and out-going of the breath. We will talk about this because it is the method the Buddha himself used and through which he became enlightened. It is suited to all personalities, and we can carry it with us into every aspect of our daily lives. There are many variations of this practice. I will explain just one simple method. Many people teach that we should concentrate on the inhalation and exhalation of the breath. This conjures up a picture of standing back from the breath and looking at it. But actually we need to become one with the breath, to become the breathing in and the breathing out, to not make this division between self and breath.

One of the problems we Westerners encounter in meditation is that on the one hand, we have the object of meditation, and on the other hand, we have ourselves trying to meditate upon it. Right from the start we have this dichotomy. There is me, and there is the practice, and I am going to do the practice. It's like two mountains facing each other. And then people wonder why they don't make progress. We need to dissolve the boundary between the subject and the object. In other words, we have to become the meditation. Once we become the meditation, the results come immediately because the mind merges with its object. If we keep the mind separate from the practice, it's never going to come together, no matter how long we do it.

When we are doing a practice involving the breath, for example, we should drop all thoughts about the breath. We are the breath that we breathe in, we are the breath that we breathe out, and there's no separation. If we can do that, we will attain levels of peace, tranquility, and one-pointedness very quickly. The importance of developing the one-pointed concentration is that the mind becomes very malleable. Some people claim that a mind that is one-pointed and concentrated becomes rigid. But this is a curious idea. Actually, when the mind is totally concentrated and absorbed in its subject, it becomes soft and fluid. If you want the mind to think this, it thinks this. If you want it to think that, it thinks that. It's just like a body. If a body is rigid, it can break. But if the body is supple, even if it has an accident, it is not hurt so easily. It can recover. Likewise, if our mind is supple and pliant, it will be able to cope with extreme traumas and difficulties. On the other hand, if the mind is stiff and rigid, it will snap.

We need to develop a mind which is tranquil, one-pointed, and tamed. Then if we want to take that mind and apply it to this or that practice, it can adapt easily and the results will come quickly. We can say mantras for a million years, but if our mind is not one-pointed and fully absorbed in what we are practicing, they will have no effect. On the other hand, if our mind is fully absorbed in our practice, even a few mantras will be effective. First we have to learn how to make our minds workable. The Tibetans use the word *le su rung wa* which means exactly that, workable. The mind has to become workable so that it can accomplish whatever task we present to it with ease. This is what shamatha is for. It is not the goal in itself. The goal of Buddhist meditation is not just to be peaceful or happy, or even just to be concentrated. But if we have a peaceful, concentrated, supple mind, we can use it as an instrument to develop wisdom, compassion, and understanding. Practicing shamatha is all about learning to use the mind. We all want to be peaceful, happy, compassionate, and kind, and we find ourselves agitated, stressed, irritable, and frustrated. We all have the potential to have a peaceful, happy, patient, and wise mind. But we have not exercised this potential. Shamatha works with the mind in this way. It makes the mind malleable so that we can use it to benefit ourselves and others. But it takes time.

If we really apply ourselves, it can be extremely helpful. If we hear a sound, it's just a sound, let it go. If thoughts arise, they are just thoughts, just waves on the ocean of the mind, let them go. Don't give them any energy. The important point with shamatha is not to be curious. Curiosity belongs to insight meditation. First we are just concentrating on getting our minds quiet and one-pointed. If we become fascinated by the content of the mind, the mind will get distracted. So we don't do that. Nothing in all the world is more important at this moment than being one with the breathing. That's all we have to do.

Practicing shamatha, even for short periods at a time, is beneficial. If the mind begins to get restless, we can open our eyes, look around and then come back to the meditation again. The mind gradually begins to understand, and we can train it progressively. It begins to remember that all it has to do during the meditation is be with the in-going and the out-going of the breath. We are intelligent beings, and the mind can learn. At the moment the mind is learning how to be distracted, how to think, how to intellectualize, how to rationalize. The mind has had a lot of training in the art of chatter. Now it has to be reprogrammed. This takes time and patience, but it can be done. When the mind begins to experience and appreciate peace and tranquility, it starts to generate its own enthusiasm, provided we don't push it too hard.

One of the advantages of using the meditation on the incoming and outgoing breath is that we take the breath with us everywhere. We are always breathing. So even during the day, and especially when we are feeling stressed, we can bring our attention back to the inhalation and the exhalation of the breath. That's all. We don't have to think about it, we don't have to do anything with it. We don't have to judge whether it's nice breath or nasty breath. We just breathe ourselves out and breathe ourselves in. We can do this all day.

We have countless opportunities during the day to bring ourselves back to the breath and get ourselves centered. We should be grateful for this.

Another way of generating one-pointedness is to give the mind lots of things to do, instead of trying to empty it. Tibetans are fond of this. Personally, for most Westerners, I think emptying out is a very good idea, because our minds tend to accumulate so much junk as it is. It is nice to have a chance to let some of it go. We can think of our mind as a garbage heap and slowly start throwing out some of the garbage. This other method involves making our thinking extraordinarily complicated, but in a disciplined way. In Tibetan Buddhism this entails doing extremely intricate visualizations of mandalas, deities, lights, mantras, and this sort of thing, which totally occupy the mind so that there is no room for distraction.

I remember being given a practice in which we had to visualize one hundred and twenty-four deities, all in consort relationship, all with six arms and three heads. None was synchronized with the others. They were each holding different things. The consorts were all different colors from their partners. And all of them had to be seen in an area which was between the top of the skull and the hair line. At the same time, they all had to be seen inside the heart of a small deity sitting at the center of one's chest. All hundred and twenty-four at the same time. That's actually two hundred and forty-eight. By the time I went to see my teacher, I was cross-eyed. He told me to try to see them as clearly as possible. "If you can visualize them clearly," he told me, "your mind will become high and vast." He told other people to think about it just vaguely and roughly, but I wasn't lucky enough to get that instruction. I was told to see them very clearly. So I really tried. I remember throwing myself into this totally impossible task and really trying to see all these infinite mandalas within a space the size of a pin head. Of course, my mind became totally immersed in its impossible task. Trying to do this gave me a lot of energy. I wouldn't say my mind became vast and wide, but it did develop a kind of clarity. So this the other method. We either occupy the mind totally or empty it totally. For some people one works better, for others, the reverse. Sometimes it's good to alternate between the two. Tibetans usually alternate. We'll go into this more when we deal with Vajrayana.

Right now we are dealing with more straightforward kinds of shamatha practice. Again, as they say, the important thing is to understand why we are doing this. Of course we would all like to be more peaceful and happy, and that is not a bad motivation for learning to meditate. But it's not the ultimate motivation. The ultimate motivation is to become enlightened. Being enlightened means uncovering our infinite potential for wisdom, compassion, purity, and power in the sense of infinite energy. We actually possess all of this. We just have to uncover it and discover what lies within us. The way to do this is to meditate.

Why do we want to be wise and compassionate? If it's because we would simply like to be wise and compassionate, we are off course, because the "I" cannot attain wisdom and compassion. Wisdom and compassion can only be revealed once the "I" has disappeared. When we reach this level, we will be able to benefit others. In the meantime, it is the blind leading the blind. All true religions seek to gain access to that level of consciousness which is not ego-bound. In Buddhism, it is called the unconditioned, the unborn, the deathless. You can call it anything you like. You can call it atman. You can call it anatman. You can call it God. The fact is, there is a subtle level of consciousness which is the core of our being, and it is beyond our ordinary conditioned state of mind. We can all experience this. Some people experience it through service, others through devotion. Some even think they can experience it through analysis and intellectual discipline. Buddhists usually try to access it through meditation. That's what we are doing. Breaking through to the unconditioned in order to help others break through to the unconditioned. But we have to start where we are, from right here. We start with these minds, these bodies, these problems, these weaknesses, and these strengths.

We are each unique, yet our underlying qualities are strikingly similar. When people sit, they face two basic problems: either they become extremely distracted or they become sleepy and slothful. If our minds become too active, and this is a continual problem, we are usually advised to calm down. The methods for achieving this include sitting in a warm room, closing our eyes, eating heavier food, and by various means trying to bring the mind to a state of greater relaxation. The essence of meditation is to induce a mind which is totally relaxed and at the same time totally aware. If you get into a lovely, dreamy, peaceful state where you don't want to move and you feel you could just sit for hours, completely blissed out and peaceful, but in a vague fog, you have gone completely astray. It is very easy to do this. It feels very pleasant. Some people even think they are approaching samadhi, but actually this is a state known as mental dullness.

If the mind is distracted, we have to learn to relax it. Just think of dropping everything and keep the eyes down. It is said that it also helps to eat a little. That grounds the mind, because blood goes to the stomach, rather than up to the brain. On the other hand, if we have the problem of becoming sleepy, the answer is to be in a slightly cool place, keep the eyes open, and eat very lightly. Sometimes it is also helpful to stare into space. If the mind is distracted, one can visualize a black spot at the abdomen. Black dulls the mind. Also, bringing the mind down to the abdomen tends to make the mind more stable. If the mind is too sleepy, one can visualize a white light at the center of the forehead. This raises the mind and lightens it. Somebody I knew who had a continual problem of sleepiness during meditation dealt with this by sitting on the edge of a well. He soon stopped feeling sleepy! Even Milarepa had this problem. He used to put a lighted butter lamp on his head. A friend of mine used to meditate with a bowl filled with water on top of her head. This straightens the posture and reduces the likelihood of keeling over.

The important thing is for the mind to be relaxed but alert. If you find that your mind is becoming more and more awake and more and more alert, it is like finding something inside you unfolding, waking up and becoming much more light and spacious. Then you know you are on the right track. After all, this is all about waking up. The word Buddha means "Awakened One." Anandamayi Ma, who was a very great Bengali Hindu saint, said it doesn't matter what meditation stage you get to, if you do not have clear awareness, it is the wrong state. The important thing is to maintain this awareness, consciousness, or knowing. This is enormously important in meditation.

We need to develop a balance. The Buddha said that if you take a stringed instrument and tighten the strings too much, you will produce a harsh sound and the strings might even break. On the other hand, if the strings are too loose, they don't make any sound at all. You have to tune your mind as you would tune an instrument. Not too tense, and not too slack, but just right. Balanced. It's like being on a surfboard. If you are too tense or too loose, you will fall off. You need to be poised. If you have that balance, then no matter how high the waves are, there is no problem. The mind is like that. We have to attain that level of balance.

It is also very important to have a regular time to meditate. I don't really have time to go into this now. I am not talking about shamatha from the point of view of your own practice, because you can always go to teachers to learn the methods. This is just a general overview. However, it is important for all practitioners to have a regular time and place to practice. We are creatures of habit. If we do the same thing every day, we get into the habit very quickly. We get up, we go to the bathroom, then we do our practice. We sit down, we light incense or whatever. Very soon, the mind begins to remember this is meditation time. It settles down quickly because it remembers what to do, whereas if we keep switching the time around, meditating a little bit here and a little bit there, then again and again we have to keep reminding the mind what this is all about and it takes longer to settle down, at least at the beginning. We should try to establish a rhythm. It's good to do even ten minutes at a regular time if you cannot manage more than that.

In the early morning just after you get up, if possible, sit for ten minutes, twenty minutes, half an hour, an hour, however much time you can give to it. It is good to start the day by centering yourself. Bring the mind into the room, into the body. First connect with the body, then connect with the breathing in and the breathing out. It doesn't matter what your religion is or if you have no religion, this has nothing to do with that. It's dealing with how to come to terms with our mind. It's also a very good idea to sit for a while before we go to sleep at night, and if we have time, review the day. How aware were we during our day? How kind were we? What did we do that we think was nice? What did we do that we think was perhaps not so great? We are not judging, just having a look at it. What have we actually done with our day? Then we make the resolve to do better the next day, to become more aware, more conscious, more kind, more patient. And then we just sit for a while with our breath. Five minutes, ten minutes, just being with the breathing in and breathing out. Emptying our mind, letting it all drop away. Just being present.

We need to ask ourselves what we are doing with our lives. What we are doing with our days. What we are doing with the hour. What we are doing with this moment. Nobody is stopping us from meditating. Nobody is stopping us from becoming Buddha. We are stopping ourselves. We are dealing basically with mind practices, because in the end, everything is our mind. Whether we are happy or sad, whether we are peaceful or agitated, it's nothing out there. It's in here. We cannot transform the world, but we can transform our attitude to the world. Once we have transformed ourselves, that will have ramifications for everything around us.

Once when I was in Switzerland, I spent time with some Catholic monks and nuns, Jesuits and others. They have a large institution in Zurich. The founder of this institution and also the people who are working with him, the nuns and monks, spent many years in Japan studying Zen Buddhism. Now they are in Zurich, where they have been for many years. They are very well known in Switzerland. Originally their area of influence was in human rights and helping drug addicts and street people. But now their main concern is teaching meditation to economists, politicians, bank managers, and a lot of top people working in the United Nations and so forth. Their belief is that these people should learn how to access their own wisdom mind and their own clarity and calm, because they are the ones who control the economy and the world political situation and can therefore do tremendous good. I asked them how successful this program was, and they said it was successful beyond their wildest dreams. These monks and nuns are organizing lots of courses and programs which are attended by hundreds of people. These people have great enthusiasm to learn how to practice meditation, even just to lower their stress levels, to develop more peaceful minds. This is not a selfish practice which helps only the individual. It has vast benefits. As long as we are entrapped within our own ignorance, greed, and anger, everything we touch is polluted. If we want to save the world, we have to save ourselves first.

Now I would like us all to sit quietly for about fifteen minutes. If your mind has strayed away, bring it back into this room. Then bring it into the body. If there are sensations in the body, just note them. Don't comment on whether you like them or dislike them. Just know that they are present. Know the body. When you have become settled in knowing the body, bring your attention to the in-going and out-going of the breath. Just be one with the breath as it flows in and flows out. Don't try to make the breath longer or shorter. This is not really concentrating, in the sense that we are not looking at the breath from a distance. We are just becoming one with the breath, knowing it as it comes in and as it goes out. When thoughts arise in the mind, don't be concerned. It is the nature of the mind to have thoughts. Don't give them any energy. Don't get caught up in them. Ignore them. If people try to attract our attention and we ignore them, eventually they will give up and go away. Thoughts may come and go, but we are not interested in them. We just bring the attention back again and again to breathing in and breathing out. We will do this for about fifteen minutes. When sounds occur, they are just sounds, just vibrations moving across space. No problem. Sounds are naturally there, and it is natural for the ear to hear them. Don't give them any energy. Go back to the breath.

Questions

Q: What do you suggest for people who have breathing problems?
TP: If a person is having problems with his breath, some other form of meditation would be more appropriate. There are so many methods. The breath is very accessible for most people. But some people who are highly stressed experience a lot of agitation focusing on the breath, even if they are not ill or dying. In such cases, it would be more appropriate to do some other kind of visualization or concentrate on something else, like light, or whatever. Christians might visualize Jesus, for example.

Q: Would you tell us something about meditation posture?
TP: The back should be straight, the shoulders back, but at the same time relaxed. Although the spine is straight, the weight should be low, not up in the shoulders. It's very important to support the weight just below the navel, rather than hunched up in the neck and shoulders. The back is kept straight even if you are sitting in a chair. It is important for the feet to be flat on the ground. Don't lean back in the chair. The hands should be either joined in the lap or resting lightly on the knees. With regard to the eyes, there are many different ideas. Some people think it's okay to gently close the eyes. The Tibetans and the Japanese insist that the eyes should be slightly open and focused a few feet ahead. Drop the eyes slightly and look down the nose. This gives you the position at which the eyes rest. They say if you close the eyes, it darkens the mind. In the beginning it might be more difficult to practice with the eyes open. But of course, you do not focus the eyes. Eventually you will find that it is better to leave your eyes open if you can. This also prevents too much inner fantasy from taking place. In Buddhism, we are not trying to dissociate ourselves from the senses, but just let the senses flow without responding to them. We are aiming for a meditation which flows, without any clinging. If you hear or see anything, just let it go. Don't try to close things off, though.

Q: How does one calm the mind if one is angry?

TP: There are a number of ways. Traditionally, one does a meditation on lov-ing-kindness. The idea is that we replace one mental state with its opposite. So if we are feeling angry at someone, we sit and generate thoughts of loving-kindness towards him. We start by generating thoughts of loving-kindness towards ourselves. Then when that warmth, that sense of acceptance even of the anger, arises in the heart, you can give it out to others. Another way, depending on what kind of meditation we are doing, is to look at the anger itself. First you quiet the mind. Then you look at the anger to see what it feels like. Where is it? What is the physical reaction to it? What is anger? When we say "I am angry," what does it mean? How does it feel? That's one way. Another way is to replay what made us angry and observe it from a dis-tance, the way we would watch a movie. Then try to see whether we can replay that scenario in a different way.

Anger is a very interesting emotion because we usually want to get rid of it. In this way it is unlike desire and attachment, which most people, pro-vided they can fulfill their desire, are happy to have. Anger hurts us. It often doesn't hurt the person we are angry with, but it hurts us, and we don't like it. It makes us feel uncomfortable. So therefore, we want to get rid of it, which is good. I am not saying this is bad. But our motivation is that we don't like it. There are an infinite number of ways to deal with anger. Another way is to realize that patience is one of the very greatest qualities to develop on the Buddhist path. The Buddha praised patience again and again. It is one of the qualities required in order to attain Buddhahood. Now unless there is some-one around who irritates and annoys us, we can never learn patience. If every-body is lovely towards us, if they all say and do just the right things, this may make us feel great, but it will not give us the opportunity to extend ourselves. So people who annoy us, who do things against us, who hurt us, far from being a cause of resentment, should be a cause for enormous gratitude. These peo-ple are really our helpers on the path. These are the people who enable us to develop our spiritual muscles. They give us the opportunity to practice under-standing and patience. They are our gurus. If we have this attitude towards people who drive us crazy, it transforms the whole relationship. Instead of being an obstacle, they become our great opportunity. You see? It is all in the mind. The outside world hasn't changed at all, but our mind has changed. This is the whole point. It is not about changing people and situations, it is about changing ourselves. This includes anger towards ourselves, of course, which is extremely destructive and useless. We need to have lots of compassion and patience towards ourselves, because we are also suffering sentient beings.

Q: Do you think it is necessary to get rid of desire?

TP: It depends what you mean by desire. Desire for enlightenment is a good desire. We don't want to get rid of that. The problem with ordinary desire is that it fools us all the time. We always imagine that if we can just satisfy our desires, we will be happy. But worldly desires are like salty water. The more you drink, the thirstier you get. The problem is not so much the desire itself, but our attachment to it. You can live in a palace, you can live in a mansion, you can have ninety-nine Rolls Royces. And if you don't care about them, if you lost them all tomorrow and said "so what," that's fine. But if it really troubles you and you spend all your time trying to get things, defending them, trying to stop others from taking them, trying to get more and more, then that's a big problem. It's not what we have and how we enjoy it that's the problem. The problem is the way we cling to things, and our inability to let go. That includes people.

Of course we can enjoy relationships. But the person we have a relationship with may leave us or die—this is the nature of things. We are all going to have to leave one another at some stage. How we react to that is the point. It is about whether we are able to hold our experiences and possessions lightly, so that when they come it is a joyful thing and when they go, that's also okay. But if we hold onto things tightly and are distraught when we lose them, this is a problem. What holds us to the wheel of birth and death, to this state of delusion, is the fact that we hold onto things. We are not bound to the wheel. It is we who grasp it tightly with both hands.

There is a story which is often told about a particular way of trapping monkeys in India. There is a coconut with a little hole in it. Inside the hole, which is just big enough for a monkey's hand to fit through, there is a sticky piece of coconut sweet. The monkey comes along, puts his hand through the hole and grasps the coconut sweet, because he can smell it. He forms his hand into a fist to grab the sweet, but when his hand is in a fist, he cannot get it out. Then the hunters come and take him. Nothing is holding the monkey there. There is no trap. All he has to do is open his hand and he could get away. He is held there only by his desire and attachment, which will not allow him to let go. That's the way our mind works. The problem is not the coconut sweet. The problem is that we can't let go. Do you understand? The problem is not what we have or don't have, but how much we cling to things.

There is another story about a king who lived in ancient India and had a large palace with a harem full of beautiful girls. He possessed many jewels and gold and silk fabrics. He had a huge treasury. He had a guru who was a Brahmin, and the only thing this Brahmin possessed in the world was a begging bowl made from a gourd. One time the king and the guru were sitting outside in the garden under a tree, and the guru was giving teachings to the king. Then a servant came running towards them, shouting, "Your Majesty, come quickly, come quickly, Maharaja. Your whole palace is on fire!" The king replied, "Don't bother me. I am taking teachings from my guru here. You go and attend to the palace fire." But the guru jumped up and cried, "What do you mean? I left my gourd in the palace!"

Do you see? It's not what you own that is the problem. The problem is how much you are attached to it. The problem is not so much desire, but clinging. If you want to hold water, you have to hold it with cupped hands. If you make a tight fist, it runs away. Clinging and attachment bring us great suffering. We think attachment is love, but it is not.

Q: How can we develop patience and compassion towards ourselves?
TP: I think we have to realize that patience and compassion are for all sentient beings, and we are also sentient beings. As it happens, we are the one we have responsibility for right now. If we don't have patience and compassion towards ourselves, for our ignorance, delusions, stupidity, anger, and greed, we are not really going to be able to have compassion towards others either.

7
Vipashyana, or Insight

THIS TALK CONTINUES the theme of meditation begun on the previous talk. Now we are going to discuss vipashyana. As I mentioned, shamatha makes the mind focused and single-pointed. Vipashyana uses that one-pointed mind to focus on the mind itself. Maybe I should begin with a short anecdote. This is apparently a true story, told to me by an old Tibetan yogi who was my meditation teacher when I was first in India. He told me that when he was in Kham in eastern Tibet, one of his disciples was a Tibetan trader. This trader used to take salt to China and then from China he used to bring back tea. He was very keen on mahamudra meditation, but he especially enjoyed the tranquility of shamatha practice. The yogi would say to him, "Now it's time for you to change. You've done enough of that. You should move on to insight practice." Of course, insight practice requires us to think. We have to analyze and look inwards. But the trader wasn't interested. He wanted to remain in this peaceful and blissed-out state, so he just carried on with shamatha.

Once this trader was traveling to China with his friends. One day, they came to a large forest where they decided to settle down and have some tea. The trader went off to look for wood. While he was wandering around collecting branches and twigs to make a fire, he decided to sit down for a few moments and do a little meditation. He sat down and went into what is called samadhi. This is a very profound state of absorption, almost like a trance. In the meantime, his companions were waiting for him. They started calling him, but he didn't answer. They looked everywhere for him, but couldn't find him, and finally they gave up and made camp for the night. The next morning they looked again, but to no avail. They thought he might have been killed by wild animals. In any case, they couldn't remain there searching for him forever. Regretfully, they continued on their way to China. There they did their trading, bought their tea and headed back home. A year later, they were back again, in that same forest. They decided to try at least to find some of the lost man's clothing which may have been left behind. By this time they were certain their friend had been killed by wild animals. Again they started looking around the area. They found him, still sitting in meditation. They shook him. He opened his eyes and said, "Oh, is the tea ready yet?" When they explained that a whole year had passed since they had stopped for tea, he was shocked. He realized that he had just wasted a year of his life. That kind of absorption is of no benefit. Some religions think it is remarkable for people to remain for months on end in this trance-like state, but the Tibetans disagree. They call it "frozen meditation," and regard it as useless. After his experience, the trader was eager to develop insight and stopped playing around with these heavy, tranquil states.

Say that we have been doing shamatha for a while now. Our minds are peaceful and focused. When we want to focus on the breathing, we stay on the breathing. When we want to stay on the visualization, we stay on the visualization. Our minds are becoming trained. If we go back to the early teachings of the Buddha, we learn that he made this progression from shamatha. It is not the end, but it is a very important beginning. Nowadays most people don't have the conditions for this kind of practice, which requires a very tranquil, safe environment and lots of time. Because such conditions are so rare nowadays, there is a whole movement emphasizing vipashyana meditation to the exclusion of shamatha. This is also known as "bare insight." In other words, we just practice insight meditation right from the start without ever learning shamatha. The problem with this is that, because our minds are so ill-trained, it is very difficult for us to achieve any deep level of insight. All we ever see is the thoughts bubbling away. Earlier we discussed the example of a lake. Trying to do vipashyana without the preparation of shamatha is like trying to look into a lake agitated by waves. The surface is choppy and broken up and the water filled with mud. It is difficult to see to any depth.

So although it takes time, it is worthwhile to at least try to quiet the surface waves of our mind and develop some ability to focus. This is how it has always been done. There is another profound reason why we are supposed to develop calm abiding first and then seek to develop insight. Insight meditation is intended to peel away the layers of the ego. If we begin such a practice while our egos are in a fragile state, we can end up becoming more neurotic, more disjointed or even more psychotic. In order for us to reach a state of being calm and one-pointed, all the psychic factors have to be in balance. If they are not, we are not ready to enter deeper states of meditation. During our shamatha practice, the mental factors slowly begin to balance themselves. Once we reach a state of profound peace and one-pointedness, we have achieved inner balance. When we have that inner balance, the sense of ego is also in balance. Once that inner center is established, it is time to undo that center. But we can't do this until we have something there. We have to see through it, but we can't see through it until we have it.

Countless Westerners come to meditation hoping that it will resolve a lot of their psychological imbalances and problems. But this won't happen unless we first go through this nurturing period of learning how to make the mind quiet and calm. People often freak out during the long vipashyana courses because they don't have the emotional stability to cope with that level of insight. So the traditional approach, which is first to get the mind calm, centered and balanced before we start probing inside and peeling off the layers, makes a lot of sense. It's not a waste of time. It's a safe and grounded method. It doesn't mean that we have to proceed to very advanced, deep levels of shamatha. But we should ensure that the mind is more centered, quiet and balanced before turning it in on itself.

What is vipashyana, or insight meditation? In the Tibetan tradition it is looking into the mind itself with a great big question mark. What are the things closest to us? They are our thoughts and emotions. But our thoughts and emotions are so close to us that we never even look at them. Our senses are directed outwards, so we are always lending our attention to what we hear, what we see, what we taste, and so forth. But we rarely ask ourselves the question, "What is the mind?" It's surprising how few people ever do that. We all say, "I think this, or I think that." But what is a thought? Have we ever seen it? Where does it come from? How long does it stay? Where does it go? Some people believe in their thoughts so strongly that they will die for them. Whenever we think something, we really believe it to be true, even though next week we might think something different. We all identify with our thoughts intensely. We think, "I am angry. I am an angry person. I am a depressed person. I am a lovely person. I'm so kind. I'm so generous. I'm so this, I'm so that." But what is this "I"? We don't even ask ourselves.

Vipashyana shifts the beam of our attention from what's going on externally and refocuses it on our internal universe. There are many methods of practicing vipashyana, just as there are many methods of practicing shamatha, but all of them involve this big question mark, the inquiring mind. A mind which doesn't have the answers, but has lots of questions. Of course, the great question is, "Who am I?" We think: I like this. I don't like that. I'm Australian. I'm Chinese. I am an angry person. I am a depressed person. I am a woman. I am a man. I am a teacher. I am a bus driver; I, I, I, I. But who is this I? Our entire lives are based on this sense of "me" and "my." My country, my husband, my wife, my children, my house, my car, my ideas, my emotions, my depression. Who is this "me" who owns so much? This is what the meditation is about. It's not about making us feel better, although it might have that effect. On the other hand, it could also make us feel worse. It is not really about being peaceful, although we might become peaceful, but then again we might not. It's certainly not about blissing out. Vipashyana is about looking inside and finding out who we really are and what the mind really is, finding out how the mind works, how it functions, and then reaching a level of consciousness which is beyond the mundane. In Buddhism this is known as the "unconditioned." By its very definition it is beyond thoughts, beyond words, beyond concepts. But it is the deepest layer of our being and of all beings. It is what connects us to all beings. That's what meditation is.

As I said before, there are many approaches to this. One is to focus on the in-breath and the out-breath. When we are practicing tranquility, or calm abiding meditation, we ignore whatever thoughts, feelings or sensory perceptions come into our consciousness. We just let them go. This is because we are trying to make the mind calm and one-pointed, so we don't become distracted either by thoughts or external disturbances. But when we are doing vipashyana, we have curiosity. Instead of just letting the thoughts flow out, we bring up this question mark and ask, "What is a thought? What does it look like? What color is it? Does it have any shape? Where does it come from? Where does it stay? What does it feel like? What is the mind? Is a thought and a mind the same, or are they different?"

When the mind is in a state of complete tranquility, containing no thoughts, is that the same state as when thoughts are present, or is it different?

Is the awareness which sees all this, which looks at the thoughts and at the mind, different from the thoughts or is it the same? In this way you look and you question. You peel off layer after layer, looking for the mind. We talk about mind, mind, mind. But what is the mind? What is anger? What does it feel like? Say someone has done something bad to you and you feel angry with that person. Now drop the person. Drop the object of your anger and look at the anger itself. What is it? Where is it? How does it feel? How does the body feel? Just experience that. Don't judge it. Don't think about it. Just know it.

Our problem is not the fact that we have thoughts and emotions. Thoughts and emotions are natural to the mind, just as waves are natural to the ocean. The problem starts when we believe in them, identify with them and hold onto them. If we could recognize thoughts and emotions as passing mental states, transparent in nature, the play of the wisdom mind, there would be no problem. They would just rise and fall again like ocean waves. But we don't do that. If an emotion or a thought comes up, we immediately jump on it. We elaborate on it, we go into it, we keep going over it again and again. We identify with it, we regurgitate it over and over. We worry about it. We blame ourselves if it's not good. We don't let it go. We believe in it. We do the same thing with our memories. We are extremely attached to them because we believe they define who we are. Even if they are painful, we still don't want to let them go. We think, "This is me." However painful memories may be, they are in the past. They are gone now. Why do we need to hold onto them and make them our identity? But we do, and because we do, we suffer.

Most people sitting here right now are perfectly fine. Nothing awful is happening to any of us right at this moment. And yet there must be many of us here who are troubled by worries and anxieties, memories and confusion. Each of us thinks, "This is my problem." We cannot be fresh in the moment. Yet every breath we take is a fresh breath. We are not breathing old breaths. Likewise, every thought should be a new thought. Then there would be no problem. One of the aims of vipashyana meditation, at least in the Tibetan system, is to begin to understand the nature of our thoughts and emotions. How does the mind really work, and how can we gain access to more and more subtle levels of our psyche? This takes time. Meditation is not instant. There is no pill we can take to give us insight. We can take pills to give us psychedelic experiences, but there is no pill to show us the real nature of the mind. Pills may open up our minds to get us interested, but they are not going to do the work for us. There are machines which help us to calm down, and get us onto alpha waves, or whatever. But no machine can give us inner realization. This only comes from sitting patiently.

Meditation is hard work, but it is also the most rewarding thing we can do with our time. As we begin to see the mechanisms we previously took for granted and start to understand them, the knots inside our minds begin to loosen. We feel a tremendous sense of freedom, space and release inside us. As we begin to understand our warped thinking patterns and our neuroses, we see them directly. We begin to develop compassion for ourselves, for our pain and confusion. Now that we start to look with clarity, we can see the pain and confusion in the eyes of other people, and we naturally develop compassion for them. It doesn't matter how outwardly successful people may appear, we can see their pain when we look into their eyes. It is very rare to come across people whose eyes are truly sparkling with joy.

I don't think it is always necessary to sit and develop all these complicated Tibetan meditations on compassion. What we really need to do is to start looking into our own confusion. Then we can see the confusion in others. As deeper and deeper levels of our psyche open up, this naturally releases our innate compassion. We have both clarity and compassion within us, that is the nature of our mind. All we need do is uncover it. It's like a spring of water hidden by stones and mud. We have to uncover it by clearing the rubble away. When we clear away the mud and the stones, the spring will gush to the surface, clean and pure. There are vast reservoirs of love and compassion lying frozen within our hearts. We have to access these and begin to warm them up so they can flow. We can do this by looking into our own heart and seeing the pain, confusion and false identification. We can use that discovery to realize that everyone is in the same predicament. That's why people are so awful. They are awful because they are suffering, because they are confused. A person who has peace, love and compassion in his heart is not going to be awful. He is not going to hurt others, or be obnoxious, prejudiced or violent. He is going to be open.

As we practice first this calm abiding meditation and then insight, a certain quality of the mind becomes highly developed. It is called *she shin* in Tibetan. It means a kind of alert awareness which watches. When we are meditating, even when we do calm abiding meditation, there is a part of the mind which stands back and watches. It is able to see when we are falling into one extreme or another, in other words, if we are becoming agitated on the one hand or sinking into a sleepy state on the other. This part of the mind knows. It can redress the imbalance. This quality of the mind is very interesting. When we begin to look into the mind itself, this is traditionally compared to someone sitting on a river bank watching the water go by. Another traditional analogy is that of the shepherd watching his sheep. There is at once the sense of standing back and looking.

Once when I was in Lahoul, the usual shepherd was sick, and a young boy was sent up instead of the experienced older man. This young boy had obviously never done this job before and was very nervous. He brought up the sheep which he had gathered from the villages below, about a hundred of them, and probably realized that he would be beaten to a pulp if he lost any. So he was extremely concerned that they didn't wander away. He kept them all together in one big group, and moved them continuously from place to place. He ran around with these sheep all day, until finally when night came and he went back down, he was totally exhausted. The sheep were also exhausted. They had had very little to eat, because they had been kept in such a tight bunch, and they had also become very agitated. They were miserable, the shepherd was miserable and nobody had a good day!

The next day, the experienced shepherd came back. He drove the sheep to the pasture land, then climbed to a small hillock above, got out his bottle of chang and lay down to watch them. He didn't fall asleep, but kept a quiet watch. The sheep ambled about, nibbled away, and as the day progressed they sat down. At the end of the day, he gathered them all and took them back down. They had all had a quiet, peaceful day. The sheep had had enough to eat and everybody was happy. This is a perfect example of the wrong and the right way to look into the mind. Remember this when you try it. As the Zen Master Suzuki Roshi once said, "The best way to control your cow is to give it a wide pasture." When we look at the mind, we should not be like someone who is about to pounce on something. We shouldn't sit there and try to catch every single thought. If we try to do that, we make the mind tense and rigid, and prevent it from wandering at all. We exhaust ourselves, and if anything goes wrong, we snap.

Sometimes you can see this happening with meditators. They sit grimly, with an expression that says "Buddhahood or bust!" That attitude is counterproductive. We must learn to look at the mind while remaining very clear but totally relaxed. Just let the mind go its own way. It doesn't matter what it thinks. It can think incredibly brilliant thoughts, or incredibly stupid ones. It doesn't matter. These are just thoughts, just the play of the mind. The important thing is not to be fascinated by the mind's play. You think, "Wow, that's really an interesting thought," and then suddenly you're sucked into it. Then you realize you've been completely caught up within some memory or fantasy and the awareness has disappeared.

If we make our awareness too rigid, our thoughts become awkward. It's just like when somebody knows he's being watched and becomes so self-conscious that he can't even drink a cup of tea properly. The thoughts themselves lose their natural quality and the body and the psyche become overly tight. At the other extreme, if we are too loose, we continually lose our awareness. What we need is to be interested and to watch, but not interfere or be caught up in what we are thinking. Don't think of the past, don't anticipate the future, don't get fascinated by the present. See it as it is. Just be there with it. A thought is just a thought. An emotion is just an emotion. It is like a bubble. It will burst and another one will come up.

When we first begin to put this into practice, the mind appears to split. We develop what is called the observer, the witness, the knower. This is an aspect of the mind. It is still just mind, conceptual mind, but it is a mind which is standing back and looking at what is going on as if at a distance. In itself, this is not ultimate reality, because it is still a dualistic mind. But it is a vast improvement on the way we normally think, because it gives us the space to see a thought as a thought and an emotion as an emotion. Then we can decide whether this is a useful thought or emotion or not. We know it for what it is, rather than being absorbed in it. We no longer identify with it.

If we develop this inner awareness, which is like an inner space, we can ride the waves of life. People imagine that to be a meditator you have to always live in very tranquil situations and that you are likely to be inundated if a turbulent situation arises. This is true for beginners, just as it is for someone who is learning how to surf. At the beginning, they have to stick to the small waves otherwise they will be bowled over. But an expert surfer looks for the big waves. The greater the waves, the more fun, once you have your balance. The secret is to be balanced, to be poised. To be a good surfer you need to be neither too tense nor too relaxed, just balanced. This is what we need in our practice, too.

When we develop this inner space, everything takes on an almost dream-like quality. Not dreamlike in the sense of being sleepy, but in that it is no longer so solid, so real, so urgent. It has a quality almost like an illusion. You don't take it quite so seriously any more, because you are not so totally involved with it. Now when we have that sense of stepping back and seeing life with a degree of clarity, we are able to respond to situations which arise with freshness and spontaneity, instead of our usual automatic response, which is like pressing a button on a machine. We begin to respond naturally and in an appropriate manner. We have been filling our minds with junk since we were tiny children. Junk comes in through television, books, movies and idle conversation, and we never clear it out. We are so careful about keeping our houses clean. We are alarmed by even a bit of dust. But our mind, which is our real home, we do nothing with. We never clear it out.

Meditation is also about cleaning out the mind to make space for nicer, cleaner, purer things. All of us can start by putting aside some time every day to just quietly look inside. It is best if we can find a teacher to give us personal instruction, and there are also books. We must be determined. The twin aids of any meditator are patience and perseverance. It's not an overnight thing, but the rewards are infinite. Nothing is as rewarding as getting our minds into order and acquiring an understanding of the nature of the mind. This benefits not only ourselves, but everyone, everywhere. Eventually, when our minds are simultaneously aware and relaxed and open, it can happen. Just for a microsecond perhaps, the whole thing falls apart, and we catch a glimpse of the unconditioned.

As the Tibetans love to say, our minds are like the deep, vast, blue sky. Normally it is covered with clouds, which are all we can see. So we identify with these clouds. But for a moment, there can be a break in the clouds, and we see can through to the sky. We see that there is a sky there. It is always there. However dark the clouds may be, the sky itself does not become sullied. However white and fluffy the clouds may be, they do not beautify the sky. The sky is just the sky. It is this big sky mind which connects us to all other beings. This big sky mind is not just a cute concept, it is something we can actually realize. In that moment of realization we know we are that knowledge, because the realization is non-dual. There is no "I," and there is nothing to be seen. In that moment there is just the seeing. At that moment we wake up.

The real aim of the practice is to gain access to the unconditioned mind, to be able to recreate this more and more often and to prolong it further and further until we are continually in that state of absolute non-dual awareness. Then we are Buddhas. That's what being a Buddha is about.

QUESTIONS

Q: Sometimes when I meditate I see this void and I become fearful. What can I do about this?

TP: I don't think it's bad to experience fear. It is quite common to feel fear when we meditate. It is the ego, which is afraid it might die. And it is right to be afraid, because it will die. The ego fears that its games will be discovered, and so it panics. When we are on the crest of some new understanding, it always panics. But this panic is not a bad thing. Rather than following the panic, be it by throwing a tantrum or whatever, we can try to be present in the moment with that panic, with a very compassionate and gentle mind, allowing the fear to arise, acknowledging it, accepting it and being with it. The important thing is not to try to distract ourselves from it. It is natural for us to want to do something to distract our minds away from the fear. But whenever we do this, we are setting ourselves up to go through similar experiences again and again. It is better to just sit quietly and try to face the fear. Ask it where it comes from and who is afraid? That's a great question to ask if you have fear.

Q: I've always been a fairly placid non-violent person, but nowadays I encounter recurrent dreams with violent situations. Where do they come from?

TP: From your psyche. Maybe this is good. I don't know, I'm not a psychiatrist. But I know that sometimes when we think we are peaceful, placid people, it's only because of this cloud layer. We've never actually been challenged. Underneath it there is all this other stuff waiting to come up. Sometimes when we do certain practices, and meditation is one of these, all this gets churned up. One of the first reactions people get when they start to meditate is, "Oh, but I thought I was such a nice person." This is because we are churning the depths of our psyche, and it is like disturbing a stagnant pool. We cause all the muck to rise to the top. Of course it is necessary for the muck to rise. The important thing is not to identify with it. All we need do is to see the muck as muck, and rest the mind in the midst of this. We need to remember that all this is just thoughts, just emotions. Good thoughts, bad thoughts, they are all just thoughts. They are not me, they are not mine. Maybe it's not a bad thing. Maybe this is a new stage you need to go through. Don't resist it, just be curious.

Q: You said before that the ego has to die. What happens to the psyche?
TP: What we mean by ego in Buddhist parlance is this tight little sense of solidity in the center of our being which is "me," and which therefore makes everything else into "non-me." We all do it constantly. *I* think, *I* feel, these are *my* memories, etc. This tight, closed, solid consciousness is always identified with the past. We are always identified with our habitual responses—how we have always done things, this is me, I have always liked this, I don't like that, I want this, I don't want that, etc. It's very stale. This means that when we come across anything new, it's difficult to have a natural open response. That's why life becomes so boring for people. Actually, life is fascinating, but we bore ourselves because our minds have become so conditioned and therefore so stale. We are trying to see through that conditioning.

Why is this conditioning such a problem? The problem is that it obscures the real nature of the mind. When we first see something beautiful, we think, "Oh, how beautiful." Then the next time we think, "Oh, that's nice." Then by the third or fourth time we don't even notice it any more. We are totally caught up in these conditioned reactions to everything. When we begin to look at our thoughts, we realize how utterly boring the mind is. This is why meditation is so difficult, because it's such a bore. The same old thoughts keep coming up, again and again. This is the ego. Bringing these up constantly makes it feel secure, that somehow we are a unit—something unique. This is my little set of conditioned reactions. But that completely blinds us to what is actually happening in the moment. This is the problem. All religions try to get beyond this little ego, this little "I," and gain access to a higher level of being. The Christians say it is not I that moves, but Christ that moves in me. The Muslims and the Jews also try to sidestep this little "me" and gain access to a higher level of consciousness where things manifest perfectly and spontaneously.

In this state we have access to an enormous source of flowing energy, because we are not caught up in all the friction of our conditioned thinking. After we reach that level of consciousness, which we call the unconditioned, the nature of the mind, Dharmakaya, or whatever, we come back to the foundation of our being. Of course we can keep our ego. But now we know it's just a game. When I said "psyche" before, I meant inner mental factors. I use the term loosely. Once we become realized, we still use our inner mental factors, but we are no longer fooled by thoughts and emotions.

There is a big difference between having thoughts and emotions and being absorbed in them and identifying with them. We can still have thoughts and emotions while seeing their rainbow quality. In other words, although we don't really believe in them wholeheartedly, we can play with them. When we see a rainbow, we don't think it's real. Rainbows arise from certain causes and conditions, such as moisture in the air coming into contact with sunlight at a certain angle, and so on. If all these causes and conditions come together, we get something which is very beautiful and very solid-looking which we call a rainbow. It doesn't really exist, yet it does exist. We can all see it, yet we can't reach out and grasp it. This is very much like our external reality and our emotions. They are there, but they are not there in quite the way we perceive them. When we realize this, we gain tremendous freedom. We can enjoy the rainbow without trying to grasp it. It's not my rainbow. Nobody can buy that rainbow and put it in their own backyard as their own private rainbow. We need to be free from this tyrannical slavery to the ego. If we look for this ego, we will never find it. In this way we can deconstruct this fiction.

Q: Children seem to accept their thoughts, feelings and emotions as they come up. There is a kind of lightness about them, yet it would be horrible to have to be a child forever! Is it necessary for us to try to recapture that child-like nature?
TP: I think it's a mistake to confuse a naive child's mind with an enlightened mind. Children are not enlightened, although they have certain qualities we need to develop. They are non-judgmental, they have an openness and a lightness, as you mentioned. But at the same time, a child is extraordinarily caught up in the grip of its emotions. When we look at a hungry baby, we see that it is convulsed with greed. It becomes furious if it is not fed on time.

When you see children playing, you can watch the ego operating in its most brutal form. When the child gets what it wants, it is all sunshine and smiles, but if it's thwarted, it quickly becomes furious. This comes from beginningless time, from when our original non-dual awareness split off into "I" and "other," "self" and "other than self." This is our primordial ignorance. This belief in a separate identity is our problem. We need to develop certain childlike qualities, such as freshness, openness and curiosity. Young children are full of why, why, why about even small details we wouldn't notice. They are very aware and curious in that sense. They haven't yet acquired a conditioned response to everything that's happened. That fresh, spontaneous quality of mind is something we certainly need. But we don't need to go back to being slaves to our greed and anger.

No one is more egotistical than a small child. As far as they are concerned, the whole world exists to fulfill their wants. They have no sense of consideration for others. We shouldn't be too sentimental about children. They are also caught up, as are we all, in this realm of birth and death. We can see the human condition very clearly in children. They are so naked. They haven't yet developed the social finesse to cover up their naked greed and anger. It's all out front. I have found living with friends who have small children to be quite an education. I have seen children brought up in the nicest circumstances, with loving parents, a nice house, toys, being very pampered and cared for. Still, we can see how traumatic their lives are. If they are thwarted in the slightest, there is a tremendous intensity of emotion.

Q: What are some of the positive qualities of a childlike mind?
TP: An example of a childlike quality is when children are in the midst of intense grief and then someone gives them a lollipop. The tears disappear and they giggle and smile. They have completely forgotten that a few minutes ago they had been grief-stricken. A childlike quality of the mind really means a mind which is fresh, which sees things as if for the first time.

Once someone did a test on meditators which was rather interesting. You know, when they stick all these electrodes and things onto people's heads to test their brainwaves. They tested someone who was doing a formal Hindu style meditation and a Zen master. This was to find out what the difference was, because they both said they were meditating, but each was doing a very different kind of meditation. They also tested a non-meditator. Every three minutes, they made a sudden loud noise. It was regular. The first person they tested was the one who didn't know how to meditate. The first time this person heard the loud noise, he became very agitated. The second time he was less agitated. The third time there was some vague agitation, and then the fourth time he more or less ignored it. The person doing the Hindu meditation didn't react to the noise at all. He didn't hear it. When the person doing the Zen meditation heard the noise, the mind went outwards, noted the noise and then went back in. The next time, the mind noted the noise and went back in. The next time, noted the noise and went back in. His reaction was unchanged. Each time, the mind noted the noise and went back in.

That tells us a lot about the quality of mind we are talking about. This is a mind which responds to something with attention and then returns to its own natural state. It doesn't elaborate on it, doesn't get caught up in it, doesn't get excited about it. It just notes that this is what is happening. Every time it happens, it notes it. It doesn't get blasé. It doesn't become conditioned. In this way, it is like a child's mind. When something interesting happens, it will note it and then let it go and move onto the next thing. This is what is meant by a childlike mind. It sees everything as if for the first time. It doesn't have this whole backlog of preconditioned ideas about things. You see a glass and you see it as it is, rather than seeing all the other glasses you have seen in your life, together with your ideas and theories about glasses and whether you like glasses in this or that shape, or the kind of glass you drank out of yesterday. We are talking about a mind which sees the thing freshly in the moment. That's the quality we are aiming for. We lose this as we become adults. We are trying to reproduce this fresh mind, which sees things without all this conditioning. But we do not want a mind which is swept away by its emotions.

Q: Is that why life gets shorter as we get older?
TP: Yes, because we become more and more robotic. When we are small children, everything is so fascinating that life seems to go on forever. Every day is huge, because there are so many fascinating things happening and we are so interested. So childhood seems like a very long period. But as we become dulled, as our minds get less and less curious, as we go onto automatic pilot more and more in our relationships, in our social life, in our work, even in our intimate relationships, we become increasingly somnambulant. Therefore life

loses its vivacity and seems shorter. Has anybody here read a book entitled *The Magic Mountain* by Thomas Mann? It's about somebody who has tuberculosis and is living in a sanatorium in Switzerland. This is a very thick book. By the time you have read a third of it, you realize that nothing is going to happen. Mann will take a whole chapter just to talk about taking someone's temperature. He deals with the quality of time and our subjective perception of it. Because basically, nothing does happen in the sanatorium. So for the first two months or so, as you are getting into the routine, it seems like a normal length of time. But as the weeks and months go by, and it's the same thing, the same meal, with the same people, the same walks, the same dull discussions, day after day, the whole perception of time closes in on itself and two years and two months begin to feel the same.

This is an extreme example. When I became a Buddhist at the age of eighteen, my life turned around. My whole way of thinking was being reevaluated. It was an intense period. When I look back, it was an enormous period. I think, oh yes, the time when I was Theravadin, it lasted years and years and then eventually I came to Mahayana. In fact, it was just a few months. But because it was such an intense time and so many things were happening inwardly, the time stretched out. But when nothing much is happening, it's the same job, the same relationships, the same this, the same that, we become more and more conditioned in our responses, and time seems to get shorter and shorter. This is very sad, isn't it? Because actually, it is the same time. It seems to speed up. This is an indication of how we are becoming more and more robotic in our responses. In a way it is a warning sign for us to wake up and reestablish that original childlike curiosity and fresh quality of mind.

8
Awareness

As we have already discussed, we need to develop the mind if we really want to practice the Dharma. This means developing the clarity and insight to see things as they really are. We have talked at some length now about the need for a daily meditation practice to help us develop clarity and insight. The great benefit of maintaining a daily sitting practice is that it helps stabilize the mind and gives us the space to let go, fall silent, and gradually begin to understand what is going on inside. But there are limits to the amount of time most of us can spend in formal meditation. Fortunately, meditation is only one of a number of tools available to us. In addition, we need to learn to practice awareness during the greater part of the day when we are off the mat, that is, in the course of our everyday lives. The present talk will focus on techniques to help maintain awareness throughout the day.

First, we need to become more conscious. Usually we give only half of our attention to the things we do. We often think we are doing things whole-heartedly when in fact we are probably thinking about a hundred different things at the same time. We are not usually conscious of this. We are a bit like the person who thinks he is walking his dog, but ends up following the dog wherever it leads him. He is so busy trying to keep up that he does not notice whether or not the dog is going in a straight line. One of the first things to realize is that our minds are totally untamed. The Buddha compared an ordinary mind with a wild elephant in rut. Not one of those nice tame elephants we see in the zoo or in the circus, but a wild elephant. Sometimes he went so far as to say a drunken wild elephant! These days we hear news reports about even the most important statesmen behaving in completely uncontrolled ways, causing terrible problems for an entire nation, not to mention the harm they cause to their families and themselves. It is frightening to think that despite having so much at stake, many people in public office are apparently unable to control their behavior. When people cannot control their behavior, it is because they cannot control their minds. We all have this problem to some extent. How often do we do things impulsively, without giving a thought to the consequences? We want to do it, so we just jump right in. We don't know how to control ourselves, either. Our minds are obscured by anger, desire, jealousy and confusion. We can't see the wider implications, and consequently, we often feel no sense of responsibility for what we do.

How can we begin to take responsibility for our actions? A good way to start is by learning to understand our mental states. One of the easiest ways to train in this is to take some simple everyday action such as combing our hair, brushing our teeth, shaving, or drinking our morning coffee, and bring our attention fully to what we are doing. Just be with the action. Know that we are doing it. That's all. We will see how long the mind can remain in a state of wordless knowing before we rush in with all our commentaries, justifications, and interpretations. "Oh goodness, this is really stupid. What am I doing cleaning my teeth and having to think about it?" Or, "Wow, now my life is going to be really good, it's easy to be mindful about cleaning your teeth."

When we rush in with this mental chatter, we are no longer being mindful. We are just thinking about being mindful. Mindfulness is not thinking about, it is being present and actually knowing in the moment without any mental commentary. If commentary begins to happen, we simply ignore it and return to being present in the moment. Think about this. There are so many things happening in our lives that we never really experience. We experience only ideas, interpretations, and comparisons. We dwell on things that happened in the past or anticipate future events. But we almost never experience the moment itself. It is for this reason that we often find our lives boring and meaningless. What we need to realize is that this sense of meaninglessness does not come from our lives, but from the quality of awareness with which we live our lives.

There is a Vietnamese Zen master named Thich Nhat Hanh who writes about the benefits of washing dishes to wash dishes. This is a very important point because normally we wash dishes in order to have clean dishes. Whenever we do anything, we do it to get a result. We write a letter in order to produce a letter which we can then send; we are washing dishes not to wash dishes, but so we can have clean dishes and go on to the next task. As we wash the dishes, we are thinking about what we will do next, how we will have a cup of coffee, what somebody said to us this morning, what TV program we watched last night, what our kid is doing, or what our husband said to us before he went to work. The last thing on our mind is the dishes. Then when we come to drink the coffee, we are thinking that after that we have to go shopping, and what are we going to buy, and things like this. We are drinking the coffee now, but we are not really drinking it because our mind has gone forward onto something else again. Our entire lives pass in this way. Even when we are doing something nice, like eating a delicious meal, we are thinking about dessert. We never even enjoy the good things. We experience the taste for a few seconds, and then we are off again.

Thich Nhat Hanh asks, "Why not wash dishes just to wash dishes?" We get clean dishes anyway! But it means that while we are washing the dishes, we are completely with it. There is no action in the world more important at that moment than washing the dishes because that is what we are doing. Everything else is just our thoughts. But the thing happening in the moment is the actual reality and, therefore, the most important thing. If we miss it now, we miss it forever, because we can never get that "now" time back once it has passed. So let's try to wash the dishes and just know we are washing dishes. It's not a big deal. We are conscious that we are standing at the sink. Now the hand is picking up a dish. We can feel the water. We can feel the soap suds. We are conscious of what we are washing. We are completely attentive to what is happening in that moment. In this way we become centered in the moment. And that moment is all we ever really have. Our whole life is made up of moment after moment after moment. If we miss these moments through thinking about something else, they are gone forever. If we bring our consciousness to the task at hand, whatever it is, the mind itself is washed clean. There is no stress attached to doing this. The mind actually finds it quite a pleasant experience.

The Zen tradition places a lot of emphasis on being present in the moment. They teach that every action performed with awareness is a profound activity, but even the most seemingly exalted activity is meaningless if we do it mindlessly. We might be an abbot sitting up on the teaching throne, but if we are teaching without being conscious, it is a meaningless activity. Or, we could be outside the temple, sweeping the leaves, scrubbing the floor or chopping vegetables. Provided we do it with consciousness and presence, even the most mundane activity becomes a profound meditation.

Some people think, "I'm pretty conscious, I know what I'm doing." Try taking a simple action like drinking, combing your hair, brushing your teeth, or shaving—any action which we normally do quite automatically, while thinking of other things. Instead of thinking of other things, bring all of your attention to that task. While you are combing your hair, just comb the hair. Know what is happening. Know what the body is doing. Know what the mind is doing. Be with it. This is not as easy as it sounds! Almost invariably, we start not just thinking about other things and bringing in other comments, but also thinking, "Oh, this is easy. I'm very mindful." As soon as we think, "I'm being mindful," we are no longer mindful. We are just thinking about being mindful. True awareness is nonverbal.

Bringing presence into our tasks as often as possible will help us to transform our day on a very deep level. It's easy. The main problem is that the mind is so deep in its inertia, so deep in its desire to stay asleep that we keep forgetting to be mindful. Actually, the meaning of the word mindfulness in both Sanskrit and Tibetan is "to remember." It is akin to the Christian idea of recollection and to Gurdjieff's concept of self-remembrance. It is about remembering where we are and who we are and what's happening in the moment. Because mindfulness is akin to recollection, its direct enemy is forgetfulness. I often tell people about this quality of mindfulness, and they say, "Yes, that sounds good. I'll try it." The next day they really try hard to be more conscious at work and with their families. This immediately adds a special new dimension to their lives. People begin to notice and say, "Wow, you are so much nicer. What happened?" They come back and tell me about how great this mindfulness is and what a marvelous effect it's having on every aspect of their lives. I say, "Okay, tell me about it in a few months' time." Then about six months later, I meet them again and ask how the mindfulness is going. They usually reply, "Oh, I forgot all about it!"

This is the main problem. We are so used to being asleep that the effort to wake up is very hard for us. Otherwise there is no problem. It doesn't require any time, or any particular talent. It doesn't require us to be great geniuses or yogis or to do years and years of advanced training. The minute I say to you to just be present, just know the body in this moment, you can know it! The mind steps back and suddenly you know what the body is doing. Right? It's very easy. The main challenge is to remember. If you are learning how to play a musical instrument, for example, you don't begin to learn by playing Beethoven sonatas. In the beginning you do very simple exercises, like scales. But you keep practicing until eventually the technique takes over. If you keep going, you come to a point where you are not even conscious of the technique any more. The music just flows through your fingers to the instrument.

It's the same with the mind. Our minds are full of bad habits, and we need to reprogram them by developing good ones. In the beginning it is very difficult and there is lots of resistance. But if we are patient and persevere, the awareness will grow stronger and stronger. Gradually the mind begins to understand what it means to be aware. Then the moments of awareness begin to prolong themselves. Then, one day when we are not even thinking about it, in the midst of total confusion, we suddenly become totally present. We see everything clearly, yet inwardly our minds are silent. Then the commentaries and the judgments come flooding in again and we've lost it. But as time goes on, there are more and more of these moments of clarity and inner silence, when we really see things, and everything becomes very vivid. It really is a process of waking up. Normally, because we are sleeping, we have lots of dreams. Some are pleasant; some are nightmares. It is all very fascinating and entertaining. But when we wake up, we see that that was actually a lower level of consciousness, however fascinating it might have seemed and however much we may have believed in it. Now we know we are awake and that this other consciousness was only a dream. Nobody else can wake us up. We have to do it for ourselves. But if we decide we prefer to be asleep, so be it.

Sometimes people ask me about the difference between awareness and concentration. Awareness is not the same as concentration. To use an example, suppose you are reading a fascinating book, and you are completely absorbed in it. You don't see anything else; you don't hear anything else. That is concentration. But to know that you are absorbed in the book is awareness. Do you understand the difference? Being aware does not mean thinking about being aware. As long as we are thinking about being aware, we are not really aware, but just thinking about being aware. At first, we will only be able to be aware for a few seconds at the most. Then our conceptual mind starts bringing in all sorts of thoughts, ideas, comparisons, and commentaries, and we drop out again. When this happens it is important not to be discouraged.

With practice and perseverance, we will inevitably improve. We must learn to be patient not only with others, but with ourselves!

The Buddha taught four basic levels of mindfulness, starting from the very gross to increasingly subtle levels. The first of these is mindfulness of the body, including the breath. The second is mindfulness of feelings. This does not refer to emotions, but to bare sensations. When any stimulus is received through the sense organs, the eyes, ears, nose, mouth, skin, or mind, and processed by the sense consciousness, there is a sensation. That sensation is either pleasant, unpleasant, or neutral. We'll go into this later. The third is awareness of the mind itself. The fourth is awareness of the external environment as it impinges on us through the sense organs. This is what connects us in this very panoramic awareness.

When I first started training with an old yogi at my community, I said to him, "I sort of know what to do in formal situations, but I don't know what to do during the rest of the day." He said, "That's easy. You just realize all thoughts and emotions which arise are the dharmakaya." Dharmakaya means ultimate reality. I said, "No, that's too difficult, I can't do that." He replied, "Yes, you can, you are just lazy!" But actually, it is quite difficult. It's not easy to look directly at the mind itself, and it is especially difficult to realize it as the play of wisdom, especially if you don't know what wisdom is! But the Buddha was kinder to us. He started by focusing on the physical, because the physical is very obvious to us. He said, "When we are sitting, we know we are sitting. When we are standing, we know we are standing. When we are walking, we know we are walking. When we are lying down, we know we are lying down." Think about that. So often when we are sitting, walking or lying down, we are totally unaware of our bodies. We don't even know what we are doing. Try to become conscious of the body, of its posture, of what the body is doing in this moment. Not thinking about it or comparing it or commenting on it in any way, just knowing what the body is doing, what it is feeling. If we can do just that, we are present. This is a very skillful way to bring us into the moment.

Another way of using the body to bring us into the here and now is to bring the attention during the course of the day to the inhalation and exhalation of the breath, as we do in our meditation practice. We cannot breathe in the past or in the future. We can only breathe now. The breathing is always with us. It is a skillful practice for bringing the mind back into the present, because breathing is closely related to our state of mind. Depending on whether we are angry, fearful, passionate, peaceful, happy, or depressed, our breathing changes. The breathing reflects our state of mind in this moment. Bringing our attention to the in-going and out-going of the breath actually helps the mind to settle down. Even in common parlance, when someone is upset we tell him to take a few deep breaths and count to ten. We can do this quite easily during the day whenever we think of it, or whenever we feel the need to calm the mind. Even in the busiest life, there are times when we need to be still.

When the traffic lights are red in New Delhi, they display the word "relax." Every time you come to a red light, instead of sitting grinding your teeth, try seeing it as an opportunity for practice. Connect with the in-going and out-going of the breath. Be one with the breathing. Then, something which usually causes us stress will actually help us to relax without anything in our surroundings needing to change. The red light is still there, but our response has changed. This principle applies throughout the day. Try to see things which normally trigger stress as warning signs. Imagine a warning, a red traffic light with the word "relax" written right across it! Just let it all go. Just be present in the moment. We can all do it.

The second level of awareness is awareness of sensations. By "sensations" we mean the process that occurs when we receive stimuli through the five sense organs or the sixth sense, which is the mind. The stimulus is immediately interpreted by the mind and felt as pleasurable, unpleasurable, or neutral. Everything we perceive, whether it comes from outside or inside, is based on this pain/pleasure principle. Our normal reaction is to be attracted to what is pleasurable and to try to avoid what is unpleasant. We do this constantly. Even while we sit, we remain in a certain position for a while, and then we begin to get a bit uncomfortable. We start to feel unpleasant sensations, so we wriggle around until we are comfortable again. Then it's okay again, but only for a while.

Everything we do from one moment to the next is based on this process of trying to bring on and maintain pleasurable feelings and to ward off and avoid unpleasurable ones. We are attracted to sounds, sights, tastes, smells, and contacts which we find pleasing, and to pleasant thoughts. On the other hand, we try to avoid things which are considered unpleasant. Consequently, we are trapped into swinging on this continual pendulum between attraction and rejection. We seem to believe that if we can move fast enough, we will get more of the pleasurable things and avoid the unpleasant ones. We do this almost unconsciously because it has become automatic. We are ruled by this process. This applies to people, things, situations, emotional states, thoughts, whatever. As long as we remain unconscious of this, as long as we fail to see that this is the underlying substructure of our fears, interpretations, judgments, and biases, we are no different from Pavlov's dogs. We are totally conditioned.

Developing an awareness of sensations helps us become conscious of the first tremor, that initial psychic tremor of pleasure and non-pleasure before the mind takes over, elaborates and blows it out of proportion. Once this tremor happens, we are caught up in "I like it, I want it, I must have it; I don't want it, I don't like it, I've got to get rid of it, I've got to get out." This whole response is constructed upon the first tiny tremor of pleasure or non-pleasure. If we can catch it at that moment and see what is actually happening, we give ourselves space to choose how to act. If it is something pleasurable, we might respond by saying, "Yes, I like that, I'll have it." There is nothing wrong with making that choice. If something is unpleasant, we might say, "No, I don't want that," and avoid it. We are not trying to become masochists. We are trying to create the space to see the situation accurately. Then we can make a clear response rather than a conditioned one.

Our likes and dislikes seem so real, so true, so permanent that we forget that they are often quite arbitrary. For example, one week we might decide that purple is the best color in the world. We love purple, and we think everything purple is beautiful. We cannot understand how anybody could possibly bear to be seen in green! Then, a couple of years later, it becomes fashionable to wear green, and you can't imagine why anybody would want to be seen in anything else. We forget that a while ago we hated green. The point is not whether we like purple or green. The point is that our likes and dislikes fluctuate continually. They are often dictated by the society we live in. Even in art, things which are considered the height of beauty and aesthetic perfection in one century are considered kitsch in the next. You can't tell how tastes will change. We have to look at what is happening to us and become conscious of that subtle "feeling tone." Then we can decide what to do about it.

This brings us on to the next level, which concerns bringing awareness to the mind. Personally, I think that the only way to bring the attention to the mind, to the thoughts themselves, is to establish a regular sitting practice. It's almost impossible during the hectic activities of the day to have the space to see what is going on inside. A sitting practice is indispensable for bringing our attention inside the mind. An hour or two a day would be ideal, but if we cannot have that much time, I think half an hour or twenty minutes would be okay. Anything less would be insufficient, because it takes about ten minutes for the average mind to calm down. If you rise from the meditation then, you do not have time to experience that settled state.

The early morning is generally considered to be the best time to meditate. We could all get up half an hour earlier if we tried. Another good time is just before going to bed. For at least ten minutes before we go to sleep it is very beneficial to empty out the mind and let everything go—all our worries, concerns and stresses. Just drop it and let the mind be quiet, spacious, and empty. If we sleep in that state, we will rest more deeply. On the other hand, if we sleep with our minds churning over with worries about what has been happening during the day, we are likely to wake up in the morning feeling as though we haven't slept at all. Even while we were asleep, the thoughts were churning around. So it's good to have a period of sitting before going to sleep, when the mind can just relax and be quiet, and then go to sleep in that state.

One of the funny things about learning to look into the mind is that normally that's the last place we ever look! If you consider the way we normally think, we carry on an endless dialogue with ourselves full of memories, justifications, anticipations, commentaries, fantasies, daydreams, and so on. We just keep thinking, comparing, and analyzing. And we believe what we think. I have my beliefs, they are true because that's what I believe! What I like must be good because I like it! And what I don't like must be bad because I don't like it! And when we have emotions, we believe in them, too. We believe in our anger, we believe in our depressions, we believe in our memories, we believe in our fears, and we think this is "who I am." People who have had very traumatic childhoods often believe in their memories quite emphatically. They never let them go. They clutch onto them, even though they are painful. This is what gives them their sense of identity: "I am an abused individual."

The aim of the various meditation practices is to first teach us how to quiet the mind and then to look into the mind itself. They teach us how to distance ourselves from our thoughts and emotions, and to see them as just thoughts and emotions. They are just mental states. They arise for a short time, then they disappear, then another state arises. They are like bubbles. Our problem is not the fact that we have thoughts and emotions, but that we identify with them. We think, "These are my thoughts, my emotions, my memories." We have no space. It's like being in the middle of the ocean, engulfed by giant waves which roll over us and pound against us again and again. Awareness gives us a peaceful space from which to observe all this without becoming engulfed by it.

While I was in Malaysia, I saw a T-shirt depicting a surfboard aloft huge waves. Sitting on the surf board was a figure meditating cross-legged. The slogan read, "Riding the waves of life, be mindful, be happy." That's it. Awareness. Being present. Knowing thoughts as thoughts, emotions as emotions. It's just like riding a surfboard. You gradually develop the poise to cruise along on the roughest seas until, no longer immersed in the waves, you are riding on top of them. Of course you have to start with small waves until you get your balance. Then the higher the wave, the better! Likewise, when we begin to train in awareness, it is better if we have an atmosphere which is nonthreatening and peaceful. That's why people go on retreat. That's also a reason why people set aside regular sitting periods. But once we learn how to be balanced, we become like a surfer who finds that the bigger the wave, the greater the fun.

As we begin to develop awareness of the mind, the mind itself appears to divide into two. A new aspect of the mind arises. This is referred to variously as the witness, the seer, the knower, or the observer. It witnesses without judgment and without comment. Along with the arrival of the witness, a space appears within the mind. This enables us to see thoughts and emotions as merely thoughts and emotions, rather than as "me" and "mine." When the thoughts and emotions are no longer seen as "me" or "mine," we begin to have choices. Certain thoughts and emotions are helpful, so we encourage them. Others are not so helpful, so we just let them go. All the thoughts and emotions are recognized and accepted. Nothing is suppressed. But now we have a choice about how to react. We can give energy to the ones which are useful and skillful and withdraw energy from those which are not.

All this is very liberating, don't you think? The point is that we can all do this. It is not impossible. It is not even especially difficult. It is part of the nature of the psychological factors to be able to make this split. It is not something we have to manufacture or bring in from outside. It is already part of our mental makeup. If we learn how to become more and more conscious of the thoughts themselves, the mind will quite naturally create this inner space.

The stronger the awareness becomes, the more obvious the separation will be until it is there all the time. Even when emotional problems arise, there will always be this inner space. We are all capable of this because this is the way the mind works once we develop the ability to stand back and look at it.

Thich Nhat Hanh used to have what he called a "mindfulness bell." During his retreats he would designate someone to go around and every now and then, whenever he felt like it, ring the bell. As soon as the students heard the bell they had to stop what they were doing. Stop, absolutely in that second. In that moment they were to become conscious not only of what the body was doing, but of what the mind and emotions were doing. They had to be aware of everything that was happening in that moment. We need to make our own inner mindfulness bell to wake us up. Even during our busiest days, we can take ten seconds out to become aware of what the mind is doing. Then as our skill develops, the mind learns what it has to do. The moments of clarity become longer and longer until spontaneously, when we're not thinking about it, the mind will snap into it. It's like when you have a camera which is out of focus. You turn it and turn it until it's suddenly in focus. Everything becomes so clear, and for the first time you realize how blurred it all was before. Then we lose focus again because we start thinking about it and get caught up once more! That's fine. But whenever we remember, we can just bring it back. In time we will establish the habit of being conscious. It is very easy to form bad habits and extremely difficult to create good ones. So in the beginning it takes a lot of dedication and commitment. But once we begin to taste the benefits, this encourages us to keep on.

Most of us feel that our lives leave something to be desired. The solution lies not in getting the perfect partner, the perfect house, the perfect car, or the perfect country. Nothing is ever perfect. There is always going to be dissatisfaction, there will always be something wrong. If we are always trying to change everything out there, to change everybody around us, change the society, change the culture, thinking that things are going to be wonderful and perfect, we are suffering from an enormous delusion. In past times it was believed that universal education, universal health care, and provision of proper food and housing would produce utopia in this world. Yet look at what has happened. Almost everybody in the West has education and some kind of health care. You live in these beautiful places. You have everything you need. You have all the clothes you need, all the food you can eat. You have nice homes. But are people really happy? Do they wake up each day thinking, "Oh how wonderful life is! What bliss!" Never have young people had so many material goods, so much education, and so much power, yet never have they complained as much as they do today, and never have they felt so deprived, so frustrated and so angry. This should be a strong clue to us that maybe the answer is not just on the outside. Maybe part of it is on the inside.

However hard we may try to make this the best of all possible worlds, it is not happening, is it? So maybe each one of us should try changing the quality of our own consciousness. The results are amazing! Everything transforms! As we find more clarity in our lives, our hearts will also begin to open up. We will be able to deal easily with stressful circumstances which we find so difficult today. We experience everything through the mind. Do you realize that? Nothing we know can be experienced except through the mind. Everything outside is transmitted to us through the senses, the sense consciousnesses, and the mind. Without a mind, we would be dead. We would be like chunks of wood cut at the base. You might say that we actually live within our own minds, rather than in this country, this house, this body.

We pay a lot of attention to our bodies. We clean them, adorn them, feed them, and exercise them. But how much attention do we give to our real home? How often do we clean out our mind? How much do we exercise it? How much do we adorn it? How much nourishment do we give it? Think about this seriously. All experiences come through the filter of our mind. If our minds are in chaos, it doesn't matter where we are, our lives will be in chaos. If our minds are at peace, it doesn't matter where we are, we will be at peace.

I would like to give you a very simple example. Once I was staying with my mother in London. At that time she was housekeeper to a very wealthy Canadian who lived in a luxury flat just off Hyde Park. They all went off for a while, and I had the flat to myself. There I was in London, living in this luxurious flat, with two huge color television sets and all the food I could possibly eat! I had enough money for whatever I wanted, lots of records, lots of everything. But I was so bored! I told myself, "Please remember this. If you are ever tempted to think that physical comfort gives happiness, remember this." But then, another time I was staying in a cave, not my cave but another cave, which was very small. It was so small that you couldn't stand up in it, with a tiny box you could only just sit in, and that was the bed as well. It was full of fleas, so I was covered in flea bites. There was no water. You had to go half a mile down a very steep track to bring up water. There was also almost no food at all, and it was hot. But I was in bliss. I was so happy. It was a very holy place, and the people there were wonderful. Although from a physical point of view the situation was difficult, so what! The mind was happy. I remember that whole place as being bathed in golden light. Do you see what I mean?

It is one of the great lies propagated by our culture that getting more and more physical and material prosperity will lead to greater and greater happiness. This is simply not true. Genuine happiness lies in not wanting. If we think about it, we will probably all agree that our times of deepest happiness were times when everything was just fine as it was. Endless wanting is such a burden to the mind. So if we really wish to be happy and create happiness for those around us, our task is to clean, aerate and order our minds. If we all had a loudspeaker attached to our minds and everybody could hear what everybody else was thinking, people would really want to learn to meditate, and quickly! We can start ordering our inner house by throwing out the junk. Pick each thing up and ask, "Is this useful or not? Why have I been carrying this around for so long?" Get rid of it. Have a nice big spring cleaning. The mind will feel so much cleaner and more spacious. Clean the windows so you can see out clearly. This should be our number one priority. Why do we treat the mind as if it were something unimportant?

The fourth object is known as awareness of dharmas, which, at least in the Mahayana school, refers to external phenomena as perceived through the senses. As I said, we can only know something as it is interpreted through our senses. We perceive things the way we do only because of the particular senses we have. If we possessed different senses, we would perceive things differently, but they would be equally real to us. We never actually perceive what is there, only what is related back to us through our senses. The reality perceived by a fly, with its very differently structured eye and antennae, is very different from the reality we perceive, but it is equally valid from the fly's point of view. We don't see things better than the fly does, we just see our own version. Take this glass, for example. It's very solid. If I were to hit somebody with it, he would feel it. But modern physics tells us that this glass is composed mostly of space, with just a few electrons, protons, and neutrons zooming around in it. Yet we don't perceive it that way. And if I were an ant, or an elephant, or a dolphin, I would perceive something else again. Each of these perceptions is valid. Our version is no better than anyone else's.

The problem is that we grasp onto stimuli we receive from external phenomena. Because it gives us this pleasure/pain reaction, we proceed to elaborate on it and interpret it. We don't see it as just a series of stimuli. There is a story from around the time of the Buddha about a *sadhu*, or Indian holy man, who was living somewhere in south India. He had an experience in his meditation and thought he had attained enlightenment. But the tree spirit living in the tree under which he was meditating said to him, "No, you are not enlightened." He said, "I'm not?" And the tree spirit said, "Definitely not." So he asked the tree spirit, "Who is enlightened?" The tree spirit replied, "Well there is this guy called the Buddha who lives up in north India. You could try him. He is enlightened." So the sadhu thought, "Okay. If this is not enlightenment, I've got to find someone who is enlightened and really knows what enlightenment is."

He set off and traveled for weeks, if not months, around the north of India asking people where he could find the Buddha. Eventually, early one morning, he arrived at the town where the Buddha was staying. But the Buddha was out on his alms round. The sadhu found the Buddha and raced up to him, prostrated at his feet and said, "Please tell me how to get enlightened. Give me teachings." The Buddha said, "This is not an appropriate time. I am doing my alms round. Come back later." But the sadhu insisted, "You have to tell me now. Give me some teachings." The Buddha replied, "It's really not appropriate right now. Get off my feet." "No, no," replied the sadhu, "You've got to give me a teaching." So the Buddha said, "Fine. In the hearing, there is merely the hearing; in the seeing, there is merely the seeing; in the sensing, there is merely the sensing and in the thinking, there is merely the thinking." By the time the Buddha had finished speaking, this guy had got it. He became an arhat. He then rose into the air, bowed to the Buddha and self-combusted. So that was the teaching. Did you get it?

QUESTIONS

Q: Did he get *shunyata?*
TP: In one way it was shunyata, in another way it was saying. . .

Q: There's nobody home?

TP: Exactly. It is like being in an empty house with all the doors and windows open and the breezes blowing through. In the seeing, there is merely the seeing. In thinking there is merely thinking. Everything else is our interpretation. When I was younger, just before I became Buddhist, I started to go into these states spontaneously. There would be a sudden click, and I would become conscious that I was seeing and that it was indeed just visual input coming onto the eye consciousness and being received, and that hearing was just sounds and that thinking really was just thoughts coming up in the mind, up, down, next thought, up, down.

When the mind entered this kind of consciousness, I would look at all the people around me—at that time I was working in a library—and I would see how incredibly involved they were all in their ideas, their emotions, the daily news, their relationships, and whatever else was happening. There was no space: they were completely involved. It was like they were suffocating. I realized that I was normally like this, too. Enormous compassion arose. I saw how much pain and suffering we create for ourselves and those around us. Yet we don't want to. We want to be happy. We want to be peaceful. We want to make people around us happy. But we do everything to create the opposite effect. When I saw this, I felt unbearable love and compassion. I am telling you this because I don't want you to think this focus on awareness makes us cold. Sometimes when I talk about topics such as detachment, non-attachment, being conscious, seeing thoughts and emotions just as thoughts and emotions, not being involved, and that sort of thing, people think it sounds cold. But in fact it is not like that. The true emotions such as love, compassion, and empathy are free to rise because they are part of our innate nature, and there is no longer anything obstructing them. Earlier on we were talking about opening up the heart. Learning to become more present and more aware like this is really another way to open up the heart.

Q: I have a question about thoughts. We are all good at various times either at experiencing our thoughts or actually going out and having to act on them. It seems very compelling to go and do something about a thought. So I guess my question is, From where do thoughts arise? I would be terrified to think that some of the thoughts that arise within me actually came from me.

TP: Where did you think they came from?

Q: Well, that's my question. Are there are a finite number of thoughts skate-boarding around in the universe, waiting to get onto my screen of conscious-ness or are these things like weeds which arise from a field?

TP: We manufacture our own thoughts. They don't come into us from out-side. They come from within. And we are capable of every kind of thought. We have the whole spectrum within us, from the infrared to the ultraviolet. We have the potential for everything—to be demonic or to become Buddhas. It's all there. Whether we hover down closer to the infrared than to the ultra-violet is up to us. But we need to recognize that we have everything within us. That doesn't mean we have to act on all our thoughts. However, we need to recognize that we are perfectly capable of being demons as well as angels. As long as we are unenlightened, as long as the roots of delusion, aversion, greed, and desire are still in our hearts, we are capable of just about everything because we are worldlings. Worldlings are like that. When thoughts come up, we need to recognize them, accept them, but not give energy to them. We certainly don't have to think that there is a force outside implanting them within us. The Prince of Lies is within our hearts. That's why we need to purify our hearts.

Q: With the example of washing dishes and being with the washing of the dishes, do you think sometimes doing an activity you don't have to think about is actually a chance to think about things you need to think about? You are being mindless, but you are actually using this as an opportunity to think about something else.

TP: Sometimes in a busy day this is necessary. But one should be aware that one is doing that. If we do it all the time and apply it to all of our actions, we are never present. As our awareness becomes clearer with practice, we are able to do an activity, know we are doing it, and at the same time plan some-thing else. Sometimes we need to go on automatic pilot. But if we are always on automatic pilot, our entire lives just slip away from us!

Q: A little along the same lines would be creative inspiration. I've appeared in a community theatre. I have wanted to be present, yet at the same time to release my mind to be creative.

TP: Then you know that now you are releasing your mind to be creative. Being aware does not mean that you don't think. Being aware of thinking is one of the areas of being aware. For example, after his enlightenment the Buddha spent forty-five years organizing a community and a doctrine which has remained more or less unaltered for 2,500 years. He was certainly thinking, but he knew what he was doing. He was thinking with a mind which was very clear. In Zen, they are very creative in poetry, art, and theatre. But they do it with a mind which is like a still lake, not a turbulent ocean. When the mind is centered, knowing and clear, great creativity arises. It's not murky. It's pure because it's coming from a much deeper level. All great artists and musicians are able to access that deeper level. It's not the surface mind, but a very deep pure stream of inner creativity, which is non-ego.

Q: You spoke before about the mind and consciousness being like a sense of space. I've heard it spoken about before as a sky-like mind. Do we exist in that all the time?
TP: Yes, we do, but we don't recognize it because we always identify with the clouds. Black clouds, white clouds. We don't see that space-like nature of the mind. That's what we have to reach. That's what we have to recognize.

Q: When you are speaking, are you in that same state?
TP: On an ultimate level, we can never leave it, because it is the root of our being. Whether or not we recognize it is another matter. To actually recognize the space-like nature of the mind is considered a major breakthrough. The idea is to learn how to develop that genuine non-dual awareness more and more often and in more and more activities. When it is present the whole time without a break, one is a Buddha. Most people don't access it at all. People whom we regard as being realized go in and out. When they want to see it, they do. For most of the time, they are in ordinary states of consciousness. That underlying consciousness is the energy which fuels the computer. It is always there. If we turned it off, we would be dead and the consciousness would depart.

Q: Sometimes I have so many thoughts that I find it hard to sit down and meditate, I find it hard to get into that awareness.
TP: Because you are agitated?

Q: Yes, because I get waves of thoughts.

TP: Everybody gets waves of thoughts. If you wait until you have no thoughts before you sit down to meditate, you will never meditate. The whole point of meditation is to learn to acknowledge this chaotic mind and to work with it. But if you are especially agitated at some particular point, it is a good idea to go out for a walk, look at the sky, the flowers, and the trees until the mind settles down a little.

Q: It's best to try to sit down for a while?

TP: Just bring the mind quietly to the in-going and the out-going of the breath. Basically this is all that's happening in this moment. Whatever happened before that we are so worried and agitated about, whatever might happen in the future that is worrying and agitating us, let go of it. At this moment we are just here. The breath goes in, the breath goes out. That's what's happening. The rest is all our mental commentaries and interpretations. Just bring the mind back into the present. Let everything else drop away. Don't give any energy to it. Just be present in the moment. That calms the mind. And if the mind doesn't calm down, it doesn't. That's okay, too.

Q: With the breath meditation, I've learned so many, I don't know which to do.

TP: It's good to stick to the one you like best. There are many different ways of doing this. You can bring your consciousness to the rise and fall of the abdomen. You can be conscious of the whole breath going in and the whole breath going out. Some Tibetans talk about lights going in and going out. It doesn't matter. Just find the one that you are most comfortable with and stay with that one. They all lead to the same thing. You see, nothing is stopping us from being conscious. Nothing is stopping us from being aware. On one level we are always aware, otherwise we would be unconscious. But we are not conscious of being conscious. We forget we are conscious. So it's not something we have to develop. We already have it. We just have to acknowledge it.

The inertia of our minds is so great. We get locked into habits and it's very difficult to break them. One of the most profound habits is this mental inertia. We might think we are very mentally active, we might think we are very intelligent and outgoing and clever and always thinking of things. But basically, we are escaping from being present in the moment, from really wak-ing up. We are all asleep. We are sleepwalking and dreaming this dream. For some it is a nightmare, for others a wonderful dream. But we are all just dream-ing. And the urge to wake up is covered by this heavy inertia. It's too much trouble to wake up, so we keep on snoring. This is the problem. This is why I suggest starting with little things to try to overcome our habitual pattern of inattention. We must try to develop the practice of giving everything we do our full attention. The thing that we are doing in this moment is the most important thing we could possibly be doing, because it is what we are doing. Everything else is just thinking "about." It's just memory or anticipation. The only reality we have is what we are doing in this very moment. And if we miss that, we've lost it, because it's gone. Do you see? Every person we meet is the most important person in the world to us at that moment because he is the person in front of us.

Q: Is that the ultimate reality you were talking about before?
TP: No, it's not ultimate reality because it is still within the realm of duality. There is still subject and object. Ultimate reality is non-dual. It is beyond subject and object. We live in this subject-object dichotomy, this "I" and "non-I." But this is the path leading to the realm where there is no subject and no object, to attaining non-dual awareness and being able to sustain it. When we attain this state, great unconditioned love and compassion arise naturally.

Have any of you met the Dalai Lama? Whether you are the Pope, President of the United States, or a road worker from Nepal, it doesn't matter. He will take your hand and look into your eyes. At that moment you will know that only you exist for him. At that moment, you are the most fascinating and important person in his life. This undercuts everybody, even reporters, politi-cians, and high churchmen. They are not used to being related to as another person. They are accustomed to being related to as a reporter or as a politi-cian or whatever. But he cuts through all that. He just relates from heart to heart. That's why people find it so moving, because he is so totally genuine. He is not meeting them as the Dalai Lama. He is meeting them as a simple monk, as he says. And he is talking to the person, not to the various masks they are wearing for the world. It is that kind of naked attention which really fuels unconditioned love. It is this total non-judgment. When we meet peo-ple our first thought should be "May you be well and happy." Not whether or not we like the person or whether or not we think they are good looking, or whether we like what they are wearing.

This is especially important with the people we are close to. We need to try to relate to them as if we had never met before—to see them freshly in their genuine potential instead of seeing this hard mold we have pressed everybody we know into. We are always changing, moment to moment. We have so many different potentials. We can never see the same person twice, nor are we the same person not seeing the same person twice! Not only can we never step into the same river twice, but the same person can never step into the river twice. Everything is constantly changing from moment to moment. But we stamp our prejudices and our interpretations onto everyone until we don't see them any more. Sometimes when I was staying in my cave, although it was small, I would go to another part of it or sit on the step. I would close my eyes and try to empty my thoughts and then open my eyes and see the cave as if I had never seen it before, and really see it.

We become dulled by the force of habit. We no longer see, and we think that everything is boring. Little children are fascinated by everything around them because everything is interesting to them. We should have a mind like a small child in a temple looking at the frescoes. He is not thinking, "Hmm, these are not as good as the frescoes I saw last year—the artist is not so great, or I think he has used too much blue, or I prefer the other kind of green." He is just seeing it, fascinated. Children don't have preconceptions, they don't make comparisons or interpretations. They are just looking at all those pictures with a fresh mind. This is what we are trying to achieve.

Q: Some days might be quite routine and tasks like the dishes don't feel very important or deserving of my attention, it's just the dishes, it goes on every day. Do I try to think, "Okay, when I do the dishes I should really concentrate and do a good job"?

TP: It's not, "I've got to pay attention and do a good job." It's not aggressive like that. It's just realizing and knowing you are washing the dishes. Every dish you wash is a new dish. Every time you wash the dishes it is a new experience. But because we have dulled our mind so much it seems like it's not important. It seems like it's mundane, and our lives seem dull. Our lives are not dull. We make them dull because our minds are dull. Do you see?

We are attempting to do everything with our whole being, from the center, just knowing—very easy, very relaxed, not trying to concentrate—just knowing, just being. What am I doing right now? Right now I'm washing the dishes. Okay, I'll wash dishes. If you bring that quality to everything, it makes the mind very light, relaxed, and unstressed. Actually there is joy in washing dishes!

Q: Yes, I can see that it's not demanding on your emotions or anything like that, compared to certain other things.

TP: That's not the point. The point is that whatever you are doing, even if you are doing something very demanding of your emotions and your intellect, you do it in a state of awareness. We are not talking about being goal-oriented or having aims. The results will take care of themselves. Our society is very result-oriented, that's why we are so competitive. That's why we are always stressed, because we are always looking at something in the distance. If you are always looking at the top of the mountain you are climbing, you cannot be aware of the grass and flowers growing at your feet. We are always looking ahead, aren't we? And then the actual thing, the actual living, passes us by. We are locked inside our brains, cut off from the present moment, always centered on something beyond our reach. We are imagining this mirage of happiness, satisfaction and fulfillment which will magically appear once this and this and this happens. But what's happening right now is "it" and it's the only "it" we have. The rest is just fabrication. If we lose this moment because we are thinking about something else, we've lost it forever. Just know what's happening right in this moment. That's enough. This moment will turn into the next moment, which will then transform into the next. It's not spectacular. It's not lights, music, and bliss. But it will transform your life.

Q: With the judgmental mind type of thing, is the best way to deal with that to let it go?

TP: One recognizes that is what the mind is doing, but one also recognizes it is just the mind. Our problem is that we believe our mind and identify with it.

Q: You were talking earlier about inertia and apathy and seeing the clouds rather than the sky. Fear seems to have a lot to do with that. Do you know what people are scared of and why they are scared?

TP: Fear is a very deep issue. But where does fear come from? Fear basically comes from our wrong identification, our identification with something that we think is "me" and "mine." This ego. And because we think of the ego as being "me" and "mine," it creates this whole web to protect itself. One of the main ways it does this is through fear. When we are fearful, the important thing to ask ourselves is not "What am I afraid of," but, "What is fear?" How does it manifest, what does it look like, where does it come from? And then beyond that, who is afraid? If we say, "I am afraid," then who is this I? So much of what we do is motivated by hope and fear. It's not something I can explain in two minutes. It's a vast topic.

Q: It just seems that many people have a fear of spirituality, of themselves.
TP: Yes, they do, because the ego doesn't want to be discovered as non-existent. It is very afraid of that. It sees a genuine spiritual path as its death, and it is right. Of course, it never really existed from the start, but the psychological forces move very rapidly to give the impression that there is something behind it all. It is afraid of being revealed as the charlatan that it is. So of course, many people are afraid to meditate, because of what they might find. But that is the whole point, dealing with these fears. The only way to overcome them is to confront them. Otherwise, we will be driven by this fear for the rest of our lives.

Q: I'm fascinated by the notion of omnipresence. You know the bodhisattvas with the arms, are they present everywhere?
TP: The Buddha mind is omnipresent.

Q: How do the bodhisattvas work?
TP: The bodhisattvas work in whatever way is most appropriate. They can manifest as many different kinds of beings. They can be reborn in many different situations. They can even apparently manifest as inanimate objects, such as bridges and boats for people who need them, depending on the circumstances which arise. The Bodhisattva Chenrezig has a thousand arms. This is his reaching out in every situation. In each of his hands there is an eye. This means that not only does he give help, he sees the situation with clarity and therefore gives the appropriate help. This appropriate help is given according to the karma of beings. We are very short-sighted. Take the

example of genetic engineering. We can now see whether a baby is malformed within its mother's womb. If it's going to be malformed, our present short-sighted compassion says it's better that the child not be born. We will abort it. That seems very compassionate to both the baby and the mother.

When I was a child I had some sickness that nobody could diagnose. I would very often go and stay in a hospital. In the hospital there were many children with all kinds of diseases. Some had hydrocephalus, some were spastic, some had other really ghastly things wrong with them. Even as a child, and I was the only one who was sort of normal, what struck me was the wisdom and maturity that those children had. They were so sweet. Their eyes had such understanding, such compassion in them. And how much their parents loved them! There was this incredible relationship between these sick children and their parents.

Who knows how much they were all learning from that! Would it be better to have broken that relationship by aborting the "imperfect" child beforehand? What I'm saying is, a bodhisattva does not necessarily rush in to stop something which seems terrible. Maybe it's necessary for these beings to experience this. We are not here just to have a good time. We are here to learn, to grow, to wake up. One of the reasons why a heavenly rebirth is not regarded as being a good thing in Buddhist theology is that there is no challenge involved. Everything is so nice in heaven that you never learn anything there. A human rebirth is considered the best because there is a balance between pleasure and pain. Therefore we can make choices, we can grow, we can be developed. A bodhisattva would have the wisdom to see what would be the appropriate response. But it might not be what we, with our undeveloped compassion, would consider appropriate.

Q: Is your approach to living with pain just to be with the pain?
TP: Well, if you have a headache and you take an aspirin, that's fine. But if you have pain and it is unavoidable, then yes. Pain itself can be a wonderful meditation. I remember once I was in my cave chopping wood. The axe slipped and I almost cut my thumb off. I bound it in a white Tibetan scarf. It was quite painful. It wasn't like cancer, but it was painful enough. The initial reaction is aversion, "How can I get rid of this pain?" But instead we can bring the attention to the pain itself. First of all, it's very compelling, so it's easy to focus on it. But then, what is pain? It is not this big solid block. When we go

into it, it kind of undulates. And there are many strands. Once I had an eye infection which lasted for a few months. That was extraordinarily painful, and I couldn't see. I had to be in the dark. The pain was interesting. It was like a symphony. There were violins and percussion. It wasn't just one kind of pain. There were stabbing pains, wrenching pains, raging pains. And as I got into this, there was no longer this vision of "I am feeling pain." It was no longer pain. I was completely absorbed in these varying sensations. If you go into it even more deeply, behind that cacophony, the noise of the pain, there is this underlying silence. So it can be a great practice, actually.

Q: What about if you have blocked the pain for a long time. How do you bring back an awareness of it?
TP: You mean emotional pain?

Q: No. I mean physical, spiritual, or emotional. Any sort of pain.
TP: One can become conscious again. One can give it the space to reappear, accept it and be compassionate towards it. Give it the space just to say what it wants to say. We spend our life within this pleasure/pain dichotomy—trying to avoid pain and to attract pleasure.

Q: With regard to transforming one's emotions, Venerable, how does one transform painful emotions into useful fuel for the spiritual path?
TP: In a way, one could say that the whole of the Buddhist path is about transforming negative emotions into positive ones, and there are many levels on which we can do that. So it's a big question. In brief, first we have to recognize what is happening. Then we have to accept it. It doesn't mean we have to approve or disapprove. If we have feelings of anger, first of all we must recognize these feelings, then we have to accept that we have these feelings. If we don't accept this and instead reject the feeling, we cut off any further dialogue.

From there it depends. If we take anger as the example, there are many different ways of dealing with it. We could replace a negative emotion with a positive one. This is said to be like removing one wedge of wood by inserting another, finer one. The other wedge will fall out. If we have a lot of anger, it makes sense to practice loving-kindness. There are many books and teachings on the meditation on loving-kindness. Now in the meditation on loving-kindness, the first person to whom we direct this love is ourselves. I think this is very relevant in the West because, as His Holiness the Dalai Lama has remarked, one of the main differences between Westerners and Tibetans is that on the whole Tibetans feel quite good about themselves, whereas most Westerners he encountered did not really like themselves. Sometimes they hated themselves and were very unforgiving towards themselves. He thought this strange. So, when we are trying to eradicate anger, the first thing to do is to become at peace with ourselves. After all, if we harbor anger towards ourselves, it is no good imagining that this anger is not going to be translated into anger towards others. It is no good just deciding to love our enemy if we hold onto the fundamental cause of this anger, which is our own inner conflict—our own self-hatred, guilt, or blame. First we have to work at acceptance and really feel friendly towards ourselves and have compassion towards ourselves. We are supposed to have love and compassion towards all beings, and we are also beings. The first being towards whom we have responsibility is ourselves. We must be kind to ourselves. In the West, I don't know why, people are so harsh towards themselves. They see all their faults but they don't want to acknowledge the goodness within them. They are happy to tell people, "I am such an angry person." But even to themselves they won't say, "I am angry, but I am also generous."

So in dealing with a negative emotion such as anger, we first have to make peace with ourselves. There are meditations for doing this. When we have generated a genuine sense of friendship towards ourselves, we generate that again and send it outwards, firstly towards someone we care about. We should not focus on someone to whom we are sexually attracted because, whereas the far enemy of loving-kindness is anger and hatred, the near enemy is actually desire. This loving-kindness has nothing to do with grasping and attachment. It is all about unconditional love, which just wishes for others to be happy. So when we are practicing how to give loving-kindness, we should begin our practice with someone we are fond of. In classical terms, such a person is called the "benefactor." This is anyone who has been kind to us at any time and to whom we feel warmly. With this person in mind we think, "May you be well and happy." Wish them to be free from troubles. Try to really feel this for the person.

Once we manage to generate these feelings, we next apply them to somebody who is quite neutral—somebody we see from time to time, but don't have much feeling about one way or the other. Then we try the same exercise on somebody we find difficult to deal with, someone who arouses a lot of anger in us. We just keep trying to generate this feeling of loving-kindness towards that person. If the feeling doesn't come, that's fine. We go back to working on somebody we like, then someone neutral, etc. until it works for us.

This remedy for anger is 2,500 years old. The Buddha said, "Hatred does not cease by hatred. Hatred ceases only by love. This is an eternal law." But we have to work on it. That's the traditional way of dealing with anger. There are traditional ways of dealing with other emotions, too. Each has its antidote. Each has its opposite emotion to help counterbalance it. For example, people who are troubled by excessive sexual desire may be advised to contemplate the unpleasant aspects of the body, visualizing it from the hair of the head to the soles of the feet, with all of the skin removed. We see the brains, the heart and the guts. None of it is beautiful or desirable. Think of everything which emerges from our body, such as sweat, snot, feces, and urine. None of these substances are cherishable, even if they come from the beloved. We begin to see that the body is much less attractive than our desire would make it seem. This is the antidote to attachment to the body or to experiencing excessive sexual desire for other people.

Another way of dealing with negative emotions, once we have developed strong mindfulness, is to see thoughts and emotions in their essential nature as they arise, instead of jumping in and getting caught up in them. When we look into them, we see they are not solid. They are transparent and fluid. Their nature is empty. If we can see this at the moment the thoughts and emotions arise, then in that very moment, we transform them into a source of tremendous clear energy. Such moments provide us with extremely sharp insight. At their source, all these negative emotions are a form of wisdom energy. It is wisdom energy that has become distorted. For this reason in the Mahayana, and especially in the Vajrayana, these negative emotions are not uprooted. They are understood in their true nature. This gives us access to very deep levels of clear energy. But this presupposes a strong degree of awareness. If we have that level of awareness, whatever comes up is naturally liberated in the moment. Then there is no problem.

Q: You talked about how important it is to be with people close to you, like family, to practice this loving-kindness. But if you have a lot of conflict, are you actually saying it's better to be with those people than to be away from them until you develop that?

TP: If you are in a situation which is difficult to handle and you are feeling vulnerable or fragile, then it would help perhaps to be away for a time in order to develop these skills. Of course, if that isn't possible, then you have to practice in the midst of the lions. But it might be easier in the beginning to be in a more peaceful atmosphere, where you are not feeling so threatened.

Q: Are you saying that ultimately it is better to face up to these situations?
TP: Yes. The fact is that ultimately we will be able to deal with whatever comes up. I am not saying that we need to seek out people who are especially annoying and difficult. They will come. But if you are in a situation where they are already there, yes. The point is to develop enough inner strength and clarity to be able to deal with the situation. When we learn how to deal with situations skillfully, they no longer seem so difficult.

Q: So you don't need to seek out difficult people?
TP: Absolutely not. They will come. The Buddha praised good companionship. It was one of the things he stressed over and over. He said that we should seek the company of good friends. Good friends refers to people who are morally and spiritually superior or at least equal to ourselves. We should have friends who inspire us to develop the good in ourselves, and as much as possible we should avoid bad friends—people who influence us in a negative way.

Q: I thought the whole point of this was to be able to deal with anybody, however difficult?
TP: When we are spiritually strong enough, we can. But as long as we are not, as long as we are easily influenced by the people around us and we have a choice, it makes sense to choose to be with people who help us spiritually. Of course, once we achieve a state of inner strength, we can benefit others. Then we can be with whomever. But as long as we are weak and easily influenced, we don't benefit other people and neither do we benefit ourselves.

Q: So it's all right to walk away from certain people if they are disturbing us?
TP: Yes. Until you reach a point where you can genuinely benefit others without getting involved, why be involved? It is better for us to choose to be with people who make us feel inspired, happy, and harmonious and who foster the development of these nurturing qualities within us.

Q: How do you know whether your actions are going to benefit others or not? You were talking before about perception being different for everyone.

TP: We have to examine our motives. Of course we can try to justify almost anything. Even Pol Pot claimed to be innocent. He maintained he had done nothing wrong and wondered why everyone was so angry, and this was after having caused the deaths of two million people! But, if we want to be honest, we should check to see whether our actions—actions of mind as well as speech and body—are motivated by delusion, confusion, greed, clinging, aversion, anger, jealousy, or pride. Or on the other hand, are they motivated by understanding, love, generosity, and so on. We have to ask ourselves what is really behind the action. If the motivation is positive, the action will probably be positive. If the motivation is negative, even if what we do looks good to others, the results will probably be negative. Also, we have to take a long-term view. It is like tossing a stone into a lake. If there are any ripples, what is likely to be the outcome? How will it affect people? We should look at the larger picture. We should be aware that our words and actions do affect other people. It is not enough to say, "It's okay, I bear the responsibility."

Q: I guess in some situations you would have to learn to be very skillful to know whether or not some people might be hurt, but some others might not be hurt by the same action. If you want to look after someone, for example, someone might be hurt by that but you don't know.

TP: We need to try and develop a kind of clarity in seeing the situation and judging whether or not our intention is really to help. Of course, we are all learning, and we all make mistakes. But the whole point is to develop the ability to see the situation clearly and meet it with the appropriate response. Of course, we need to take responsibility for what we do and not blame it on somebody else. There will be many times when it is difficult to make a choice. But we should not just rush in impulsively. We should look at the options and try to do the wisest thing.

Q: Are there levels of non-dual perception? And if there are levels, what are they? There are times when one can feel the no-oneness. Are there levels of non-dual perception or awareness?

TP: Non-dual awareness is non-dual awareness, just as the blue sky is the blue sky. But some people get just a glimpse. For a moment the clouds part, but then they form again. For some people the clouds part and stay apart for quite a long time. For a very few, they part and don't come back together again.

Q: How do they do that?
TP: Presumably they have had very deep experiences in past lives. In this lifetime they are just reestablishing their prior realizations. I think that can be the only reason, because it comes to them spontaneously, naturally, and the mind never returns to the state of ignorance. They remain with that awareness. Like Ramana Maharshi in this century. He had an experience when he was about sixteen and it changed him permanently. Most of us get just a glimpse. For a short period we see with great clarity, there is neither seen nor seer, and there is this panoramic awareness. But then it fades.

Q: Why does it fade?
TP: Because the conditioning of the mind is so strong. Our state of ignorance, of not knowing, of being asleep is very profound in us.

Q: You mean you go back to old thinking patterns?
TP: Yes. The point is to try as much as possible to understand and reproduce those glimpses until we gradually prolong them. There are many Tibetan books about these meditational techniques. You might have a very thick book. The first few pages deal with what you do before you have a glimpse of the nature of mind, and the rest is what you do afterwards. Then you need to learn how to understand it, how to prolong it, and how to integrate it into your thinking and into daily life and so on.

Q: You know with these glimpses, if there's that much before you get to the glimpse, and that much afterwards, does that suggest that it is quite achievable for people?
TP: Once I was told this story by an American nun who was living in Lahoul. It seems she was sitting on a roof with some monks in a Himalayan valley and the monks said to her conversationally, "When did you first realize the nature of the mind?" And she said, "I've never realized the nature of the mind." And then they said, "It's okay, you can tell us. We are your Dharma brothers, come on." And she said, "No, I never have." And they just looked at her as if to say, "What?"

Q: Had she actually had the realization?

TP: No, she hadn't. But the monks didn't believe her. They thought she was just being coy. You can't tell just by looking at someone. They were not Buddhas. They were just ordinary monks, but they were ordinary monks who had done a lot of practice. For them, it was nothing special. That's why they couldn't believe she had not realized it. Our minds are so complicated that we make even the simplest thing extremely intricate. We analyze it and pull it apart and so on. It is extremely difficult for us to find a space to see the nature of the mind, because we have clouds on top of clouds on top of clouds. Whereas in the case of the monks, there was no television, no radio, no novels, no magazines, and they almost never read a newspaper. Their minds were really quite simple and empty, in a good sort of way. If somebody says to them, "You do this," they just do it. They don't have to analyze or understand it or get into all sorts of emotional relationships with it. But Westerners can also do this. The nature of the mind is the nature of the mind. It's not Tibetan versus Western. Sky is sky, whether it's over Australia or over Tibet.

Q: I struggled with the idea of there being no one home in meditations in the past. I have reached a point which I can only call a void. I mean, I was perfectly calm and without desires. But the void seemed cold and a bit heartless. And when you said true emotions of loving-kindness and compassion arise out of that emptiness, I wondered if I didn't actually embrace that emptiness because I was afraid of losing my personality or something like that. But the void that I did face in meditation was not a pleasant thing to me.

TP: Perhaps that's true. Perhaps the ego put up this barrier of fear. It's like standing on the edge of a chasm and being afraid to jump.

Q: I felt that if I went into this any more, I would keep sinking and not come up.

TP: Well, probably the ego would keep sinking and not come up.

Q: But then what is it that experiences that?

TP: Something other than the ego. When one experiences the unconditioned, one does not cease to exist or turn into a cosmic blob. In some ways, one becomes really vivid for the first time. As I said, it's like waking from sleep. But it is an awakening which is not connected with this ordinary association of "I" and "me." It totally transcends all that. It is far greater and more vivid. Instead of the "I" and "me" which separate us from all beings, this connects us with all beings. The ego understands that this is death, and therefore it generates great fear.

Q: Does everybody who enters that path feel that fear?

TP: Most people do. Fear is the last barrier of the ego. This is why when we meditate in a Buddhist context, we always start by taking refuge in the Buddha, in the Dharma, and in the enlightened Community, and we take the Bodhisattva Vow to attain enlightenment not for ourselves, but for the sake of all beings. Then we do a Guru Yoga in which we visualize the teachers and the lineage going back to the primordial Buddha and we absorb that into ourselves. This gives us protection. It is like being held in the palms of the Buddhas. Nothing can hurt us. With that kind of inner assurance, we gain the courage to jump.

Q: What causes emotions during meditation, like crying and other kinds of energies coming through?

TP: We are creating the space for all these energies, these tight little hidden knots, to unravel. These are emotions, fears, anxieties, and joys which we somehow push down, and because of our superficial mental chatter, manage to ignore. When you are meditating, the mind becomes quiet. It gives that space and that permission for things to start coming up to the surface. Then all sorts of emotions come up. Some people start laughing. Some start crying. Some have fear. Some have elation. All sorts of things can come up. You just let them come up, recognize them, accept them, and let them disappear.

Q: How about the energies rising through the body? Are they all part of the same thing?

TP: Yes, that's part of the same thing. While you are meditating, your mind and the *prana* or *chi*, in other words, the internal energies of the body, are very closely connected. As the mind becomes more concentrated this also affects the chi, or prana, of the body, which begins to gather together and activate. In the Tibetan tradition, they have a twofold way of doing this. First of all, by consciously manipulating these energies in order to affect the mind and second, by using the mind to affect the energies. The two go together.

Q: What if you have an out-of-mind experience or an out-of-body experience while you are meditating?

TP: I would say if you had feelings like that and you felt threatened, it would be a good idea to keep the consciousness very firmly within the body. For example, concentrate on breathing in and breathing out. While you are concentrating on breathing in and breathing out, you are not going to go anywhere.

Q: Do you think that in a crisis it's a good idea to sit down and try to meditate?

TP: I think it's a good idea to sit down, connect with the breathing in and breathing out, and try to just let the mind let go. If Buddhism ever had a slogan, that slogan would be: "Let go."

Q: How does anger relate to the ego?

TP: It's one of the great ego boosters. It makes the ego feel simultaneously great and awful. When anger arises in the mind, we should be conscious of it. We should recognize it. If possible, not identify with it. Not think this is "my" anger. But just recognize it for what it is, a mental state. Then, if possible, just let it drop. If we see it with great clarity, then in that moment of really seeing it, it will naturally transform. That requires a very sharp degree of insight. Otherwise, the important thing to understand with anger is that there are a number of methods available for dealing with it. One way of dealing with anger towards a certain person is to remind ourselves that the person is acting that way because of his own causes and conditions. We can appreciate why people behave the way they do if we take into account their background, upbringing, ideas, and what motivates them. Then we begin to understand more clearly the space they are coming from. We begin to realize that anger is not an appropriate response. Maybe there is a more appropriate response, a more helpful response than anger.

Q: How would you help someone who is very fearful of dying?

TP: You know, since coming to Australia, I have come to visit about six or seven people who are just on the verge of dying. The people I met have all been incredibly wonderful. One of them had some kind of neural disease, and she could communicate only by typing with one finger very slowly, and then it came up on a computer screen. I have met others with cancer or other diseases. All of them were very active people with families. One was a yoga teacher. And then suddenly, one day they discovered they had a life-threatening disease and only a very limited time to live.

Just a couple of days ago, I met a woman who was dying of cancer. She told me she had only about three weeks left. I said, "Well, you know really, you are very fortunate because we all have to die. The only thing certain in life is death. Whether we will take another breath or not, who knows? But we are going to die. That's for sure." Most of us never think about death until we are suddenly faced with it. And people don't know what to do. They have never given any thought to it. They have all these untidy relationships which they never dealt with, because they thought they were going to live forever.

If you have the chance, the great opportunity to know, suddenly, that you are going to die, then that is a wonderful opportunity to decide once and for all what is important and what is not important. What is important to think and what is not important to think. What emotions it is necessary to cling to and what it is not necessary to cling to. It's a wonderful opportunity to come face to face with what matters and what does not matter. Death is not a bad thing; we all have to go. But we must use this opportunity to grow up and to clear our relationships. Not clinging, just loving without attachment. To really face who we are. To die without regret. To feel that we have lived our lives in such a manner that it's okay to go now. And if we are faced with the fact that we are going to die within a short time, remember that we are all going to die within a short time anyway, but we just don't realize that. If we are forced to face this fact, then this is a great opportunity for enormous inner transformation. All these people had done that. They had started with blind panic, progressed to great remorse, then anger and bitterness, because they were leaving behind children and partners. Most felt that they hadn't lived very long. Most of them were in their forties, and felt that they still had so many things to do. But they had worked through it all and reached the point of saying, "Now I'm ready to go. I cry a bit every day, but it's okay."

Q: How do we approach the fear when somebody is very fearful of dying? Some people may have finished all the business they need to finish, but still they can be frightened of death.

TP: Personally, I would tell people who are fearful of death that they honestly have nothing to fear. This is a great adventure. We have lived and died so many times. This is just natural; like trees and plants, we are constantly being recycled. It is ecologically sound, even. If you have lived a basically decent life, a life in which you did not deliberately harm people, if you were basically a kind, honest, decent sort of person, you have nothing to fear when you die. What we receive after death will be the projection of what we hold in our own minds. The beings we meet will be the kinds of beings who are on much the same level as we are.

It's not a big deal. The consciousness does not die. It's only the body that dies. And we are not the body. We are afraid only because we identify with the body. Once we realize we are not the body, what we identify with will actually go on. Then what is there to fear? People who have had near death experiences or who have had clairvoyant experiences all agree that it is nothing terrible at all. That is, unless you have been a really awful person. If you have lived your life full of hatred and anger, delighting in hurting others, then you have cause to fear. But for ordinary people, there is nothing to fear.

I think when we are with people who are fearful of death, it is important to talk to them about death because they are likely to be in a state of denial. But when you start talking about it to them, it frees them to talk also, and they are usually relieved to be able to do so, because everyone else around them has also been in a state of denial. Death is a big taboo. In general, people don't want to talk about it. They will tell you about their multiple orgasms and all sorts of things, but they won't talk about death. They are ashamed to mention it. To mention the unmentionable is an enormous relief, especially for someone who is facing it!

Q: Are suicide and euthanasia short-cutting a process we are supposed to go through?
TP: Both suicide and euthanasia may deny people the time to transform. All right, it's awful if you have a terrible disease, and of course there is the panic and the pain and things like that. I had a friend who was a nurse, and she used to work in a cancer hospital. She said that on the one hand it was extremely depressing, because you would see these beautiful little children coming in with cancer. It was heart-rending. On the other hand, you also saw so many people coming in with cancer in a state of denial or of anger and bitterness. But as time passed, you could see more and more of this inner transformation.

And she said that most people were glowing at the end. If you cut that short when you are still in a state of panic or denial, you don't give yourself the chance to make this transformation.

Q: There is also this idea that you can transform a lot of death sentences into life again as well.

TP: That's great. Then you take life really seriously. Then life becomes very precious. You don't waste it any more. When I went back to England after my first trip to India, I met my cousin for the first time. He was eight years old. He had been born after I left for India. He had cystic fibrosis, which meant that every day for about two and a half hours he had to be upside down with my aunt pounding him on the back to get rid of this phlegm which comes up—his lungs would fill up with phlegm so that he couldn't breathe. He couldn't eat most things because they created phlegm. He was often in a lot of pain, often choking, and he was being pounded on the back every day. But he was such a joyful little boy! He was so bright, so intelligent, so friendly.

The first time I met him he was making little plastic molds of insects. He asked me what I wanted. And I, looking at the scorpions and the spiders said, "I think I'll have a frog." He said, What color." I said, "Green." So he made me a nice green frog. He was so friendly, so happy, so joyful. Shortly afterwards he got very sick, went to hospital, and died. But the point is, because he was sick and because he knew he had only a very short time, he couldn't waste it being negative, moaning, and groaning. He didn't have time to be negative. He just had time to enjoy himself, make friends, and find out as much as possible before he left. It was also a great experience for my aunt. She learned a lot.

Q: We are all conditioned by our upbringing and our environment. Are these things that make us unique?

TP: From a Buddhist perspective, we are individuals because of the huge backlog of past births that we have. A baby doesn't come into this world as a complete blank. When you look into a baby's eyes, that baby is already a person. We have all the conditioning and habit patterns of past lives plus the conditioning and habit patterns from this life. But the point is to see that these are just conditioning and not think this is "me."

Q: So when you have reached that state, does that mean you have reached something universal? Or are you still an individual?

TP: You are universal and individual at the same time when you reach the unconditioned nature of the mind. The Buddha said, "I too use conceptualization, but I am no longer fooled by it." In other words, we can still use our personalities, but we are not used by them. I'll give you an example. Say we are all looking at this big white screen. On this screen there is a movie playing. We are watching the movie. The action is moving fast. You have all the characters, the hero, the heroine, and the villain. You are thinking, "Oh my goodness, is the heroine going to get the hero?" No, he's gone off. Now he's back again. There are tears and laughter, then a happy ending, and everyone comes out smiling. We are totally engrossed in this movie, which we believe in while it's happening.

But instead of looking at the movie, if you turned around and looked at the light coming from the projector, you would know that the light is actually being shone through transparent frames. These frames are moving so fast that it looks like people moving, and we're fooled, even though it is only a two-dimensional image on the screen. So meditation takes our focus away from this projection on the screen and turns it round to observe the frames. As we begin to look at the frames, they start to slow down. As our attention gets keener and clearer, the frames eventually split apart.

The frames are our mind-moments, which are linked together like a chain. The chain falls apart and then we see the light which is in the projector behind. Once we realize that we are the light shining from the projector, we can still watch the movie. But now we don't really believe it any more. We know it's just a movie being shown on the screen through these transparencies. Do you understand?

Q: Are there spiritual beings who guide us through our lives and from death to a new life? Do we have angels with us?

TP: Oh, you are talking to an ex-spiritualist here! I personally believe, and it's not just my belief, Buddhists in general believe it too, that there are many levels of beings who are not seen by us with our ordinary perception. They live on varying vibrational levels, you could say. Some of them are profoundly enlightened and these we call Buddhas. The Buddhas and bodhisattvas are there to help us. They are not judging us. They are not manipulating our lives. They are just there to help. If we open ourselves and call on them for help, they help us, provided it's within our own karmic possibilities. Then there are lower beings, not so enlightened, but nonetheless with good will, who are also trying to help. The Buddhas and bodhisattvas give spiritual help. You ask them for spiritual blessings. The other lower beings may be asked for more mundane blessings.

There are also beings in this universe who are quite malignant and want to harm. But if you take heartfelt refuge with the Buddhas and bodhisattvas, because their blessings are so great, these harmful beings cannot hurt you, regardless of your spiritual path. This is because light instantly destroys darkness. Then some people believe that there are disembodied beings who are quite ordinary, but in order to train in love and wisdom, they volunteer to try to help people here on earth. Again, if you are open to them, they are more able to help you. I think we are indeed surrounded by these beings. We are not alone. We just have to ask. If it's possible and useful—because sometimes what we want is not what we need—they will help.

Q: What do you think is the greatest lesson that Christians can learn from Buddhism?
TP: The greatest lesson that Christians seem to want to learn from Buddhism is how to meditate.

Q: Is that what you think as well?
TP: Yes. The Buddhists have very good techniques. They have a profound understanding of psychology, especially spiritual psychology. It doesn't presuppose any belief system. It can be used by people with all kinds of beliefs, and it benefits everybody. Certainly when I was living in Italy, I met many Christian monks and nuns who were practicing Buddhist meditation very happily, and teaching it.

Q: Why do you say you are an ex-spiritualist?
TP: I was brought up as a spiritualist. We used to have séances in our house every week. Now I'm not involved in that. But some of the spiritualist views on death and the after-life are still retained and kind of fitted in with my Buddhist ideas. So you are warned. They are a little bit unorthodox, but not very unorthodox. Buddhists also believe that when we die we go into an

intermediate state. Again, there you meet beings on the same wavelength. Therefore, it is important that in this lifetime we cultivate the mind and raise our spiritual level so that when we die we project something that we would really want to meet again.

Everything is a projection of our minds. Just as in the physical realm, we are all projecting. We are each living within our own projections. There is some physical basis. It is not completely arbitrary. But everybody sees things with their own interpretations. We are all projecting our own movie. When we no longer have a physical base, after the death of the body, our mind will create the seeming external appearances. Therefore it is important to write a good script while we have the chance, because we are going to be fully involved in the movie afterwards!

9
Difficult Points for Westerners

THIS TALK IS ABOUT areas which pose difficulties for some Westerners when they first come to the Dharma, and which may continue to be problematic for them further along in their practice. I would like to begin by talking about doubt. Perhaps because of our Judeo-Christian background, we have a tendency to regard doubt as something shameful, almost as an enemy. We feel that if we have doubts it means that we are denying the teachings and that we should really have unquestioning faith. Now in certain religions, unquestioning faith is considered a desirable quality. But in the Buddhadharma, this is not necessarily so. The Buddha described the Dharma as *ehi passiko*, which means "come and see," or "come and investigate," not "come and believe." An open, questioning mind is not regarded as a drawback to followers of the Buddhadharma. However, a mind which says, "This is not part of my mental framework, therefore I don't believe it," is a closed mind, and such an attitude is a great disadvantage for those who aspire to follow any spiritual path. But an open mind, which questions and doesn't accept things simply because they are said, is no problem at all.

There is a famous sutra which tells of a group of villagers who came to visit the Buddha. They said to him, "Many teachers come through here. Each has his own doctrine. Each claims that his particular philosophy and practice is the truth, but they all contradict each other. Now we're totally confused. What do we do?" Doesn't this story sound modern? Yet this was 2,500 years ago. Same problems. The Buddha replied, "You have a right to be confused. This is a confusing situation. Do not take anything on trust merely because it has passed down through tradition, or because your teachers say it, or because your elders have taught you, or because it's written in some famous scripture. When you have seen it and experienced it for yourself to be right and true, then you can accept it."

Now that was quite a revolutionary statement, because the Buddha was certainly saying that about his own doctrine too. In fact, all through the ages it has been understood that the doctrine is there to be investigated and experienced, "each man for himself." So one should not be afraid to doubt. Stephen Batchelor wrote a Dharma book entitled *The Faith to Doubt*. It is right for us to question. But we need to question with an open heart and an open mind, not with the idea that everything that fits our preconceived notions is right, and anything which does not is automatically wrong. The latter attitude is like the bed of Procrustes. You have a set pattern in place and everything you come across must either be stretched out or cut down to fit it. This just distorts everything and prevents learning.

If we come across certain things that we find difficult to accept even after careful investigation, that doesn't mean the whole Dharma has to be thrown overboard. Even now, after all these years, I still find certain things in the Tibetan Dharma which I'm not sure about at all. I used to go to my Lama and ask him about some of these things, and he would say, "That's fine. Obviously you don't really have a connection with that particular doctrine. It doesn't matter. Just put it aside. Don't say, 'No, it's not true.' Just say, 'At this point, my mind does not embrace this.' Maybe later you'll appreciate it, or maybe you won't. It's not important."

When we come across a concept which we find difficult to accept, the first thing we should do, especially if it's something which is integral to the Dharma, is to look into it with an unprejudiced mind. We should read everything we can on the subject, not just from the point of view of Buddhadharma, but if there are other approaches to it, we need to read about them, too. We need to ask ourselves how it connects with other parts of the doctrine. We have to bring our intelligence into this. At the same time, we should realize that at the moment, our level of intelligence is quite mundane. We do not yet have an all-encompassing mind. We have a very limited view. So there are definitely going to be things which our ordinary mundane consciousness cannot experience directly. But that does not mean these things do not exist.

Here again, it is important to keep an open mind. If other people with deeper experiences and vaster minds say they have experienced it, then we should at least be able to say, "Perhaps it might be so." We should not take our limited, ignorant minds as the norm. But we must remember that these limited, ignorant minds of ours can be transformed. That's what the path is all about. Our minds do become more open and increasingly vast as we progress. We do begin to see things more clearly, and as a result they slowly begin to fit into place. We need to be patient. We should not expect to understand the profound expositions of an enlightened mind in our first encounter with them. I'm sure we all know certain books of wisdom that we can read and reread over the years, and each time it seems like we are reading them for the first time. This is because as our minds open up, we begin to discover deeper and deeper layers of meaning we couldn't see the time before. It's like that with a true spiritual path. It has layer upon layer upon layer of meaning, and we can only understand those concepts which are accessible to our present level of mind.

I think people have different sticking points. I know that things some people find very difficult to grasp were extremely simple for me. I already believed many of the teachings before I came to the Buddhadharma. On the other hand, some things which were difficult for me, others find simple to understand and accept. We are all coming from different backgrounds, and so we each have our own special problems. But the important thing is to realize that this is no big deal. It doesn't matter. Our doubting and questioning spur us on and keep us intellectually alert.

There have been times when my whole spiritual life was one great big question mark. But instead of suppressing the questions, I brought up the things I questioned and examined them one by one. When I came out the other end, I realized that it simply didn't matter. We can be quite happy with a question mark. It's not a problem at all actually, as long as we don't solidify it or base our whole life on feeling threatened by it. We need to develop confidence in our innate qualities and believe that these can be brought to fruition. We all have Buddha-nature. We have all the qualities needed for the path. If we don't believe this, it will be very difficult for us to embark because we have no foundation from which to go forth. It's really very simple. The Buddhadharma is not based on dogma.

But why is it so difficult for us? Basically it's because of our state of mind, because we lack knowledge of who we are and our role here in this life. Because we don't know who we are, we feel separate from everybody else. There's this sense of "me," which creates all our fears, angers, attachments, jealousies, and uncertainties. But the Buddha said that it doesn't have to be like that. Our inherent nature is pure. All we have to do is rediscover who we really are, and that's what the path is for. It's very simple. It's not based on faith, but rather on experiment and experience leading to realization. It's not a matter of learning what this lama says, or what that tradition says, and then believing it's going to save us. It's not going to save us. Of course we need to know what the Buddha said. We need to know what great teachers in the past have said because they have been there ahead of us and have laid down maps for us to follow. But it's a bit like reading a travel book. You can read a travel book and feel you're already there, but in reality you're not there. These are somebody else's travel experiences. And when you do go there, you will have your own unique experiences. Following the path is about experiencing it for ourselves. It's not taking on what other people have described. It's not based on blind faith. Of course, you need a certain amount of confidence to buy a ticket and start on your journey. You have to believe that the country exists and that it's worthwhile to go there. But beyond that, the important thing is to just go. And as you go, you can say to yourself, "Yes, that's just the way they described it. That's right. It does look like that."

One area of difficulty for some people is the notion of karma and rebirth. It is not easy for me to talk about this area, because I cannot imagine not believing in karma and rebirth. I remember when I was a small child asking my mother if she believed in reincarnation, and she said it seemed to her perfectly logical, and why not? And I thought, "Right. That's what I think, too." So I don't ever remember a time when I didn't believe in it. You see, for me, the joy of believing in rebirth is that it gives you this enormous panorama, backwards and forwards and, in a way, from side to side. There is an immense space of time. This lifetime is just a tiny thread in the whole tapestry. This means that we do the best we can in this lifetime, but we don't have to do everything. We've probably already done everything anyway. We have had so many different roles in so many different lifetimes. We've experienced everything. We don't have to experience it all again this time. In this lifetime, we need to experience the things that really matter. Some people who believe there is only one lifetime feel they must pack every kind of experience in before they die. You can relax. You don't have to fear that you might miss out on something just because you don't experience it this time around. You can do something else this time. It's just a game, anyway.

The problem is that we identify completely with the role we are in at the moment—"I am a woman," or "I am a man," or "I am a mother," or "I am a wife," or "I am a nun," and so forth. Identifying with something so ephemeral as our present role is our big mistake. When we understand this, we don't need to cling to our present role thinking, "This is me," because the role itself is not important. People get so worked up about feminism and women's rights. But in our last lives we were probably men, and many who are men now would have been women. It's very fluid. Sometimes we play at being women, sometimes we play at being men. What's the big deal? We can play at being anything. It's like what Shakespeare wrote about being a player on a stage. You go on and play your part and you're totally convincing. But you come off, and the next night you're playing another role. A skillful actor identifies with his part just enough to play the role, but he is aware that he is only playing a role. Understanding rebirth gives us power over the future because we can direct things in this lifetime the way we want them to be in the future. This consciousness will keep going. The vows we take in this lifetime will continue to bear fruit in future lifetimes. Of course, from a Buddhist point of view, we can question who the actor is. But right now we are talking on the relative plane. It is better to identify with the actor than to identify with the role. Then we come to the question: who is the actor, anyway?

Accepting rebirth also gives us space to see that the conditions of the present life are just passing states. We don't know who we were in our past lives. We would have identified totally with whoever we were at the time. Next time we will be someone else with whom we will again identify very strongly. Our basic problem is not the role, it's our identification with it. So even if rebirth is not true, it is a very helpful world view because it enables us to find equilibrium and space in the midst of our daily preoccupations. Without a belief in rebirth, Buddhism doesn't make sense, because the path is based on the concept that we are trapped in ignorance. We don't know what we really are. Because of our actions of body, speech, and mind and our attachment to these actions, we are caught in this subject-object duality which propels us from rebirth to rebirth. The Buddhist path teaches us to realize that there has never been any one person performing these actions. It helps us break that connection, to see the vast, spacious quality of the mind instead of this very tight, ego-centered identification.

Once we see that all other beings are equally caught in the trap, we develop a deep compassion which makes us determined to be of benefit to beings throughout time and space. You can't do that if you've got only one lifetime. You can't vow to save all beings if you've only got the here and now, can you? How otherwise do we answer the question of, "Why are we here? Why are we experiencing the things which we experience?" If we only have one lifetime, anything that happens to us is just coincidence or accident. If we think in this way, life is aimless and has no real meaning. We might just as well settle down and make ourselves comfortable and simply try not to harm people. We want to be nice people. We want to make ourselves comfortable, and be kind to our neighbors. But to actually undergo rigorous spiritual disciplines and practice to attain Buddhahood for the sake of all sentient beings would seem insane. It wouldn't make any sense. Why would we bother? Why go to a Dharma group? Go home. Lie out in the sun. Read the Sunday papers.

The path of Dharma is not easy. It is only when we see the larger picture, stretching over endless rebirths, that we become truly motivated to transform ourselves. If we see things within the framework of eternity, it all makes sense. This perspective also helps us understand what is happening to us right now and how this very moment is the result of causes we have laid down in the past. Once we realize that everything we are experiencing now is the result of past causes, we can understand that what happens to us now is not so important. What is important is the way we respond to whatever happens, because this will shape our future. With this knowledge we can become responsible for our lives instead of being helpless victims. Isn't this good news? It gets us away from the habit of blaming everybody else, our environment, our parents, or the government for everything that goes wrong in our lives. We can take responsibility because we understand that what we have in this lifetime is the result of causes we created in the past. We know it is no use sitting around bemoaning our fate. The issue becomes, "How are we going to deal with this?"

There is a film called *Groundhog Day*, which is really a Buddhist movie because this is exactly what the plot is about. For those of you who haven't seen it, it's about somebody who had to relive the same day again and again until he got it right. He started out with an extremely negative attitude, and so throughout the first day he created a lot of negative causes. People related back to him from his own level of negativity, and so he had a very bad day. Then the next day he had to experience the same day all over again. Then again, and again. He became desperate to find a way out. He attempted suicide many times, but the next morning, there he was again in the same room and the same bed. The date hadn't changed, and the same song was playing on the radio. His attitude underwent many, many changes, until in the end he spent most of his time trying to help people. He forestalled tragedies he knew were going to happen because he had lived the day over so many times, and his whole attitude gradually turned around into working out ways to help others. As his inner attitude transformed, the day gradually got better and better. Finally, he was able to break through to a new day.

The important thing is how we respond to our situation. We can transform anything if we respond in a skillful way. This is precisely what karma is about. If we greet situations with a positive attitude, we will eventually create positive returns. If we respond with a negative attitude, negative things will eventually come our way. Unlike the scenario in the movie, it doesn't always happen right away. We can be very nice people but still have lots of problems. On the other hand, we can be awful people and have a wonderful time. But from a Buddhist perspective, it's just a matter of time before we receive the results of our conduct. And usually it is true that people with a positive attitude encounter positive circumstances. Even if the circumstances do not appear positive, they be transformed through a positive view. On the other hand people with negative minds complain even when things are going well. They also transform circumstances, but they transform positive ones into negative ones!

Both our present and our future depend on us. From moment to moment, we are creating our future. We are not a ball of dust tossed about by the winds of fate. We have full responsibility for our lives. The more aware we become, the more capable we are of making skillful choices. As we make more and more skillful choices, our lives become increasingly smooth and easy. Awareness and clarity of mind are so important because we have produced many of our problems through our confused mental states. Taking responsibility for our lives doesn't mean that we have to blame ourselves for everything. Indulging in feelings of guilt and self-flagellation is useless. Often people tell themselves, "This only happened because I'm such a stupid, worthless person." That is just a waste of time. We need to use our increasing clarity of mind to make positive choices about the present and future rather than focus on the past and wallow in self-blame. We all have innate intelligence. We just have to develop it and gradually detach ourselves from our confusion.

Karma is all about choice. As humans, we have choice. That is why this human birth is so incredibly important. You see, on the whole, animals don't have much choice because they are primarily creatures of instinct. It's hard for them to develop a wider view. We human beings are also driven by our instincts to some extent. Some people are very instinctual, and basically are no more conscious than an animal. I mean, anyone who's spent his life only thinking about food, comfort, sex and having a nice time is no different from a cat or a dog. What creates our human potential is our intelligence and our consequent potential for discovering our innate awareness. This is what enables us to make skillful choices. If someone hits us, we don't have to hit back. We can hit back if we want to, of course. That is our instinct. But we can also see it from another point of view. Instead of attacking the other person, we can try to calm them down. We can try to understand why they're attacking us. There are many ways that we could act. We're not computers. We can learn how to reprogram ourselves.

Karma is not the same as destiny. It's not fate. Even though most of what happens to us is created by causes from the past, it is how we respond that will create what comes into our karmic path in the future. We are masters of our own destiny. Rather than leading us to be heedless, this fills us with a sense of our individual responsibility. This is very important. The Buddha said we should use our discernment in everything we do. We always need to look at our intention. According to the Buddhadharma, the most important component of any action of body, speech, or mind is intention. We need to continuously examine our motivation. Are our actions based on ignorance, aversion, anger, greed, or desires, or are they based on understanding, an open, generous heart, and loving-kindness? We need to be very vigilant and honest with ourselves, because the true intention is not always the one we ascribe to ourselves. Of course we can always claim to have wonderful, fine, and sound motives for everything we do. But the true underlying intention behind any action is what determines the nature of its results. So we have to be very discerning and very careful.

If we lead our lives in this way, taking responsibility for our body, speech, and mind, using discernment and awareness, our lives will take on a new sense of meaning and direction. And I think you will also find that your mind becomes clearer and life begins to simplify. This is very important, not just in this life, but in future lives. This consciousness goes on and on, interacting with all those around us. We are not separate. We are all, each one of us, interconnected with everything else on this planet. This gives us very wide responsibilities. Some people imagine that Buddhism is a passive religion. On the contrary, we have to become increasingly conscious, increasingly aware, and increasingly responsible for our lives and for the lives of those around us, especially those to whom we are intimately connected.

I could talk on about why I believe in rebirth. But at this point, you either see it or you don't. But I think the principal significance of rebirth is that it gives us a totally different perspective on this lifetime and what we are here for. Those of you who have doubts about it, I think, should go away and read about it. There are many excellent books written by academics on the topic of reincarnation. It has been studied by parapsychologists and other such people. Some people might be convinced by their findings. I think that if you had had contact with some of the very young incarnate lamas you would find the idea of rebirth quite compelling. You would have no doubts that you were in the presence of a great being. Many of these young lamas not only recognize people from their past lives, but they also recognize them by name. I could tell you endless anecdotes about this, but I won't. Personally, I think the most important thing is to see the advantages of studying the Dharma in this life. It transforms our everyday existence from a string of meaningless and arbitrary occurences into part of a vast and meaningful pattern.

Knowledge of the Buddhadharma allows us to see into our own ignorance and suffering, and through this into the ignorance and suffering of those around us. And it's unbearable because we are not separate from those beings. Their suffering is our suffering. Then we understand for the first time what we are doing here. We are here to discover who we really are and use that knowledge to benefit beings throughout time and space. This is the real meaning of our lives. There is no instant salvation. We have to work at it.

As I don't know what your doubts and difficulties might be, I think it would be a good idea to take questions now.

QUESTIONS

Q: When you were talking about karma, there was nothing I could find to object to. But I don't find some of the traditional teachings about karma very helpful. I find them very oppressive and depressing. Especially in some of the purification practices, the whole perspective is that we've had an infinite number of lives, so we've had plenty of time to accumulate huge amounts of negative karma, as vast as Mount Meru. And each little seed never goes away. It's not only sitting there, it's getting bigger and bigger and bigger. It's that kind of perspective I have problems with.

TP: Yes, I know what you mean. Well, I'm going to be rather heretical. Once I was reading Shantideva's *Shikshasamuccaya*, which lists all the things you could have possibly ever done in your life and how there's a special hell for each one of them. I was totally depressed. It seemed like there was no escape. I went to my Lama and said to him, "Well, it looks like whatever I do, there's a special hell for it." And he just laughed and said, "Oh well, we talk that way in order to frighten people into being good. Actually, it is very difficult to be reborn in hell. You have to be especially evil, and particularly, very cruel. Most beings will not go to hell. But we talk in this way, making it sound very simple and making all these things very heavy in order to frighten people."

Now this is a very medieval approach. It's not that I don't personally believe in hell. I do. I think there are distorted states of mind which can project a definite hell. And when we die, we are the victims of our projections. So if you have a very distorted frame of mind, you will indeed find yourself in some very unpleasant places. I don't think they are necessarily hot and cold hells, but definitely there are some terrible states of birth. In our past lifetimes, we have done infinitely awful things. We have also done infinitely good things. Obviously, we must have done something right to be here now.

We don't have to be burdened by the wrongs we did in the past. We can do purification practices. As you know, there are "four powers" we can invoke. First, we should feel sorry for any bad things we have done, not just in this lifetime, but in past lifetimes. And then more importantly, try not to do it again. Then we perform the purification practice and take sincere refuge from the storms and tribulations of samsara. The Buddha and the Dharma and the Sangha are our refuge. If we take refuge from our heart, these terrible things we did in the past can be purified. Even if some of the results come up, we can deal with them. You see, it's not so much that we need a life which is all happiness and joy and peace. What we need is the inner space to deal with things which arise. So we shouldn't worry. Okay, you've done horrible things in the past. I've done horrible things in the past. We've all done horrible things. We're still trapped in samsara. But the important thing is not to worry. We do some purification. We feel regret. We do our very best not to do horrible things in this lifetime any more. The Buddha described his teachings as the raft, the ship to take us across the ocean of samsara. We're on the ship now, so we are no longer like a bottle being slapped up and down on the waves, sometimes up, sometimes down. Now we have something we can hold onto to take us to the farther shore.

My Lama once said, "Not everything you read in the sutras is true. You don't have to believe everything you read." One needs to exercise discrimination. The Dharma is vast. The Tibetans took from that huge ocean a few drops of this and a few drops of that and put it together into a mixture which was helpful for Tibetans. Much of it is relevant for the rest of us as well. The way they present the Dharma is wonderful. But there is no doubt that certain aspects, although helpful for them, are not very helpful for us. We can leave those aside. The purpose of Dharma is to help our mind to expand, to grow, to clarify. It should uphold us and create an inner sense of peace, joy, and clarity. If it's just making us feel more paranoid, more worthless, more frightened, tense, and closed, something's wrong. We also have to be discriminating. Some things are not so useful for certain people. There are many levels to the teachings. And the higher teachings often seem to contradict the lower teachings. This is because as we reach more subtle levels of intellect and spiritual understanding, what was relevant at the lowest level is no longer so relevant at a higher level. So some of the fundamental teachings are not helpful to us when we are intellectually slightly more subtle.

Once one has realized emptiness, one sees that the whole idea of good and bad is irrelevant anyway. The important thing is not to cling to this sense that "I" did it. A Burmese master once said that our karma is like the beads on a rosary. It is all connected. If you pull one bead, all the others will follow. However, if you cut the thread, all the beads will scatter, and even if you pull one bead, nothing will follow. This thread is the belief in an "I" which performs these actions. Once one has seen the truth of *shunyata*, of emptiness, of the non-inherent existence of a doer, everything falls apart. That's the ultimate purification. The important thing in this lifetime is to be careful about what we do, to understand why we are doing what we're doing and to be conscious of our body, speech, and mind from moment to moment. That's it. That's enough. If your intention in this lifetime is good, you shouldn't worry.

Q:: Can you please explain what is meant by "right livelihood"?

TP: Yes, livelihood is an interesting topic. Obviously, the Buddha thought it was important because he included it as a separate category in the Noble Eightfold Path. Do you know the Noble Eightfold Path? Right view, right intention, right action, right speech, right livelihood, right effort, right mindfulness, right concentration. He had already covered right action, but then he made right livelihood into a separate category. Now isn't that interesting? He could have brought something else in, such as "right emotions." He obviously made a distinction between "right action" and "right livelihood" because he regarded livelihood as very important. And that is of course because we spend so much of our day earning a living. How we earn our living affects the quality of our lives enormously. Basically, a right livelihood does not create harm to any other beings. Selling weapons, poisons, or alcohol would be regarded as "wrong livelihood." And any kind of livelihood which involves cheating people would of course be regarded as bad.

The Buddha was not opposed to business. In fact, many of his main sponsors were successful businessmen. Anathapindika, for example, who was one of the Buddha's lay disciples, was a businessman, a millionaire. The Buddha stipulated only that one should make a fair profit, but not to the extent of cheating people or exploiting them. This is an issue nowadays with these corporations which are often extremely exploitative and also with takeovers and layoffs and things like this which do create a lot of hardship for beings. But I think that if one is not part of the policy-making, if one's own job within the organization is not particularly harmful, then it's probably okay. That is, of course, provided you're not working for an arms manufacturer or any firm which, by its very nature, is going to harm beings.

Q: I work in a hospital and am very disturbed by the conditions there and the treatment of the patients. If I stay, I worry about condoning it. But I also worry about the results of my leaving. What should I do?

TP: I think it's important for you to hang in there and bring an element of compassion into the situation. I mean, if people like you abandon it, what hope is there? You don't have to approve of what's going on. And you should not approve of what's going on. But please stay there and help where you can. It's extremely important to bring some sanity and care into a situation like that.

Q: What about pursuing Dharma as a lay person?

TP: The Buddha said that the problem with lay life is that it's filled with dust. This is true. Even with the purest motivation, one has a work place, one has an environment in which one has to participate, and there are going to be things which create problems for other beings. That's the nature of samsara. Why is one doing these things? If the motivation is basically to help and to create something better, then the fact that other beings suffer is just the way things are. One can't help that.

It's like being a farmer. A farmer grows food. Along with growing food, he kills insects. Not just by spraying, but by plowing. He's pulling up the insects from underneath and putting them on top. The ones which lie on top are being churned underneath. That's very sad. But it doesn't mean that farming in itself is a bad livelihood. One tries to be as careful as one can, but one's motivation is not to cause problems for the insects. One's motivation is to grow food to feed beings. So, in a way, a higher motivation overrides the fact that animals are being hurt. And of course one tries as much as possible to harm as few beings as possible. If you really feel bad about it, you can certainly do some prayers for all those animals and their higher rebirths. In the East, people do a practice called "Saving Life." I don't know how that would work in America, but in the East, they go and buy fish which are still alive, which are to be eaten, or caged birds, and let them go. But at least you could do some prayers from time to time. Or you could get someone to do some prayers for all the animals which are destroyed. The important thing is the motivation. We're not doing this in order to harm beings. We regret that. You don't rejoice in their death. We're not indifferent to their suffering.

Q: Is it a good idea to take political action to right social evils?

TP: Obviously, in this imperfect world there are things which need to be changed, and in order to change them, there need to be people who care enough to want to change things. And that's fine. The problem arises when we take ourselves too seriously. Then we become totally identified with the role and our motivation is not so much benefiting others, but anger towards those who are obstructing us. You see this very clearly in peace movements. People talk about peace with such anger. It's "us" against "them," and it's tremendously vicious. And what is the motive? It's not peace at all. It's just an excuse for one's own innate aggression. We can always find something to be aggressive about. All this righteous indignation is just anger, really. And if it's not one thing, we're going to find something else and feel justified in being as angry as we like. There's always going to be something. So we just funnel it and pour oil on the flames of our own negativities—however "right" the cause may be.

Maybe there's a way of dealing with this, in feminism also. Obviously, women have had a hard time; although, often their problems are fuelled as much by other women as by anybody else. But nonetheless, yes there are inequalities and problems, and it would be nice for us to deal with them. But if we are setting up the other, the male, as the enemy, then it's absurd, isn't it? Identifying with being female as though this identity is "me" is equally absurd. As I said, this time female, next time male. Who knows? Political agendas are important for changing things and for changing attitudes. But we should be very careful to examine our basic motivation. Otherwise we just create more confusion and more aggression, and we don't need more of "us against them."

Q: What are the basic differences between the world view of the Semitic religions and that of Buddhism?
TP: That's a huge subject. Where to start with this one! I would say the main difference, or one of the main differences, is that the Semitic view of God is that of an omniscient, omnipotent being, separate from his creation but very involved in it, a being who existed since time immemorial and decided to create, and so he created the universe and the beings in it. While he is intimately connected with them, he is separate from them. This kind of creator is denied in Buddhism. In Buddhism, as in Hinduism, the universe is in a constant state of evolution and dissolution, with large intervals in between. It's continually either coming together or disintegrating. For inconceivably vast periods of time, all matter is scattered, and then through the karma of the beings, it comes back together again. When the previous universe devolved, all the beings in that universe took rebirth in one of the higher heavens for the time being, one of the higher spiritual levels, because they had no material form and there was nowhere for them to be reborn in the material realm. During this vast period, one of them who had created vast amounts of merit was reborn spontaneously in one of the Brahma heavens. He lived there by

himself for an immense period of time, lighting everywhere with the glory of his effulgence. Then, after a while, he thought, "Wouldn't it be nice if there were other beings? Why am I stuck here all by myself?" Now, because of the karma of those other beings out there, eventually some of them also got reborn in the same Brahma heaven. Then that Brahma, who was called the Great Brahma, looked at them and said, "Oh, I created you," because he had wished for them, and then eventually they had appeared. And because he came first, and because he was much more glorious than they were, they assumed he had. So they regarded him as their creator. Eventually, after aeons and aeons of time, the universe would come back together again, and there would be conditions for beings to come back onto the earth again. And they would come back as beings of light. At first, they lived on the surface of the earth as beings of light. Brahma didn't, but some of them did. Then eventually they started eating the earth, which in those days was sweet, and gradually, according to this cosmology, began to get grosser and grosser bodies until they turned into what we now know as beings. But many of these beings remembered that heaven in which they had been with the Brahma who said he was their creator. So they came back and started those religions which have the idea of a creator and beings created by him. According to the Buddha, this is how, when people entered into meditation, they would experience this heaven, with this god and these other minor gods around him, thinking that this was the creator of everything. And the Buddha said, "He is very powerful. He knows a lot. But he's not omnipotent, and he didn't create."

That is the Buddha's version of how the idea of the creator came about. From a Buddhist point of view, this universe is created by the karma of the beings within it. So in one way we are all holding it together ourselves. This is why we project a universe which has some uniformity. We see more or less the same universe. But other animals with different senses perceive a very different kind of universe. Yet we know, also from the point of view of physics, that how we perceive the universe is nothing like the scientist's description of the universe, which has given us a wholly different picture. Now the Buddha was a human being like the rest of us. He was a sentient being. He had gone through many different lifetimes, as animals, humans, etc. and had accumulated vast quantities of positive karma. Eventually, he was able to attain absolute, complete, and perfect enlightenment. Part of his enlightenment experience was that in the first watch of the night, he went back through all his past incarnations, into the evolution and devolution of universes. He went back and back and back and he never saw any end, because samsara is cyclic. Our whole idea of beginning and end stems from our limited, linear minds. In the second watch of the night, his mind expanded still further, and he saw all the beings in the universe coming into being and going somewhere else, being born and reborn. He saw that they were all interconnected, and that everything comes about as the results of our past actions.

That was how he came to his understanding of karma. It was not, as some people say, because that was the idea current in his day, so he just picked it up and added it to his doctrine. It was an integral part of his enlightenment experience. His mind expanded infinitely to its utmost potential, and he saw how it all fit together. That's why later, when Ananda said, "Karma's kind of difficult to understand, but I think I've got it," the Buddha said, "Don't say that. Karma is the province of a Buddha's mind only." Ordinary people cannot understand how it works because their minds are too limited. You have to have an absolutely totally open Buddha-mind to understand it. There is a story of when the Buddha was in the jungle and he picked up a handful of leaves and asked his companions, "Which are more, the leaves in the jungle or the leaves I am holding in my hand?" And of course they replied, "It's obvious. The leaves in the jungle are infinite. What you're holding in your hand is just a few." And the Buddha replied, "So it is with what I know and what I am telling you. But what I am telling you is all you need to become enlightened. The rest is not important for you to know."

To me, the Buddha is someone who realized his total potential as a human being. Everything which a human being could possibly think or experience is the potential of each of us. But our minds are too closed. The Buddha's mind was wide open. But still he taught within the milieu in which he was living, in concepts which would be helpful to the people around him. When people asked him questions whose answers were too advanced for them to understand, he explained that it was not important for them to know the answer. "It's not going to get you out of samsara. One thing only I teach, suffering and the ending of suffering."

Buddha is not a god. He's our own potential. And ultimate reality is not a being outside of ourselves, it is a state of enlightenment, of who we are. We are all potential Buddhas. We have it all. The problem is that it's covered up. We have to uncover it. According to the Buddhadharma, we are responsible for what happens to us and how we respond to it. We put ourselves at the center of our lives. We take responsibility. What happens to us is the result of causes we ourselves have set in motion, and how we deal with all this will create our future. We have responsibility for our lives. That's why the Buddha's path is perfectly feasible. We can walk it as ordinary human beings, because it was taught by somebody who had done it himself and knew the problems. If you read any of the texts on meditation, they deal with the various problems that you're likely to experience and all the different things you can do to solve them. Buddhism is non-theistic, but nonetheless it's a balanced spiritual path. It's not atheistic.

Q: It seems that now more and more beings are taking human rebirth and the earth's population is increasing. What do you think about this?
TP: I don't know what the answer is. There are many other realms apart from the human realm. And it does seem that at this time there is an enormous acceleration of beings seeking human lives. On the other hand, because the population is getting out of control, the quality of their human lives is often very low. This may be a chance for human beings to start going upwards instead of downwards. It's hard to know. It's because we see just a part of the whole pattern. It seems to me as if it were a giant tapestry and we are looking at it from the back, so we see all the loose ends and the knots and it looks like chaos. But if we could look at it from the front, we would get the whole picture. Right now, through our ignorance, it all looks very confusing, and we don't see where each thread connects to the overall pattern.

Q: Are all these realms connected to the earth somehow?
TP: Yes. They seem to be. Each inhabited planet seems to have its own structure, its own level. Traditionally this planet is described as being Mount Sumeru in the middle of the four continents, with the hells underneath, and the heavens going up. From the top of Mount Sumeru, the heavens start spreading out upwards. So obviously the traditional idea at least is that they're very connected with this planet, and it does seem that even in the spirit realms, there is a connection with this particular earth and that they're very interpenetrated. I mean, they're not really up there, but on many different vibrational levels they are nonetheless connected with us.

Q: I hear teachers talk about the dark ages. Are we still in the dark ages? Is it ever going to change?

TP: Buddhist cosmology goes on forever, but basically the idea is that it gets worse and worse, not only spiritually, but also from the point of view of such things as welfare and natural catastrophes. And then the Buddhadharma also begins to decrease, until in the end it dies out completely. This period continues until Maitreya Buddha comes and revives the Dharma and things begin to improve again. Then the whole cycle repeats itself.

In the East some people blame their spiritual laziness on the fact that this is "the dark age." What is the dark age? This is where we are. The Dharma is still with us and we still have our intelligence and our lifespan, so let us get on with it. Even in the Buddha's time, people were complaining that it was the dark age and people no longer had any spiritual potential. So since time began, people have always complained.

Q: Could you talk about the Lama as Buddha?

TP: How do you relate to the Lama? As an authority figure? Do you mean the inner Lama? You know, this is a huge question and one can answer only in fairly simplistic terms. But there are two things here. There is the very word "lama." The word lama is a Tibetan translation of the Sanskrit word guru. And so there is a guru who is called in Tibetan, Tse-rab-kyi Lama, which means "the guru for all your lifetimes." That means the guru with whom you have a mind-to-mind connection. He or she shows you the nature of the mind. You have this inner commitment from now until enlightenment, however many lifetimes that may take. Now, if, and it's a big "if," you meet a lama with whom you have that personal heart-to-heart connection and commitment, through that intimate connection and your openness, he or she is able to show you the nature of your mind.

The nature of your mind is the inner guru. This is because the nature of your mind, which is Dharmakaya—this spacious, open awareness—is the same as the Lama's mind. The Lama's mind and your mind are the same. When we are relating to the Lama in an ultimate sense, we are not relating to the personality. We are relating to his or her omniscient mind. The omniscient mind of the Lama shows us our own inner omniscient mind, if only for a second. That is the inner Lama. On the other hand, most lamas we have contact with are not on that level. They are not lamas with whom we have had a connection over many lifetimes. They are our teachers. They show us the path. They act as role models. They are advisors. They are helpers. But at that level, it's a very different thing. Therefore we are, in a way, relating much more to a human being who has accomplished more than we have on the path, who has had more experience and knowledge, and in whom, to a certain extent, we can trust. Nonetheless, he or she is like us, also on the path. Sometimes what he or she says may not necessarily be what we need to hear, and we can question it. Just because somebody is sitting up on the throne as an authority figure, however great their reputation and however vast their wisdom, we don't have to take everything they say as being Buddha's *vachana*, or the word of the Buddha. We still have to be open to what they are saying and definitely listen and be receptive. But that doesn't mean that we have to drop all discernment and discrimination. We should keep our wits about us!

∽ 10

Tonglen—
the Practice of Giving and Taking

ONGLEN is a very interesting practice! In most spiritual traditions, including New Age ones, there are meditations which
involve breathing in light, love, and bliss. We visualize these qualities coming into the heart and transforming the body. Then we breathe out all our
negativities. This seems like a very logical practice to do. But tonglen practice flips our mind and our preconceptions upside down because it does the
exact opposite. We actually breathe in all the negativities and the darkness
and breathe out all the love, purity, and light. This idea can be alarming for
some people when they first encounter it. The negativities come into us as
dark light and are absorbed into a small dark pearl at the center of our chest.
This pearl is our self-cherishing concept. It is the thing which says, "I am so
important. Other people may be important, too, but they're much less important than I am. I am basically the center around which the rest of the universe
revolves."

When we do this practice, we are chipping away at that little black pearl,
which cringes with every blow, because it absolutely does not want other people's suffering, misery, and sickness. But the little pearl takes all this negativity in and it disappears into the emptiness of the Dharmadhatu, or ultimate
reality. Then we breathe out all the joy, goodness, and light we have accumulated over aeons. We give this out to take the place of the suffering
endured by all sentient beings. This reverses our usual concept of how things
should be. People say, "I already have more than enough suffering. I don't
want other people's suffering as well."

In brief the usual Tonglen practice is to visualize another person's sickness or suffering in the form of dark light being drawn into oneself along with the inhalation. This dark light strikes back at the black pearl-like seed of self-cherishing at our heart center. This pearl instantly radiates out, along with the exhalation, the bright light of all our good qualities and merits. This radiance then absorbs into the suffering person to help them.

Sometimes instead of a black pearl, it is taught that we can visualize a crystal vajra which represents our innate Dharmakaya mind. The dark light absorbs into this and is instantly tranformed into radiance, since no darkness exists within the pristine nature of the mind.

I'm going to tell you a true story. When I was about nine years old, I caught on fire. I was wearing a nylon dress at the time, and I went near an electric fire which was not turned on, but was plugged in. My dress brushed against the fire and it burst into flames because it was nylon. Fortunately for me, at that time my mother was very sick in bed with kidney trouble, so she hadn't gone out to work in our shop. I ran screaming up the stairs and crossed the landing to her bedroom. She later told me that she heard me screaming while she was in bed. The next moment, the door crashed open, and I burst into her room, engulfed in sheets of flames. She quickly wrapped me in a blanket, put the flames out and then rubbed me with penicillin and wrapped me in a clean sheet. Apparently, my whole back was just one big blister. The entire skin of my back was burned right off along with part of my face. And at that time, I remember being in extraordinary pain. You can imagine.

Then I had an out-of-body experience. I was up above, looking down on my body, surrounded by all these beings of light who were saying to me, "Come with us. Come with us." You know, the usual thing. And I thought to myself, "Oh good, now I'm going to die. That will be interesting." I actually did not want to go back into that body. I was looking down at that body which was all burnt, and I didn't want anything more to do with it. It was like looking down the wrong end of the telescope. The appearances of this world began to recede as I traveled further and further upwards towards the light. Great! Then suddenly the neighbors started coming in because they'd heard my screams, and I was brought down into this body again.

I remember that they took me to the hospital, and I remember lying on a trolley. The doctor said to me, "You're a very brave little girl. You must be in tremendous pain." And I said, "No, there's no pain." And there was no pain. When I came back down into my body, I felt no pain at all, despite the fact that my whole back was burned. No problem! I stayed in the hospital for about two months. I had a great time. At no time did I experience any pain. Although I had to lie in bed, I wasn't sick. I was too young to understand that I might be scarred, so I wasn't worried. As it turned out, I wasn't scarred at all. Some years later I talked about this with my mother. She told me that when I was lying there, I lost consciousness and she thought I was going to die. She was a spiritualist, so she prayed to the spirit guides, "Please don't let her die. And please don't let her suffer. She's too young to bear that sort of pain. Give all her pain to me. Let me have her pain." Now she was already in agony with kidney trouble, but if she could have taken on my pain as well, she would have done so gladly. And I'm quite sure it was because of her prayer that when I came back into the body again I had no pain. What other explanation could there be?

Fortunately, she didn't get my pain, either. But the point is, not only did she pray from her heart to take my pain away, but she would have been over-joyed to have my pain transferred to her if that would spare me. This is the kind of love we're talking about in tonglen practice, the kind of intense love which unselfconsciously places more importance on healing the other person than on our own well-being. Now this was relatively easy for my mother. Not easy, exactly, except that it is in the nature of a mother to love her child like that. What the Dharma asks is that we treasure all beings without exception in the same way. As the Buddha himself said, just as a mother loves her only child, so must we extend love to all beings.

One of the advantages of being a mother is that you learn from real life what this means. You can use this experience as a basis to extend this kind of love outwards to all beings. This is what we are called upon to do in the ton-glen practice. Some people say, "Oh, tonglen is very easy." I can only gasp at their level of bodhisattva attainment. I don't think it's at all easy to sit and absorb the pain and suffering of others. It's very interesting to watch the mind and the levels of deception we can clothe ourselves in. Because of our enor-mous capacity for self-deception, we must try to be as honest as possible with ourselves. Only by fearless honesty can we identify and peel away the levels of resistance to opening up the heart.

A lot of practices can be done by rote. If we just do tonglen practice auto-matically, it's very easy to sit and think of all sentient beings as this kind of blurry mass outside and send out light and love to them and absorb all this darkness. We can even come away feeling very expansive and bodhisattva-like. But when we get to actual individuals, when we are faced with someone who is genuinely sick or depressed, are we still prepared to take on their suffering and give out our well-being in return? This is a mind-transforming practice, so the only way we can know whether we are making progress or not is by observing our reactions in everyday situations. When we meet people in everyday life who are suffering, how do we relate to them? Is our heart genuinely open to them? Are we kind? Are we getting progressively kinder?

Let us think about the way the practice works. All this negativity comes into us and attacks the self-cherishing concept. What does this actually mean? Sometimes it's easier for us just to get caught up in the mechanics of the visualization and forget what it is all about. You know, we have this dark little thing in the heart and then the dark lights start hitting it, and it all transforms into bright light. It's a very nice visualization if we get into it. But as we practice, we must really remember what this is all about. We must ask ourselves, if this were really happening, what kind of resistance would the ego put up. If somebody came here right now and said, "You can have all the sickness and misery from that person over there, and I can promise you I will free him from it. In exchange, he will have all your good health. How's that?" Would you really say, "Okay, I'll do it"? Maybe so, if it was somebody you loved—your husband, your child, or even a parent or a beloved teacher—but just a man on the street?

These are not easy practices. They are not for the foolhardy nor are they for the timid. They are intended for bodhisattvas. On no account should we take these practices lightly. We should understand what we are doing and what this training is all about. At least this is how it seems to me. Whenever I read the tonglen practices, I am astounded at what they're actually asking of us. Other people don't seem to be struck like that and I don't know why. This seems to me to be the utmost frontal attack on our ego-clinging. Doesn't it seem like that to you? And it's very interesting to try to be vividly alive and to bring specific situations into our mind while we are practicing. These can be real or hypothetical cases. How does the mind react?

Finally, of course, we dissolve everything into primordial space. This is very important. We don't keep the negativities sitting in our heart. We have to dissolve the negativities into this ego-clinging, ego-cherishing entity which thinks, "I am so important and others are naturally much less important than

I," which we all have. We dissolve that and everything else into open space. Then we really feel light and joy going out to all beings. Not just in our visualizations, but also in our everyday life, we should be able to give something to beings we meet who are suffering. Even by just being kind and friendly.

If we remain just as closed off from other beings as ever, still preoccupied with our own pleasure, happiness, and comfort, and still seeing other people as separate, remaining unaffected by their happiness or their sorrow, then, even if we have been doing tonglen for twelve years, it hasn't worked! It doesn't matter how long we do it. The important thing is to break this separation between ourselves and others. We all have this separation, and it is our primary delusion. It's a very radical practice, and if we do it from our heart, it transforms us. So I think we should do it now. I don't think there's anything more to be said about it.

Questions

Q: The thing that's a problem for me is just that it's so dynamic, it's so hard for me to imagine taking all this stuff in and transforming it. Is it okay just to have longer periods where you're just taking in, taking in?
TP: I think that's fine. I know what you mean and it's true. In fact, it's much better, especially initially, until we're really practiced at it, to spend some time not worrying so much about the breathing, but just as we breathe in, it comes in and in and in, and then it dissolves away this heavy tight sense of "I," sitting there like a spider in the middle of the web. When we feel this ego being dissolved and melted into the spacious openness, we can generate all this light and spread it out to all beings. Yes, you could do that.

Q: What happens when you have all this accumulation? Does it dissolve?
TP: It hits at this sense of self-cherishing at the center of the heart, and then that dissolves into open spaciousness, into emptiness. The whole idea of this ego, this sense of "I," is that it believes it is so much more important than everybody else, even though "I" am only one and everybody else is so many. When that accumulation hits against it, it dissolves away and we enter this open, spacious, egoless mind.

Q: How do you know that the other has received it?

TP: Well, one can imagine that they receive it. And if one's concentration and one's desire are strong enough, maybe they will. Why should they not? It's extremely powerful.

Q: I have a similar situation. My mother was supposed to have surgery for what the doctor said was a huge growth as big as a grapefruit, and I wished that it wouldn't be there. I imagined I was powerful enough to let it not be. And when they operated, it was gone. There was nothing there. It didn't occur to me at the time that I had anything to do with it.

TP: The mind is extremely powerful. It's the most powerful thing in the world. We just don't know what our potential is.

Q: If the pain of somebody else terrifies me, I do tonglen, and it destroys my fear. I do it over and over again until I find I can think of their pain with compassion instead of fear. I use it as an antidote.

TP: The thing with a practice like this is that it can be used in many ways, on many levels. Because it is such a powerful practice, it can break through so many of our barriers. That's why it's so highly valued and why at the beginning it was regarded as quite a secret practice. It is very radical. In some ways it seems to many people to be quite dangerous and threatening. As I say, in most spiritual traditions, you breathe in the light, not the dark. Somebody said it's like becoming a human air conditioner. You breathe in all the bad air and transmit it as clear, fresh air. It's rather nice!

II

The Nature of Mind

TRADITIONALLY, the Buddhist path may be divided into three stages: view, meditation, and action. First we develop the right view, we meditate on it and then we put it into action in our lives. In the Buddhist tradition, what we call view is known in Sanskrit as *drishti* and in Tibetan as *ta wa*. It means the way we look at things. It is considered extremely important. The Fourth Noble Truth taught by the Buddha is the truth of the path. The path I am referring to is the Noble Eightfold Path, which begins with correct view. We might reflect a little on why view is placed first. It is because our basic outlook on life influences everything we think and do. Even people who say they have no philosophy of life are affirming a philosophy. That understanding will influence their thinking and everything they do with their lives. This is at the core of everything. Our view determines how we see things, what we think is important, what we think unimportant, our prejudices and our biases. It will determine whether or not we place value on spiritual matters and lay the foundations for our spiritual journey.

Why are we here today? We are here because we have some inherent interest in finding a spiritual dimension to our lives. The fact that you think having a spiritual dimension is important is your view. If you didn't think that dealing with the mind was important, you wouldn't be here. Our basic outlook is the foundation. In the Tibetan schools of mind training, such as Mahamudra and Dzogchen, a division is made between our underlying viewpoint, our inner mind development which arises from this viewpoint, and how we incorporate it into our daily lives. It is not enough to hold vast views. If there is no correspondence between these views and our conduct, we are in danger.

Guru Padmasambhava once said to King Trisong Detsen, "Your view must be as vast as the sky, but your conduct must be as finely sifted as barley flour." There are people who develop vast views, seeing everything as emptiness, the vastness of space, and everything that happens as the interdependent play of bliss and voidness. It sounds wonderful. Then when they are arrogant, rude, unethical, or dishonest, they claim it doesn't matter because it's all emptiness anyway. They believe that tantra gives them a license to do whatever they want. It doesn't matter, they say, because it's all just an expression of our primordial nature, whatever that means. So we have to be very careful. We have to take care to make our view very clear and vast, but at the same time keep our conduct careful and precise. We must avoid falling into what the Tibetans call the "path of the Black Demon," thinking that since ultimate reality is vast, spacious emptiness, it makes no difference what we do.

We are using "view" to mean "understanding the ultimate nature of the mind." From a Buddhist point of view, everything is an expression of our mind. One of the problems in Western society is that we are centered in our heads. This very much affects the way we practice. When you start to do Mahamudra or Dzogchen meditation, one of the questions Tibetan lamas always ask is, "Where is the mind?" Then they ask, "Is it in the heart? Is it the stomach? Is it in your foot? Is it in the whole body? Is it inside you, is it outside you?" They rarely ask if it's in the head. It doesn't occur to them. What a stupid idea! And yet most Westerners would answer, "Well obviously, the mind is in the head." Interesting. Where is the mind? Before you dismiss this whole question and say, "Obviously it's in the brain," consider that when somebody accuses you and says, "I know you stole my money," for example, and you answer, "You mean me?" You point to the center of your chest, not to your head. Most of our sense organs are in the head, right? Our nose, our eyes, our ears. But when we say we felt something really deeply, we point to our heart. Think about that. Ask yourself why this is.

From the Buddhist point of view, the brain is only the computer. It's the part that does the programming. But what is the energy that drives the computer? Without that energy, the computer is dead. The energy driving the computer does not reside in the computer itself. Recently, I was reading a series of articles written by top brain surgeons. One of them remarked that although we now know a lot about the brain, we still have not found the mind. Tibetans know about the brain. If somebody is very traditional, unable to accept new ideas, very caught up in old ways of thinking, the Tibetans call them "green brained." The idea is that the brain has become mildewed. They understand that the brain has to do with thinking, but thinking is not mind.

When we talk about mind in Buddhism, we are not just talking about the intellectual faculty. We are referring to something much more profound. In fact, the words for mind and heart are interchangeable. They are often the same word. The underlying word, which is *chitta* in Sanskrit and *sem* in Tibetan, means both heart and mind. Here at the heart is where you concentrate. This gives the energy, the electric current to operate the computer without which the computer is dead. So when we meditate, we have to learn to bring that energy down to the heart level.

Let us return to the specific topic of the view. Traditionally stated, the view says that our primordial wisdom mind is awareness and emptiness combined. If we can break through to the unconditioned nature of the mind, the fundamental underlying condition of who we really are, we are left with non-dual awareness. We are consciousness; that is who we are. We know. If we don't know, we must be asleep, in a coma, or dead. We know. We are aware. But that awareness is not concrete. It's not something we can grasp hold of and say, "This is my awareness," or "This is me." It's transparent, open, and spacious. In Tibetan parlance, it's empty. Empty here means "like the sky."

They say the mind is like the sky. Now why do they say that? Because if you think of a deep, vast, blue sky, it's all-encompassing. It's up there, but at the same time it's down here. Where does the sky begin? It's not, "This is my sky, here's your bit, and there's my bit." It belongs to everybody. It supports us. Without space, we couldn't exist. The Tibetans compare our fundamental primordial mind with the sky or space because it's infinite and vast, yet ungraspable. At the same time, it's unlike space in that it is conscious. When we gain access to that level of our mind it is like being awake for the first time.

This awareness is non-dual; there is neither subject nor object. There is no sense of "I" doing anything. There is just total awareness, which is vast and infinite, beyond time and space. That is what supports all our thoughts and emotions. To understand that, to have seen it even for a moment, is called the view. The fact that we already have it is important for us to grasp. We don't have to bring in something extraneous. We don't even have to develop anything. We already have everything. We just need to uncover it. It's always been there. It's absolutely perfect just as it is. But we don't recognize it. It's as if we're standing in the sunshine, and then we go inside, draw the shutters, and say that it's dark. But the sun is shining the whole time. This innate wisdom mind is always present. Our problem is that we don't recognize it.

There is a story of this great but very eccentric Lama of the last century named Patrul Rinpoche. One of his disciples was a professor of philosophy who had been a follower of his for many years. He was very learned and devoted. Even after all those years, after all the searching and all the practice he had done, he still hadn't seen the nature of the mind, and he was very depressed about it. After all, what's it all for if you don't realize the nature of the mind? It's just words and concepts building upon each other. Then, one night he was at a retreat at Patrul Rinpoche's hermitage and Patrul Rinpoche said, "Let's go outside, lie on the ground and look up at the stars." The professor replied, "Okay, that sounds nice." So they went out. They lay and looked up at the stars. Then in the distance, a dog barked. Patrul Rinpoche asked, "Did you hear that sound?" And his student answered, "Yes, it's a dog barking." Then Patrul Rinpoche said, "That's it." And he got up.

Do you understand? The fact that we are conscious that it is a dog barking is it. But we don't recognize that. We think it must be something else more exciting, and so we are always looking for this something else that is higher and more thrilling. Once I asked one of the yogis in my monastery to give the oral transmission of a very famous Dzogchen text by Shabkar Rinpoche. It has been translated into English as the *Flight of the Garuda*. He was giving this oral transmission when he stopped halfway through and said, "You know, the problem with these texts is that they make it seem something so far, so remote, so incredibly vast, when actually it's so completely simple. It's so ordinary that we miss it." So we have to go through all of these hundred thousand prostrations and mandala offerings and millions of mantras and all these extraordinarily complex visualizations just to get back to where we have always been, and recognize ourselves at home for the first time.

We have established the view that the nature of our awareness is clarity and emptiness. Since primordial time, that is what we have been and that is what we are. Based on that view, we start to practice. View is so important because it underlies and underpins everything which goes after it. It is so important to understand that we already have everything we need. The Tibetan example is a person who has an infinite treasure chest, full of diamonds, gold, and all kinds of wealth, buried under his hearth. But he has forgotten about it, and he lives like a beggar, going out every day to collect a few measly coins.

That's how we are. We have everything we could possibly need. We have Buddha-nature. But we feel so poor. We feel so unworthy. We think we are failed human beings. We feel so alienated, so worthless. We think, "Other people can do all these wonderful things, but I can't do anything. I'm so stupid. I mess everything up. I had this horrible childhood, and now I'm completely warped, and there's nothing to be done. Maybe a psychiatrist can at least help me to face each miserable day as it comes along." Yet all the time we are a Buddha! All the time we have this infinite amount of wisdom and compassion within us. It's just become clogged up, so we can't find it.

It's important to understand that we are not worthless worms. We have this complete Buddha potential. It's just that it's a bit obscured at the moment. If we go out now and try to look for the blue sky, there are a lot of clouds there, so we can't see it. But the sky is there. However thick the clouds may be, the sky is always there. It's like when we are in an airplane. The clouds are there, but behind them there is this infinite deep blue sky. We all have access to it. We are not ignorant sinners. At the very foundation of our being, there is infinite wisdom and compassion. We have lost sight of it, but we can be back there in a millisecond, just as if you are in a room which has been in darkness for centuries, the minute you switch on the light, it is illuminated. Just because it has been dark in there for hundreds of years doesn't mean that it will take a long time to put the light on. The minute you switch on the light, there it is. However deep our ignorance, however profound our sense of unworthiness, however much we feel inundated by our negative emotions, however alienated and isolated we feel, the moment we access the unconditioned nature of the mind, it's all gone. It might come back, of course. Enlightenment is not usually a once-only experience as some people seem to think. But that moment of seeing transforms everything. We now realize that we have always identified ourselves with all the wrong stuff. That's not who we are at all! That's why this initial breakthrough is emphasized so much in all schools of Buddhism. My Lama used to say that once you realized the nature of the mind you could begin to meditate. Before that you are kind of playing around, trying to get it right. Suddenly you get it right and you receive a flash. Now you know what you're doing. Next you start to learn how to reproduce these flashes, and then how to prolong them. Then you learn how to integrate that understanding with everyday consciousness.

One of the problems of not having a teacher is that some people experience a profound breakthrough and mistakenly think they are enlightened. Then they set themselves up as enlightened people. It's because they don't have a teacher who says, "Yes, fine, good, keep sitting." There is a story about Gampopa. He was the chief disciple of Milarepa, the great yogi of the eleventh century. In addition to being a very great meditator, he was also a professor. He had a number of disciples, but the main two were Dusum Khyenpa, who was the first Karmapa, and Pagmo Drupa. From Pagmo Drupa came all the other Kagyupa schools. At one time, it is said that Pagmo Drupa had been meditating for a long time and nothing was happening. He was becoming disillusioned. On one occasion he meditated all through the night and had a breakthrough. He became quite excited. He rushed off to tell Gampopa. It was very early in the morning. Gampopa was eating *tsampa*, which is roasted barley ground into flour. This is mixed with butter tea and formed into balls, called *pag*. Gampopa was sitting eating his *pag*. Pagmo Drupa rushed in and said, "Oh, I've had this experience. I've finally got it." He described his experience. He was so excited. Gampopa just sat there and said, "I think I prefer my *pag* to your experience." So the pupil went back again to sit some more. That's what a teacher is for!

Of course the initial breakthrough is very important. My teacher explained it by saying, "It's as if you are going along a winding mountain path to get to a town. You are not sure that this path does actually lead to that town. You are not even sure that the town exists. But you've heard that it's there. So you have confidence that eventually this path will get you there if you keep on going. There are a few signposts. Then one day you turn a corner, and there, in the distance, is the town. This is an enormous breakthrough on your journey. You now know the town exists. You now know that this path leads there. Maybe, because the path is winding, there will be times when you don't see the town any more. But each time you see it, it gets a bit closer. However, you are not in the town yet. You are just getting glimpses of it. But one day, provided you keep going, you will arrive at the town, and you will be able to live there. Then you're a Buddha."

Another example was given by a Zen master who was living in London years ago. He said the mind is like a big mirror. It's covered with dirt. Then you get a little pin and make a pin prick in the dirt. Through this you see the glow of the mirror. Most of the mirror is still covered with dirt, but that little gleam of light is the real nature of the mirror. Of course, it's not all uncovered yet, but this is a big step forward. You now see that under all that dirt is a gleam of light. The task now is to make that little gleam bigger or make lots of points of light until they all connect and eventually the whole mirror is completely clear. That's why they say that the initial realization of the nature of the mind is the first breakthrough. It's a very important point in all Buddhist schools. At that moment, you cease to be an ordinary person. You become in Buddhist parlance an *arya*, a noble one. It doesn't mean you are finished. It doesn't mean you are a high level bodhisattva. We can fall back from this. But still, this is a big breakthrough. We now understand what is true and what is not true. We don't have to take it all on faith any more. It is a direct non-dual experience. The point is that it is very easy. It's not difficult, and it's not something that can only be attained after years and years of practice.

Our main obstacle is the fact that we don't know how to relax our minds enough to be open to this experience. In the back of our minds we keep thinking this is something so difficult and so advanced. For this reason we don't recognize what is in front of our face. This is why a teacher can be extraordinarily helpful. A teacher living within that realization is able—if the mind of the disciple is completely open—to transmit his or her experience. The problem here is that if we have too many hopes and fears, it creates a barrier. It is very hard to be open. You can't just will it.

I knew an English nun who was in her seventies, and her daughter, who was in her fifties, was also a nun. She told me that once she had been at my Lama's community in Tashi Jong for the lama dances. This was during the time when the previous Khamtrul Rinpoche was still alive. She was not his disciple at all. She had Gelugpa teachers. She was just sitting there, watching the dances. My Lama was dancing. He was a very good dancer and she was watching him. During the dance, he turned around and looked straight at her. In that moment, her whole mind fell apart, and she realized the nature of the mind. She wasn't even his disciple, but at that moment she was totally open and he knew it. It's as close to us as this, only we don't see it. This is why a qualified teacher can be very helpful. Some Tibetans say it's almost impossible to realize the nature of the mind without a teacher. I don't think that's true. Some people do realize the nature of the mind spontaneously without a teacher. But a good teacher helps.

Now I think we will just sit for a quarter of an hour. I'll tell you what I

want you to do. Just do it at your own speed. First we are going to bring ourselves into the present. Bring the mind clearly into the room. Then bring the
mind quietly into the body. In other words, be conscious of how you are sitting. Be conscious of your posture. Be conscious of any pressure on the body.
Just know it. Just note it and know that this is how it is. Then, very quietly
bring the attention to the in-going and out-going of the breath. Don't think
about the breath. Don't look at it from a distance as if you are up in your head
looking down at the breath coming in. Just try to experience it. Flow with the
in-breath. Flow with the out-breath.

While we are doing this, you are going to think thoughts. We all think
thoughts. Thoughts are just the natural play of the mind. They are like waves
on the surface of the sea. They are not a problem. It is the nature of the mind
to think thoughts, but we don't have to follow after them. We don't have to
give them energy. So drop all thinking about the past, stop anticipating the
future, and don't give any energy to the present. Just be with the breathing in
and the breathing out. When we hear noises, they are just waves impinging on
the ear organ. Noises are natural. To hear them is natural. It's not important.
Don't give any energy to that either. If you hear a noise and start thinking, "Oh
what a horrible noise," or, "I wish this noise could stop," just be conscious that
this is what you are thinking and go on. Whatever happens is fine. No problem. Whatever comes up, we recognize it, we accept it, and then we let it go.
Very simple. Stay with the breathing. When we lose it, bring the mind gently
back again. Whatever happens, recognize, accept, and then let it go.

Questions

Q: It appears as if the mind splits off and one aspect of the mind becomes the
witness, or the knower. This aspect then views the rest of the mind as an
object. How do we bring together and balance these two faculties of the mind?
TP: That's a good question. In our normal state of mind, we are completely
submerged in our thoughts and feelings. There is no inner space available.
When we think, we think we are the thoughts. When we feel, we think we
are the feelings. We are completely identified with our thoughts and feelings.
We totally believe in them. We are totally engulfed in them. This is one of

Ven. Tenzin Palmo at Tashi Jong, 2001.
Photo: Angus McDonald.

Tenzin Palmo outside her cave in Lahoul. Her possessions,
soaked from the spring thaw, are spread out to dry in the sun.
Photo: courtesy of the author.

Inside Tenzin Palmo's cave, showing meditation box.
Photo: courtesy of the author.

Ven. Tenzin Palmo with H.E. the Ninth Khamtrul Rinpoche
at Tashi Jong, 2001.
Photo: Angus McDonald.

Ven. Tenzin Palmo.
Photo: Angus McDonald.

Ven. Tenzin Palmo and nuns of Dongyu Gatsal Ling Nunnery, March 2001.
Photo: Angus McDonald.

Ven. Tenzin Palmo and some of the Dongyu Gatsal Ling nuns at the site of the new nunnery, March 2001.
Photo: Angus McDonald.

Nuns of Dongyu Gatsal Ling at the site of the new nunnery, March 2001.   Photo: *Angus McDonald.*

the reasons why we suffer so much. It's nice, of course, when the thoughts and feelings are all happiness, joy, and peace, but often they are the opposite of that. They are depressed, angry, frustrated, and consequently we feel completely enshrouded by dark feelings. So we suffer. When we begin to meditate, the surface mind starts to calm down. Then it is as if a part of the mind steps back and a kind of space, or distance, is created within the mind. Part of the mind becomes a calm, unmoved observer that just knows. And then there are the thoughts and the emotions of which that observer is conscious. This development in itself is extremely helpful. It is not ultimate reality, but it is beneficial for many reasons. One reason is that our center is no longer in the turbulence of our thoughts and emotions, but standing back in this inner space. We have this cool inner space to which we can retire.

This inner space sees very clearly. It merely observes, it doesn't judge. We can now view our thoughts and emotions as merely thoughts and emotions. We don't believe in them the way we did before. They are no longer solid. We are not identifying with them. We see them rise up like bubbles; they appear, they grow, they burst, and then new ones come up. This happens continually. This is the natural activity of the mind. It is fine. But we are no longer immersed in these thoughts and emotions. We can see them for what they are. They start to become more and more friable, more and more transparent. And we begin to understand something of this empty spacious quality as it begins to open up. We begin to understand that all of this is just like a rainbow. The thoughts are actually transparent. They are not real. You can't catch a thought and hold it.

Developing this kind of mind state is an enormous help to us on our spiritual journey. It is not difficult. It's actually quite simple. We always think these things are so difficult, we think that other people can do them, but not us. Actually, it's just like a snap of the fingers and then you've got it. Our main problem then is to keep it going. It's easy to slip back. But once you get it, even for one second, you understand that it's nothing special. It's just being present in the moment without being submerged in it.

Now we have the subject, which is the observer, and we have the thoughts, which are the objects being observed. The question is how we bring these two together. The good news is that we don't need to. At a certain point, when the mind is completely aware, completely present, and at the same time completely relaxed, the whole thing falls apart, and we find ourselves naturally in a state of non-dual awareness. Even if only for a second, at least for that moment, we get it. We cannot do anything to make it happen. We can only create the conditions so that it happens spontaneously.

Q: About three years ago I was doing a yoga course. Everything started to get wider and wider, and it frightened me. How does one deal with fear?

TP: The fact is, the mind has infinite capacities, infinite potential, and many, many states. Our ego wants to be in control of all of this. The ego becomes threatened when it seems to be losing control. It sees different mental states appearing, and it doesn't understand what's happening. So the fear arises and we panic. If you notice that happening, it's a good idea to just relax into the moment with a kind of inner curiosity to see what unfolds and where it is leading. The mind comes up with all sorts of states. It plays all sorts of games, and we shouldn't get attached to any of them. But there are also ways that the mind sometimes really wants to expand itself. It wants to go beyond its ordinary conceptual thinking, and we want to give it the space to do that. So maybe doing that yoga relaxation in some way activated other layers of the mind which wanted to be brought up into consciousness. Maybe it would be a good idea to relax and just allow that to happen.

If you have a particular belief system, you can take refuge within that. That will protect you. Before the Tibetans start to meditate, and this is probably the case for all Buddhists, they take refuge in the Buddha, Dharma and Sangha. Tibetans also do something they call guru yoga. In this practice you envision some primordial Buddha and all the masters of the lineage you belong to arranged in chronological order, ending with your own teacher. Then you pray to them for their blessings. You imagine that they all come down into your root teacher, and he melts into you, and your mind and his mind become one. The reason for doing this is primarily to invoke the blessings of the lineage, but it's also a protection, so that whatever happens in the meditation, it's okay. Then you can just relax and allow whatever is going to happen to happen, without fear. If anything disturbing arises, you again invoke the particular masters appropriate to your belief system. Then, if there is anything nasty, it will be dispelled.

Q: I understand the benefits of having a teacher, and I understand that the teacher will find you, you don't have to go searching for him. What do you think about that, especially for a practitioner or a student who is keen to progress?

TP: When the student is ready, the teacher appears. But this idea can be taken to extremes. I know people who have spent their whole lives waiting for their ideal teacher to come and say the word and then zap, they will be enlightened. In the meantime, they don't do anything because they are waiting. That's one extreme. These people believe that the only way you can get spiritual knowledge is by finding the perfect teacher, and they don't have to do anything for themselves. The perfect teacher is going to come and find them. You might ask yourself why he would bother! On the other hand, it's true that unless you have the karmic connection, you could go around the world meeting every possible guru and still end up with nothing. I think it depends a lot on karma. If you have the karmic connection to meet the right teacher, you will meet him. If you don't, you won't. But in the meantime, by gaining access to teachers and teachings, you can still learn and practice. It may be that until we get to a certain level, even if we met the Buddha himself, he wouldn't be able to help us. Maybe we need to do all the preparation so that if we do meet the perfect teacher, he can help us. It behooves us all to start preparing ourselves now. We can learn to practice, we can get our ethical life together, we can purify our motivation. There are many practices for purification and for learning how to concentrate and tame the mind, to make the mind more subtle. Then, if we have the fortune to meet the perfect teacher, we will be ready for him to give genuine teachings which will really help us, instead of wasting his time getting him to teach us the ABC's, which we could have learned on our own.

Q: How do we get a good rebirth?

TP: We get a good rebirth by having good motivation and performing virtuous conduct. Why are we here? We are here to cultivate and develop our mind at all levels and to open our heart. However we manage to do it, it is a good thing, and it is not a waste of our human birth. We need to ask ourselves what it is about this human birth which distinguishes it from an animal birth, birth in a god realm, in a hell realm, or as a hungry ghost. Why is a human birth so precious? One of the reasons is that humans have choice. We are responsible for our actions. We can choose to respond to situations on a very instinctive level, as animals do, or we can bring into play something uniquely human, which is our intelligence. Everything that happens to us is an opportunity to make a responsible choice. That is why it is wonderful to be human. If someone insults us, we have a choice. We can insult him back, we can hit him, we can go away feeling humiliated and blaming ourselves because we are worthy of everybody's insults, or we can view the situation with understanding and patience and deal with it skillfully, applying no blame to anyone. We have that choice.

One of the gains of meditation is it makes our minds clearer so that we don't just have this push-button response to situations. If we choose wisely, we give ourselves the space to see situations clearly and make the appropriate responses. If we make appropriate, skillful responses, we will have a skillful and appropriate rebirth. We must live our lives ethically. Buddhist ethics are based on not harming. Of course, we are always harming, but it's a matter of degree. If we start thinking, "Each time I eat a carrot, so many insects are being killed, this carrot also has life," and so on, we end up with this giant, extreme view in which we can't move, and we just sit and starve ourselves to death. That doesn't solve anything. By following Buddhist ethics, we don't kill. We don't take life, because life is the most precious commodity any being has, including insects. The most precious thing to an insect is its own life. It is important to respect every being's right to live. We cause such disasters on this earth because we are so arbitrary. We decide something or other is no good, and we destroy it. Then we find that something else is getting out of control because we destroyed the thing which controlled it. The earth was so balanced, but because of our pig-headed stupidity and our ideas that "This is good, that is bad," and our assumption that we can just get rid of anything that is not pretty to us, we have caused great harm. We must respect the fact that everything has its part to play—even things we don't like.

We should not steal. We don't like people to steal from us. It's very unwise to think we have a right to other people's property. It's harming. We have to learn to take responsibility for our sexual conduct. We are very irresponsible in this modern age. The number of abortions taking place is evidence of this. We do not think of the consequences of what we are doing, how other people are going to be affected, how we are going to be affected, or how society will be affected. We don't think of the unborn child, which is a human being also. We just don't care.

Why are we so miserable? We think that if we have perfect sexual expression we are going to be happy, yet everybody is so neurotic, so miserable, so messed up. It's because we don't take responsibility for our actions and their repercussions. We are harming others, we are harming ourselves. We are lying. We are not being open and honest. Then there is alcohol and drug abuse. That harms others, it harms us, and it harms society. None of these ethical rules pertains particularly to life as it was 2,500 years ago in Magadha. They are as relevant today as they were then, if not more so. They have nothing to do with culture, nothing to do with the Buddha being an Indian. They are universally applicable. It's not about what we eat or don't eat. It isn't even about who we sleep with or don't sleep with. It's why we are sleeping with them and what the repercussions might be. It's about whether it will affect anyone in an adverse way. It's about whether we harm or don't harm.

Everything has to do with cherishing and nourishing. If we lead our lives with a sense of what the Dalai Lama calls universal responsibility, there's no way we can go wrong, because we are fulfilling our role as humans. Meditation helps us to gain clarity in doing this. But our ethical conduct also helps support our meditation. The Buddha always said that if you do not have ethical conduct, you cannot meditate, because the mind is too distracted. Once we have established ethical conduct in our lives, we become inwardly more peaceful and quiet. Our mind can settle much more quickly. That aids meditation. When the mind becomes settled, it becomes clearer. Then understanding and wisdom arise naturally. They are integrated. You can't have one without the other. It's all part of the package.

People are very happy to hear about wisdom. They are very happy to hear about meditation. But they are very reluctant to hear about ethics. Yet a code of ethics is the foundation on which everything is built. It's not about "You mustn't do this, you mustn't do that." It's not commandments. Even the five precepts do not say, "Thou shalt not kill, thou shalt not steal." They say, "I undertake to observe the rule of training not to take life." They are rules of training. Our motivation must be to live in this world without harming other beings. If people could manage only that, imagine what a pure land we would be living in!

Q: What's the process of making amends if you have acted unethically at some stage in your life?

TP: There are very specific procedures. Suppose one has done something really horrible and is sorry about it. In the Buddhist tradition there is something called the four opponent powers. The first of these is remorse. Nothing is going to be purified if we are not sorry about it. If our basic attitude is, "That was kind of clever, not everybody can do that," and we feel quite pleased inside for having done what we did, there is no way we can purify it. We have to see that it is like drinking poison. This is the traditional example, that you drink poison and then think, "Oh my goodness, what have I done?"

Then we have what is called the power of reliance. This means that we use something which we rely on to help purify this action. In the Tibetan system there are a number of practices which are done specifically for purification. Those of you who know about Tibetan Buddhism will immediately call to mind the Vajrasattva practice. There is also the fasting practice of the Thousand-Armed Chenrezig, or Quan Yin. There are also practices such as prostrations to the Thirty-five Confession Buddhas, and so on. These various purification practices invoke the power of reliance.

Then we have the power of the antidote. This means doing something which is the opposite of what you did, like the antidote to a poison. For example, a friend of mine was in the Peace Corps. Her particular program was establishing chicken farms. Her motivation was to help the villagers get money and protein by raising chickens. But then when she became a Buddhist, she realized that she had wrung the necks of hundreds of chickens, and caused the deaths of thousands more. She was horrified at what she had done. Her motivation had not been bad. She had felt no personal animosity towards those chickens, but her behavior was deluded because she had not realized that those chickens had a life and that it is not right to deprive any being of the most precious thing it possesses. She became very upset about it. Since that time, which was thirty-five years ago, she saves lives whenever the opportunity arises. She buys fish and puts them into the ocean. She buys birds and sets them free. She buys sheep destined for slaughter and gives them to people to care for. She uses this as a very deliberate antidote against all the lives she took in the past. We also can try to do the opposite of whatever harm we did in the past.

The fourth power is the power to vow never to do it again. If we do something and we know it's wrong, but nevertheless know we are going to keep on doing it, we don't really have remorse. It's not wholehearted. If we really knew we were drinking poison, we would not be tempted to drink it again. So the fourth power is the power of vowing never to do it again. If this really comes from the heart, it can indeed purify.

Q: I have thought of letting birds go. I haven't done it, but I wonder whether they would be better off in the cage?

TP: There is a lot of ambiguity attached to releasing life. It is a very popular practice in Asia. But as a result, there are many people who make their living by capturing birds and keeping them in very cruel conditions, just so that pious Buddhists will come along, buy them, and release them into the wild. However, these birds are in a dreadful state, and they immediately get recaptured. Some people like to take turtles and put them into pools in the monasteries. But the pools are stuffed with turtles who are now living in a kind of hell realm. So it's not good to be mindlessly pious. We have to use our intelligence. Buying fish from those big aquariums in Chinese restaurants in order to take them back to the ocean gives them a chance to live. When this is done, lots of prayers and mantras are said for them. In Asia, one can buy sheep and goats which are going to be slaughtered and then give them to people to care for. They have a special piece of ribbon tied onto their fleece so that everyone can see that they have been saved and they are not allowed to be killed.

Q: I live in a part of Australia where a kind of borer attacks the trees every year. If I don't get it out, the trees will be killed. What would you advise in a situation like this?

TP: Okay, I'm going to be controversial here. First of all, this is samsara. It is the realm of birth and death. By its inherent nature, it is not satisfactory. And the Buddha said that the household life is full of dust. In other words, it's very difficult to maintain immaculate ethical conduct in a household life. You always have to make decisions and compromises. In this case, you have to make a decision as to which is more important, the trees or the insects. That's up to you. If you decide that the trees are more meaningful for you than the insects, that is your decision. I would personally suggest that before spraying the tree, you talk to the insects. This might sound silly. But tell the insects what you are going to do. Tell them very clearly what their options are. Tell them, "Look, I'm very sorry. I realize this is your livelihood, this is your nature. It's not your fault. But I'm very attached to this tree and I don't want it to be destroyed. So, I'm sorry, but I will have to kill you if you don't move. It's up to you. You have forty-eight hours to make up your mind."

Tell them that very clearly, from your thought as well as your words. Tell them several times. And then give them a chance. If you really are able to communicate with those insects, they will probably decide to move. It could be that you won't be able to get into contact with them. But you should at least try. Give them a sporting chance. Then even if they don't move and you have to kill them, do it with regret, and with responsibility. Don't rejoice in it. Then say some prayers for their better rebirth. These are sentient beings. They also have Buddha-nature. They all have the potential in future lifetimes just as we do. They have a right to their lives, too. So one should not take their lives negligently, but with a sense of responsibility and regret.

Q: There may be some garden sprays available that might discourage them without killing them.
TP: Yes, that's very true. I would investigate that possibility first. We have to make these decisions. It's not easy. But at least we should make responsible decisions rather than doing things mindlessly.

Q: What are the differences between Hinayana and Vajrayana in relation to eating meat? It seems to be more common in the Vajrayana to eat meat.
TP: It seems pretty clear that the Buddha ate meat. According to the Vinaya, there is no rule that says we cannot eat meat. I'm a vegetarian, so it is not my own agenda I'm defending here. The Buddha's wicked cousin, Devadatta, tried to create a schism in the sangha. His recommendation was to make the rules of the sangha stricter than they were. He wanted all the monks to be obliged to wear rag robes, whereas the Buddha said they could if they wanted to but that they didn't need to, and if somebody offered them robes, they could wear them. Devadatta said all monks should live by begging, whereas the Buddha said they should live by begging, but if someone invited them to a meal, that was okay. Devadatta said that all monks should have to live under trees, whereas the Buddha said that they could live under trees, but if somebody offered them a hut, they could accept. Devadatta wanted all monks to be strict vegetarians. The Buddha said that they could be vegetarian if they wanted, but as they were begging for alms, they should accept whatever was given. The monks went around from household to household early in the

morning, collecting cooked food. The idea was that they should be totally non-discriminating, accepting whatever was offered to them. Therefore, in Theravadin countries, where nobody's vegetarian, the monks are not vegetarian. It's a very complex situation.

In the Mahayana there are sutras, such as the *Lankavatara Sutra*, which contain whole chapters of the Buddha's diatribes against meat-eating, mostly because it's impure. Much less because of compassion for animals, interestingly. It's quite Hindu, in a way. But anyway, there is a strong Mahayana slant against eating flesh. So therefore, in Mahayana countries such as China and Korea, the monks and nuns are strict vegetarians. They are also vegans because the Chinese don't usually eat dairy products, anyway. They eat lots of tofu as their protein source. So if you go to a Mahayana monastery, you will always be given vegetarian food.

Vajrayana evolved in India in huge monastic colleges and just outside these colleges. Now I imagine that a lot of the monks in these colleges were Brahmins and Kshatriyas, in other words, high-caste people. They were Mahayana, which means they didn't eat meat. They were pure; they were celibate, they never drank, and they were vegetarians. Vegetarianism was associated in their minds with the spiritual path. Then there were these gatherings, almost covens, often at night, where they came together outside the monastic setting, often in cemeteries. Why in cemeteries? Firstly, because these were very frightening places, and secondly, because nobody else went there at night. Their presence there would be secret. In these places, they did things which broke all of their patterns. They drank alcohol. There were girls around. They ate meat. They danced. They sang. They broke through all these heavy inhibitions they had built up about what a spiritual practice should be. So it was a catharsis for them. All this was carried out in the already incredible atmosphere of a charnel ground. The charnel grounds of those days were not like our neat little cemeteries with flowers and lights and stone angels. They were places where you took a body and slung it down, then the jackals and the vultures came and ate it. They were very frightening places, where all sorts of weird things went on. In such frightening, challenging places, you could break through all your inhibitions. This is represented in the Tibetan tradition in a rather lukewarm way during the bimonthly celebrations known as *tsog*. In tsog it is requisite, in very sanitized situations within in the monastery or Dharma center, to take a little alcohol and a snippet of meat. Then they sing a beautiful, inspiring vajra song. But this is a pale reflection of a pale reflection of a pale reflection of what really went on and where this came from.

Vajrayana aims to create an inner psychic revolution in our notions about pure and impure. Indians are very hung up on purity. Tantra attempted to break that down. Some Hindu yogis do all of those original practices today. Hindu tantric yogis are very interesting people. They really live in cemeteries. They sit on corpses. They eat corpses. They are still doing this today as a means of breaking through all these inhibitions of the psyche about "can" and "cannot," to go beyond hope and fear, repulsion and attraction. They do all those things which are conventionally considered to be totally repugnant. That's what it was all about.

There is a very interesting book called *Agora*, which is about a modern-day tantrika who spends half his time as a businessman in Bombay, and the other half taking off all his clothes and living in cemeteries. It is outrageous. But when you read this, it is reminiscent of the lives of the mahasiddhas back in the eighth century. When Buddhism came to Tibet, it was sanitized and many of these tantric practices became merely symbolic. Originally there were five nectars, which I won't describe, but they were pretty distasteful. Nowadays they use herbal pills in alcohol. But in the old days, they weren't kidding. They used the original ingredients, because they were trying to get beyond all the mental conceptions about what was acceptable and what was not. That's what tantra was about. Now it's become mainstream, so a lot has been lost. Of course, the Tibetans still routinely produce great enlightened masters, so something's working! But an aspect of tantra has been lost.

So we're back to meat. OK, the whole idea of eating meat in the higher tantras was to shock. You drink alcohol; you eat meat. When Buddhism first went to Tibet, it met with this wild and barbarous people who had just finished conquering a large part of central Asia. They were very warlike. They still are, which is why they are such good practitioners. They take that warrior spirit, and they either become bandits or great practitioners. They have a lot of raw energy. So when this tantra was introduced to Tibet by Padmasambhava in the eighth century, they fell in love with it. Well, not right away. Initially they were very skeptical. They had experienced Mahayana Buddhism before. There was actually a lot of controversy at the time of the introduction of Tantric Buddhism into Tibet. But after a time they accepted that it did work and that it was a legitimate spiritual path. When they relaxed and realized that it was OK, that it wasn't demonic, they went for it with great enthusiasm. It fitted in with the Tibetan character incredibly well. It was made for Tibetans.

Every religion has its share of hypocrisy. There is actually nothing in Vajrayana which says you have to eat meat. These days, more and more lamas are becoming vegetarian, especially the younger ones, partly for health reasons and partly because they recognize the hypocrisy of talking about universal compassion and then sitting down to a steak or a chicken. But I don't believe it has anything to do with enlightenment. I think one of the beauties of Tibetan Buddhism is that they do all the things which are considered an absolute "no no" in most spiritual traditions. They were dirty. Cleanliness is next to godliness? Forget it. They eat all the wrong things. They eat meat, onions and garlic. They drink, they do everything they are not supposed to do, and they get enlightened anyway! This is actually good for us to hear about, because it reminds us not to get attached to these things. It's good not to eat meat. It's good to be clean. But these things have nothing to do with attaining enlightenment.

Q: This is the first time I've heard about garlic and onions. What is the objection to garlic and onions?

TP: In the Indian scheme of things, the higher castes like the Brahmins do not eat meat or onions. According to the ancient science of Ayurveda, there are the three *gunas*, or qualities: *sattva*, *rajas* and *tamas*. Food is also divided into sattvic, rajasic, or tamasic. Sattvic means pure. It purifies the body and the mind. Sattvic foods include milk, pure grains, vegetables, cheese, etc. Then there are the rajas. Rajas means something which is fiery and exciting, which stirs you up and gives you energy. Onions and garlic, fish and chicken, tea and coffee are rajasic. They are considered to be stimulating, and therefore counterproductive to anyone wishing to lead a pure and celibate life. Lastly there are tamasic foods. These foods are heavy and make the mind dull. They include beef, bacon, alcohol and deep-fried foods. In the Buddhist tradition according to the Vinaya, monks and nuns are not supposed to eat garlic or onions. So in the Chinese tradition also, the vegetarian food is prepared without garlic and onions.

ᔓ 12

The Role of the Spiritual Master

I WILL DISCUSS the role of the master with particular reference to Vajrayana. At the time of the Lord Buddha himself, the teacher was of course the Buddha, and he was the ultimate authority. It is recorded that when the Buddha was about to pass away, Ananda asked him who the new teacher would be, and the Buddha replied, "Let the Dharma itself be your teacher." In the Mahayana tradition, the teacher's role is described as being that of the *kalyanamitra*, which means "good friend" or "spiritual friend." Such a person must be one who has traveled further along the path than the student. The Guru must have developed wisdom and compassion to a high degree. The appropriate response by the student is that of deep gratitude toward the teacher along with trust in his or her ability as a guide.

In the Vajrayana, or Tantric, school, the guru plays an extremely pivotal role. I think there are two principal reasons for this. Firstly, a genuine teacher, or guru, is the one who reveals to us the empty, aware, clear nature of the primordial mind, our inherent wisdom and compassion. This, the mind's unconditioned nature, is always with us. It is the most fundamental aspect of our being. However, it is very difficult for us to gain access to this without help. We need a teacher who can create the psychological circumstances for us to glimpse this inherent nature. So a true guru is the one who shows us the nature of the mind. He or she is therefore an extremely important person in our lives.

The traditional analogy to describe the role of the teacher uses the example of the sun. The sun is huge and powerful, and it illuminates and warms the whole earth. Yet if one were to put a piece of paper on the ground in the sun, even in the midday sun, at the most the paper would dry out a bit and maybe get a little crinkly. It would certainly not catch fire. But if we were to place a magnifying glass between the rays of the sun and the paper, the sun's rays would be focused, increasing their intensity. Within a very short time the paper would begin to turn brown, then it would start to smoke and shortly afterwards burst into flame. Likewise, it is said that although the blessings of the Buddhas and the bodhisattvas are infinite and incredibly powerful, it is difficult for them to transform us directly without the intermediary of a spiritual teacher because of our defilements and obscurations. A qualified teacher embodies the blessings, power, compassion, and wisdom of all the Buddhas within a human form. Like a magnifying glass, he or she can condense and transmit those blessings, igniting realizations in the disciple. This is because the guru has a human form and this is a mind-to-mind transmission. You see, the guru doesn't give us anything—he or she merely allows this inner opening to take place. We will come back to this idea again later.

The second thing a guru can give us is guidance. If we are traveling through unknown territory (and what is more unknown than our own inner psychological landscape?) on our own, it is very likely we will go astray, even with the aid of a map. Sometimes we may be walking along and suddenly the path divides. Do we go to the left or to the right? When we consult the map, it's not always clear what to do. The map gives the broad outlines, but these little sidetracks are not included. We might choose the right path, but we might also choose the wrong one and end up in quicksand or a swamp!

I remember once I was practicing with this old yogi. In those days I was going to see him every day and he would just give me general indications. I would tell him what I was doing and he would say "Oh, mm, yes, okay." On one occasion, something had actually happened. I was really pleased because I had had an experience! So I went along and told him about it and he said "Mm" and looked totally bored. Then he said, "Didn't anything else happen?" So I racked my brain, trying to remember. I remembered some other minor thing, and I mentioned it just in case it was of any use. Immediately he sat up and said, "Say that again." So I repeated what I had said and explained that this and this had happened, and he said, "That's it, that's what we've been waiting for. From now on, you do this and this." Then he sent me off in a completely different direction. I would never have known about it on my own. I didn't know that was what we had been waiting for. It didn't seem significant to me at all. This is why we need a teacher. Again, if we have a guide, we can walk confidently because we know we are with someone who knows the road. If we are alone, we have to go slowly. We hesitate a lot. With somebody to guide us, we can stride along the path.

Everybody dreams of meeting the perfect master who is going to take them under his wing. From now on, no more problems! Ha! There are movies in which people go through tremendous difficulties looking for their teacher, and when they finally find the right cave, there is an old yogi sitting there. He looks at them and says, "Ah, I have been waiting for you. What took you so long?" Trying to meet the perfect master who is going to set it all up for you is a common fantasy, where all you have to do is follow the instructions and enlightenment is guaranteed. I even know people who refuse to make any kind of effort on their own behalf, because they are waiting for the perfect guru to turn up and say the perfect sentence. Then they will immediately understand it and be enlightened once and for all, without needing to make the slightest bit of effort. They believe that they're going to meet the master, and he's going to say the thing or do the thing which will solve all their problems for ever and ever.

You might ask what is wrong with this scenario. It sounds good! Well, first of all, even if we did meet the perfect master, as long as our minds remain completely deluded, would he or she be able to help us? Maybe the teacher's only advice to us would be to "go and sit." Maybe we wouldn't be ready to receive instruction. We might first need to practice a lot more. Even the greatest masters can help only when the disciples are ready. In the meantime, we need to prepare ourselves. In doing so, perhaps we will discover that everybody we meet is actually our master. This area of guru-disciple relationships is very tricky.

What are the requirements for a truly qualified guru? Well, if you are going to study physics, you will want to make sure that the person you are studying with really does understand physics. If you are going to learn anything, you want to know that the person you are studying with is truly a master of the subject. How much the more so when we are trying to discover something as momentous as our inherent enlightened nature! Obviously, nobody can reveal that to us, nobody can show us the path to travel unless they have already traveled that path themselves.

The next question is, "How do we know if someone is genuinely realized and qualified?" The answer to that is that we don't know. It's always a gamble.

But there are indications. Personally, when I look at teachers, the one question I ask is, "Is this all coming from their inherent emptiness, or is it coming from an ego?" Realizations have nothing to do with charisma. We are very taken in by charisma and by someone's ability to market himself or to be intellectually satisfying. But where is it coming from? Is it really coming from this empty wisdom and genuine compassion? Or is it just another big ego-inflation trip? We have to be sensitive enough to feel this. I am extremely suspicious of anyone who claims to be enlightened. I have never met any Tibetan lama who would even dream of making such a claim. Most lamas will say, "Oh, I'm just like you, I'm also practicing, I'm also training. Now so-and-so, that lama over there, he's really fantastic, he's amazing, he can do this and this, but me, I'm just an ordinary guy." This doesn't mean that when they are sitting on a high throne, they cannot manifest inner confidence. But the confidence should be coming from what they are teaching and not from their own ego-aggrandizement. The other thing I think we need to look at is how they are when they get down from the throne and are mixing with ordinary people. How do they conduct themselves in ordinary circumstances? How do they treat ordinary people who are of no possible benefit to them?

The Dalai Lama says we should investigate the teacher. I know it's difficult, but Westerners really tend to be too trusting and too gullible. Asians are much more exacting. They have standards by which they judge because they've been around the spiritual scene for a long time. Tibetans are not naive. Some people imagine that Tibetans are simple-minded and superstitious, but Westerners leave Tibetans open-mouthed at their gullibility. In the tantric texts it is said that one should test the guru for up to twelve years before deciding to accept him or her. The Dalai Lama even says we should spy on the gurus! How do they act when they're not in the spotlight? Are they kind and compassionate, or are they basically just rolling along, having a good time, and enjoying taking people in? When I asked my own teacher about certain lamas who were quite controversial in the West, he said, "Well, at that level it's difficult to judge, but in twenty years' time have a look at their disciples." This is a very good indication of a teacher's caliber. What is happening to their older disciples? Would we want to be like them? What is the scene around the guru like? Is it psychologically healthy? Are the disciples being manipulated? Are they unable to make decisions for themselves without running to the guru all the time? Are they psychologically dependent on their teacher?

The Tibetan word "lama" actually means "a high mother," and *ma* of course is female. So, *lama* is a female word. Tibetans don't usually mention this. So the guru is like a mother. When a mother has small children, she cares for them, nurtures them and is there to cherish them, discipline them, and train them. That's her role. Small children are dependent on their mother because they don't know anything yet. But if the mother still wants to be "mummy" as the children grow up and wants t to keep them dependent on her, tied to her apron strings, she is no longer a good mother. A good mother brings up her children to become increasingly independent and to be able to leave home when they come of age. A good mother raises her children to be autonomous beings in their own right, and to act as parents to others in the future. Likewise, a true guru trains the disciples to discover their own inner wisdom and their inner guru. He or she trains them to make decisions for themselves. Any "guru" who is merely creating a circle of adoring acolytes waiting for every nectar-like word he speaks, growing increasingly dependent on him and focused on gratifying his every wish, is just in love with the idea of being a guru. Without disciples, that person wouldn't be a guru any more, and that's the source of his power. It's quite a power trip when you can tell people to do something and they do it unquestioningly, even if they don't want to! It can become a drug.

You see this sort of thing happening around some teachers. Year by year, they create this symbiotic relationship in which the disciples become increasingly dependent upon their guru. They can't make any decisions without first going to see what Guru-ji has to say about it. If this is happening, there is something seriously wrong. In the beginning, of course, a good teacher tells the disciples what to do because he or she is there to guide them. But as time passes the teacher will begin to say, "Well, what do you want to do? What do you feel you should be doing now?" Increasingly, he or she tosses the ball back to the disciple so that the disciple can grow. When the time is right, the teacher will probably send the disciple away altogether.

Milarepa, the great Tibetan yogin of the eleventh century, kept his disciples with him, either in the same cave or in adjacent caves, until they were stable in their practice. Then he sent them away, and from time to time he would visit them to see how they were getting on. The guru is supposed to help us discover our innate wisdom so that we do not have to rely on his or her advice indefinitely. That is why we need to do our part by purifying and simplifying our minds and making them increasingly open. Then when we meet the master, we are truly present and real transmission can take place.

So what are we going to do? Here we are in the West. There are not many teachers around. There are two main questions I am asked everywhere I go. One is how to deal with anger, and the other is how to find a teacher. Both questions are very complex. There are teachers and then there are teachers. There is the heart teacher, who has vowed and committed to take the disciple to enlightenment in this or future lifetimes. That is a heart commitment on behalf of both the teacher and the disciple. It is a total commitment which requires total surrender on the part of the disciple. This is why we have to be extremely careful. If you find a true guru, that is the greatest blessing this life could give you as far as traveling on the path is concerned. If you find a false guru, then, as the Tibetans say, teacher and disciple jump hand-in-hand into the chasm. According to the Tibetans, you end up in a hell realm. There are, however, many other teachers apart from a heart guru. And it doesn't mean that we have to throw ourselves down on the ground and say, "Okay, take me, I'm yours from now until enlightenment,"every time we meet a teacher we like and feel a connection with.

We are here now, but we want to learn how to go home. We want to learn how to return from our enormous confusion back to the ultimate simplicity of our true nature. There are many who can help us on our way. There are many who can point out signposts. It doesn't always have to be the ultimate guru. Anyone who can give us valid help and guidance is a teacher. They may come in the form of a teacher who is giving teachings. They may come merely as a brief encounter. They may even come in the form of a relative or a friend. How can we know? Anyone from whom we learn becomes a teacher, a spiritual friend. So I personally think we should shift our focus from this idea of finding a heart guru and instead start seeking spiritual friends. If we think of teachers as spiritual friends, that makes everything much vaster because we can have many spiritual friends. The Buddha once said that the Dharma was to be our teacher, and the teachings are here. The techniques are here. The practice is here. There are those who have been practicing for many years and who have devoted their lives to the practice. There are many people around who know. Help is available. It may not come in the form of high spiritual masters radiating lights or sending out brochures ahead of time to tell us they're enlightened. Teachers may come in very simple forms. But if they have had the practice, and if they themselves have had valid teachers, belong to a pure and genuine lineage, and have received the fruits of their practice, they are valid teachers.

We all have a lot of work to do. We have to do a lot of purification, a lot of learning how to pacify the mind, how to clear it out, how to simplify it and begin to understand it. We don't need the Lord Buddha standing in front of us. We can manage this on our own with informed guidance. It's not much use just waiting around for the perfect master to appear. As I said, even if the perfect master appeared, would we be ready? So in the meantime, we prepare. There is an enormous amount that we can do. And then, perhaps, just a very small thing could trigger off a major breakthrough.

There are many Zen stories in which there's some hermit living somewhere, and some monk wanders by. The hermit utters some enigmatic sentence, and the monk "gets" it! But what they don't talk about, because it's taken for granted in the Asian mind, is that this monk spent thirty years sitting on his carpet before somebody came along and gave him the enigmatic sentence. It wasn't only the sentence, because we can read that sentence and think, "So?" It doesn't trigger a major insight for us. It was the preparation—all those endless hours and hours and months and years of sitting, of bringing awareness into every activity, of really learning how to prepare and train the mind to be present. Do you understand? It cannot all come from the guru. A great deal of it has to come from the disciple.

Many stories are told of the lives of the mahasiddhas, the great yogis of eighth- and ninth-century India. They were often lay people, tailors, shopkeepers, jewelers, all kinds of people with different careers who found themselves in a kind of spiritual quagmire. They weren't going anywhere. Then a master turned up and gave them some small teaching, just some small technique, then went away, never to be seen again. But they practiced that technique. They took it and transformed it into their everyday lives until they attained great accomplishments. In other words, they weren't living with their gurus. Maybe they only saw their guru once. But they worked on it. They worked on it and worked on it persistently day after day until the accomplishment occurred.

You see, sometimes this ideal of finding the perfect guru is just another form of laziness. "Well, I'm not accomplished because I haven't found my teacher yet." But in the meantime, there is everything for us to do. Because, as I said at the beginning, what we are really trying to do is reconnect with what we have always had and find the inner guru. To reconnect with our primordial nature, our wisdom mind, which is always here. In the end, the practice is our refuge. This is not perhaps what I should be saying as a Tibetan Buddhist, but honestly, merely being caught up in the circle surrounding a guru, spending all of our time jockeying for position and making sure the lama notices us, has little to do with Dharma. It's just the same old worldly emotions, gain and loss, happiness and sorrow, praise and blame, fame and disrepute. You see all of this appearing nakedly around some gurus. There is rampant jealousy and competition. It would be better to go home and just sit on our cushion, try to be kind to our family and learn to use them as our Dharma practice. It would be better for us to learn how to be loving, compassionate, kind, and patient to everyone we meet. Very often, when people get caught up in a big guru trip, they end up just serving that one organization and develop a very narrow vision. There's only the guru and that guru's sangha, organization, and teachings. Nothing else exists. If you are in doubt about your involvement with a particular group, take a good look at the people there. Do they appear to be more enlightened than people you meet every day in the street?

I believe it is better to meet a teacher who really has wisdom, who has that very special presence which some lamas and other teachers of all traditions have. There is a certain spacious, egoless quality that makes you know you are in the presence of a genuine master, not one who is just interested in self-promotion. A teacher who is totally simple, yet in whose presence you experience something special. When you encounter such a teacher, then you should gain some teaching from that person and go away and work on it. In the meantime, if you have not met someone like that, learn from whatever sources of understanding, wisdom, and genuine practice are available to you. We all have so much to do. And all of us can start doing it right this moment. We gain nothing by hanging around waiting!

This notion of "the guru" can be pernicious. It gets people completely turned upside down and leaves them standing on their heads. I had a perfect guru, so this is not sour grapes. But I honestly don't think it's what you really need. What we all need is more practice, not this fantasy of finding Shangri-la. There is a great line in the film *Kundun* where the Dalai Lama says, "You cannot liberate me General Tan, only I can liberate myself." The Buddha said that Buddhas only point out the way. Each of us must walk the path. This can seem contradictory, because it's also true that if we meet a really perfect master, he or she can accelerate our progress. There's no doubt about that. What I'm saying is that if you do happen to meet a perfect master who does that, good for you! In the meantime, just get on with it! Don't hang around waiting. And don't base your whole life on hanging around a guru scene. It is such a waste of time. From my own observations, these scenes bring out the really base parts of our nature without reconciling them. Some gurus become outrageous, and I personally think that they can go overboard. Where is the compassion, where is the skillful means? People can get so confused, telling themselves, "This has to be a teaching." It's a bit like, "Hit me harder, ouch, it hurts, it must be good for me." Maybe it isn't good for you at all! Maybe it just bruises you! Of course, this is not always the case. Some gurus have very nice scenes, but often people's energy gets caught up in the dynamics of being around the guru instead of looking within and discovering who they are. It's better for us to focus on keeping our lives plain and becoming one with our practice rather than getting caught up in all this other stuff.

A skillful guru is like a good surgeon. He or she knows just where and how to apply the scalpel. And even though it may hurt for a moment, the body knows it is being healed, and it does heal. On the other hand, an unskillful surgeon stabs away blindly and doesn't reach the vital part. Such a person leaves the patient cut, bleeding, and scarred. Creating pain is not the purpose of the exercise. The point is to reach the vital part of the body which needs the surgeon's attention so that the patient is healed and transformed.

In the final analysis, we are all our own gurus. In the end, we have to access our own innate wisdom. This can be dangerous because our inner guide may appear to be telling us what we want to hear. But we know it really is the inner guide if it tells us to do exactly what we don't want to do!

We all possess inner wisdom, and we should begin to get in touch with it more and more often. Then we will start to experience an inner poise and a sense of autonomy. After all, we are trying to grow up, not remain children forever. The Buddha called unenlightened people "the children." Sometimes that is translated as "fools," but it doesn't actually mean "fools." It means those who are still immature. So those of us who have been on a spiritual path for some time should look back to see what is happening to us. Do we feel that there really is some inner transformation, that we really are beginning to grow up? Are we gaining greater understanding? Is our inner psychological life becoming clearer and simpler, more open and spacious? Are our negative emotions, greeds and desires, angers and aversions, delusions and confusions diminishing, increasing, or remaining the same?

Palden Atisha, the great Bengali saint who lived in Tibet during the eleventh century, said that the test for whether a practice is successful is whether our negative emotions have declined or not. If they have not, then it is of no use. If they have, we know we're on the right path. We can all test this for ourselves. We don't need anyone else to tell us. The path is here. There has been so much written about it. People have walked this path. They're right here amongst us. We don't have to give everything up and rush off to India. Right here, right now, this is our place to practice. With our family, our work, our social obligations. If we cannot practice here, where can we practice? We carry our mind with us everywhere. The mind that we have in Lismore is going to be the same mind that we will have in the Himalayas. The same ego. The same problems. Why go to the Himalayas? Why not resolve it here and now? No master can do that for us. No master can ever remove our greed, anger, and jealousy. No master can remove our ego. Each of us must do it for ourselves.

QUESTIONS

Q: To what extent should we be looking for texts and Buddhist teachings to guide us, rather than relying on our own experience and on input from our teacher?

TP: Well, of course texts and books are wonderful, and they can be extremely helpful. I think it's very important, whether one has a teacher or not, to understand the whole foundation of the teachings. So if one is following a Buddhist path, one should read Buddhist texts. This will help make the path clearer. Whatever path we are following, we should read texts about it and learn to understand the teachings. After all, we're trying to uncover and remove our ignorance. One way to gain more understanding and wisdom is certainly by study and reading. In the Buddhist scheme of things, you start with what is called "hearing," but that also means reading, because in the

Buddha's time there was no written Dharma. It really covers study, reading, hearing, and investigating. And then one sits and thinks about it, and if one has any doubts, one goes to someone who has more knowledge and asks questions. We must really think about what we read, question it and practice it until we become it. You can't become it if you don't already know what it is. You have to study. And then it's very good to meet someone who knows more than we do and receive guidance.

Q: When His Holiness the Dalai Lama was here, people sometimes threw themselves at his feet and tried to touch his toes and so on, and one could see he was telling people to get up. After a while, he said to a huge audience, "Don't revere the teacher, revere the words." This really meant a lot to me. But I find it very difficult to know what to do when I meet friends who have decided Tibetan Buddhism is just fabulous, and have met a lama they think is wonderful, yet I feel doubtful about his authenticity.

TP: It's hard. Sometimes when people become involved with a lama it's like falling in love. It's no good saying to them, "The lama you fell in love with is a total rascal," because they're not interested, they don't hear it. And we have to be careful, because maybe that person actually is a bodhisattva, and it is said that to malign a bodhisattva is worse than killing all the beings in a trichiliocosm. So we could be in big trouble! When I am faced with situations like this where I don't respect the lama, I don't put him or her down, but I make sure I don't come across as overly enthusiastic, either. I might say, "Oh yes, that's nice." If the person later asks whether I know anything about this lama, I still make sure that I don't criticize. At most I might say, "Well, that teacher is somewhat controversial." I don't think it's up to us to put anybody down unless somebody comes and says, "Look, I met this person. I'm quite interested, but I'm not sure, what do you think?" If people ask me in that way, I will tell them what I think as diplomatically as possible, and perhaps even suggest that maybe they had better avoid that person. But if somebody's already in love and totally infatuated, all you can do is refrain from joining in the general enthusiasm and wait for them to cool down. It's not skillful or kind to say, "Oh, you must be crazy, everybody knows that guy's a complete dead loss." Maybe the teacher is helpful for them. Maybe he or she is just the teacher they need at this point. Obviously, even the most dubious teachers must be giving somebody something, otherwise why would people go to them? Another guru we might consider far more immaculate might even be less helpful for those people, because the or she may not have the necessary karmic connection with those students at that time.

These situations are extremely precarious. There's no single positive sign to tell you whether this is a genuine guru or not. And it's very hard, especially if someone is charismatic, for people not to fall in love, as it were. And the long-standing disciples who have already invested so much in their guru often will not allow themselves to start having doubts, because it would make them look like fools. They may be using a lot of fast footwork to avoid seeing that maybe they made the wrong choice, and be quite enthusiastically trying to draw new people into the fold, because the more people who come into the fold, the more it appears to validate their own choice of teacher.

Q: It sounds like there need to be a few more Dharma showdowns.
TP: His Holiness the Dalai Lama is very strong on this. He says that if there is anything that is absolutely known and proved against the teacher, especially certain kinds of unethical conduct, it should be publicized.

Q: I have read Krishnamurti, and he says that there's no outer guru and that each of us must find the way for ourselves. Is that what you are saying?
TP: Krishnamurti more or less said: "We're going to bake bread. Bread is delicious, it has this nice crusty outside and inside it's tasty and nourishing. It's got to do with flour and water. An oven's in there somewhere, too. Heat. You need yeast. Okay, get on with it. But if I give you detailed instructions on bread-making, you will bake stale bread." My point is that, of course you need someone to give you step-by-step instructions such as, "You need this proportion of flour, this much water and a pinch of salt. You mix it, put the yeast in, then you knead it in this way. Then you let it rise. Once it's risen you'll have to knead it again. In the meantime, turn your oven on because it's got to be really hot. Then put the dough into the tins. Don't forget to butter your tins first because otherwise the dough is going to stick. Then put them into the oven."

Nobody ever bakes stale bread. It's not possible! It was wrong of Krishnamurti to say that if someone shows you how to practice, you are going to have a stale realization. Nobody ever had a stale realization. If you achieve genuine spiritual insight, it is as fresh as the first genuine spiritual insight which ever occurred. So I'm not saying what Krishnamurti said, at all. Krishnamurti said, "Climb Mount Everest. No guide, no tow ropes, no oxygen. The road is sort of up there, go for it." Krishnamurti himself had teachers, Krishnamurti was taught how to meditate. Krishnamurti had lots of instruction, and he himself became a great guru. He said, "Don't read any spiritual books, don't read anything," then he started a publishing company to publish his books. I love Krishnamurti, but you know, he's naughty.

Q: Can I ask you something about initiations? Especially here in the West, we get so many gurus coming through offering a whole smorgasbord of different initiations. If we don't have a guru or a guide to refer to, how do we choose, how do we know whether to go for a certain initiation or not?

TP: Speaking personally, I believe that there are certain lamas, especially some of the older ones, who would be regarded as sublime by anybody in the Dharma scene, and with whom it would be very good to make a Dharma connection. But there are not many such masters. First, before receiving an initiation, you should check whether or not there is a commitment involved. If there is a commitment, and you are not going to use that practice as one of your own practices, in other words, if you will not be keeping the commitment, it will create an obstacle for you. I would ask myself, "Do I need this initiation and would it be useful in my practice?" There is no point in merely going around taking initiation after initiation. However, if a great teacher does turn up and give an initiation involving no particular commitment, that's great. You need not hesitate about taking it. But we shouldn't bow to peer pressure and go along just because everybody else seems to be going for it.

Some years ago I was at a Dharma center and the center's root Lama was there. He was going to give a highest yoga tantra initiation of Heruka. He gave a horrendous commitment with it and said only those who can keep the commitment should take it. There was a list of people who wanted to take the initiation. The first day about six people, monks and nuns, put their names down. They'd probably had it already and were doing it as part of their practice. The next day there were about twenty names. The day after that there were fifty names. At the end, when he gave it, I was the only person who didn't take it. There were hundreds of lay people there. This was not because these people were going to keep the commitments, but because of the peer pressure: "Oh but Rinpoche never gives this, this is really a big opportunity, you shouldn't miss this. . ." You need to be discerning, because when you do take a commitment, to not keep it is quite serious.

Q: If one does have a personal connection with a lama and there is some other lama coming to give an initiation with commitments, should one ask permission of one's own lama before taking the initiation?
TP: I would say so. I used to ask my Lama. I usually said to him, "So-and-so's giving this initiation, should I go for it?" Sometimes he would say, "He's a very great Lama and it would be a great blessing. On the other hand, this is not your personal deity. You are never going to keep the commitment, and it's not your tradition, so what's the point?"

Q: What happens if you don't keep the commitments?
TP: Failure to keep a commitment is considered an obstacle on the path. I think that the best way to clear this kind of obstacle is to realize that all the deities are actually the essence of one deity and to really practice that one deity, but not take on any more commitments from then on. Or to try to fulfill the commitment by going into a retreat and doing the minimum number of mantras needed for completing that commitment. But it's not good to just go on piling up commitment after commitment when you're not keeping any of them. That doesn't make sense.

Q: No, I was thinking if you take a teaching, practice it for twelve years, and maybe then decide not to continue practicing it.
TP: I think that it's good to do a little Vajrasattva purification practice and then combine this practice with the practice you are continuing with. Sometimes people accumulate all these commitments and end up with three hours of commitments every day. It just becomes a huge burden. Then they race through their practices as fast as they can to get them out the way. That is completely useless, really. It might be wonderfully heroic to try to keep so many commitments, but the Dharma is not meant to make our lives more difficult and impose heavy burdens upon us. It's meant to lighten us up!

Q: How do you create a balance between doing your practice, the commitments that you've got and meditation? Should it be the same amount of meditation and contemplation of your own?

TP: Well, I think that's one of the reasons why it's good to keep our commitments fairly simple, because it gives us the space to do sitting practice. It's quite good to do a sitting practice before the sadhana so that the mind calms down and there's some inner space available for the practice. Then we can do the sadhana, the formal practice, and at the end during the dissolution, keep the mind in that very contemplative state for as long as possible. In this way, we bring the two together.

Q: You said something earlier about an "inner guide." Could you explain that?

TP: The nature of the mind is our Buddha-nature. It is our inherent wisdom and compassion. It is always there. It's kind of frozen over, buried under all our vast mountains of confusion, but it's there. We have to learn how to uncover it. If you consider it like a kind of vast underground watershed, on the top it looks like a desert. We're pretty dry—there's not much wisdom and not much compassion. But if we start digging down, after a while the ground begins to get damp and you can feel the moisture. We realize we are beginning to gain access to deeper levels. We keep digging deeper and deeper until finally we begin to reach this fountain of innate wisdom, our innate compassion and understanding. But even before we completely access it, we can get intimations of it. That inner guru is the real guru. Any genuine outer guru is simply trying to direct us towards this genuine inner guru.

The inner guide is always within us. It's who we really are. It's our true nature. It's vast and knowing. We've just covered it up with our clouds of confusion, but it's not coming from the outside. We can think of it as if we are getting blessings from the outside coming into us to open us up, but actually what is happening is that our own clouds of unknowing part and we can see the deep blue sky which is always there. It's not that we have to acquire anything or that anybody gives us anything. It's a matter of uncovering our original richness.

When the mind is still and centered, when the confusion has died down a bit, there is space and silence which enable our inner wisdom to find its voice. And at that moment we know. It's at a very profound level. It might not even be verbal. There is just this timeless knowing. We know what is appropriate and what has to be done, from moment to moment. It has nothing to do with intellect, it has nothing to do with analysis. It's just a knowing, in that moment, which comes from a very profound source within us which is always there but which is normally cut off from us. It is who we really are. So what we're saying is that genuine practice leads us back to our own primal wisdom.

Q: Is the "outer guru" an entity separate from the "inner guide"?
TP: A genuine outer guide leads us back to our original nature. That's why I started off by saying that a genuine teacher can ignite that spark of realization. Another way of saying it is that it's as if they precipitate an inner opening through which, for a moment, we can glimpse this incredibly vast consciousness which is the unconditioned mind. That's the true guide. Because that wisdom, that seeing, is completely spontaneous but completely appropriate. It's the nature of clarity and seeing, of wisdom, of knowing what is. In our everyday life we can suddenly experience this great clarity and we know, even though we don't know where it comes from. We call it intuition.

Q: Is that what is known as "momentary insight"?
TP: Exactly. A flash.

Q: A flash, that comes from the big light source.
TP: Exactly.

Q: But that's not stable.
TP: No, it's not.

Q: What we're looking for is to get the stability?
TP: Exactly. To become completely one with our wisdom mind. And it starts by getting these flashes, then gradually the flashes prolong and multiply. That's one way of looking at it.

Q: You've stressed the importance of our own practice and the guidance of the teacher. To what extent is the ritual of Buddhism important in our growth? Or, to put it another way, how much of an impediment would it be to our growth if we find that the rituals are not actually helping us?
TP: I think people are different. Some people are helped by ritual. To be helpful, ritual must not be empty. We must understand what we are doing. In Tibetan ritual, there is always a visualization which completely engulfs the

mind. Then there is the verbal recitation and the physical *mudras*. In this way the body, speech, and mind are integrated. And this, if it's done with understanding and complete concentration, can be extremely helpful. This is why Tibetans do it. But other people may find it a distraction or not especially helpful, and of course it's perfectly valid not to do ritual, and to do other forms of practice instead. I know lamas who don't do any ritual, who do only Dzogchen meditations and things like that. I also know great Dzogchen masters who do a lot of ritual.

∿ 13
Vajrayana

ACCORDING TO the Hinayana school of Buddhism, we are trapped in this realm of endless birth, death, rebirth and re-death because we desire things and hold onto them so tightly. Even though this wheel of life brings us so much suffering again and again, we cling to it. The Hinayana school places emphasis on eradicating even the finest roots of our desire. According to the Mahayana, it is because of our ignorance that we are trapped on this wheel. We accept as real that which is not real, and we think unreal that which is the only true reality. Everything we think reflects a misapprehension of how things really are. Therefore, our task is to develop what is called "transcendental wisdom," which will eradicate the very roots of our ignorance.

According to Vajrayana, we are trapped in this realm of endless birth and death because of our impure perceptions. We believe that what we see is solid, ordinary, and defiled. We see ourselves as impure beings. The antidote to this is to develop pure perception, or pure vision. If we understand this, the whole Vajrayana path makes sense. The way to go beyond samsara is to realize that it has always been nirvana. It is our basic ignorance which causes impure perceptions to manifest so that everything appears as ordinary, suffering and defiled. We have to "clean the lenses" in order to see that what looks so ordinary is actually a pure realm of utter transcendence. This is a basic fundamental of the Vajrayana view, and can be realized only by an awakened mind. One of the Mahayana sutras tells about a time when Ananda, the Buddha's attendant, asked the Buddha, "How is it that all these other Buddhas like Amitabha, Akshobhya, and Ratnasambhava have beautiful pure lands full of realized beings, whereas your mandala, your pure land, is full of defiled beings and foul places? How is it that you are a Buddha, yet your pure land is so impure?" The Buddha replied, "There is nothing wrong with my pure land. When I look around, I see that it is immaculate. The problem is with your impure perception, which sees it as defiled."

Once His Holiness the Sixteenth Karmapa, head of the Karma Kagyu tradition, was very ill in Delhi. At that time, I went to see His Holiness Sakya Trizin, who was also there. His Holiness Sakya Trizin is the head of the Sakya order, one of the four traditions of Tibetan Buddhism. I said to him, "It's awful that Karmapa is so sick!" He replied, "Karmapa isn't sick. Karmapa is beyond birth and death. It's just your impure perception which sees Karmapa as sick." And I said, "Well, yes, but Tai Situ Rinpoche, a very high-level bodhisattva who presumably has pure perception, is nonetheless worried and concerned because Karmapa is sick." His Holiness replied, "Situ Rinpoche is not worried or concerned. It's your impure perception which sees Situ Rinpoche as worried and concerned." You get the idea! We have to purify our perception. Then we will see that this has been nirvana all the time. It is only because of our perverted view that there was ever any problem.

Vajrayana shares its philosophy with Mahayana. The Vajrayana is not a philosophy. It is a practice technique and a view, or vision. It takes its philosophical stance from the Mahayana. The Tibetans say it takes it from the Prasangika-Madhyamaka school. Actually it seems to be a combination of Yogachara and Madhyamaka viewpoints. In the Mahayana, the practice path is this: we are here, and we have the inherent potential for Buddhahood, called our Buddha-nature, which is like a seed. The path is the means to water and nurture that seed until it grows and grows and finally ripens into full Buddhahood.

We ordinary, defiled sentient beings have the potential for enlightenment. We all have embryonic Buddha-nature and we cultivate it through aeons of time. It takes a long time to become a Buddha in the Mahayana school. We have to nurture this seed for endless ages until it grows and puts out leaves and branches and finally manifests as a full-grown Tree of Enlightenment. This could be considered as a wonderful vision, but it might also be considered totally discouraging. You might think, "Well if it takes aeons and aeons, what's the point?" In reaction to such concerns, the Vajrayana takes a very radical step: it turns the whole thing around.

The Sutrayana division of the Mahayana school is referred to as the "path of the cause." This is because we start with the cause, which is our embryonic Buddha-nature, and nurture it until we produce the fruit. The Vajrayana is called the path of the fruit. This is because it maintains that from beginningless time, we have already been Buddhas. Our problem is that we don't recognize this. Therefore, why not use our inherent Buddha-nature as the path itself? So we start from the fruit, and use that as the path. In other words, we start from the opposite direction. Therefore, Vajrayana places great emphasis on visualizing ourselves as a Buddha or as a particular tantric deity which symbolizes some aspect of a fully flowered Buddha-nature.

Most Buddhist meditation focuses on the breath, on the mind itself, or sometimes on very simple geometrical designs. Vajrayana meditation depends on a faculty called "creative imagination," or visualization. This is what makes it different from other forms of Buddhist practice. Although nobody knows when the Vajrayana first entered the Buddhist stream, it was certainly in existence by the early centuries of the common era. It might have been there from the beginning. Tibetans believe that it was always there and was taught by the Buddha himself. In any event, by the fourth or fifth century it was extremely prolific, although still a very secret form of practice.

At that time there were huge monasteries in India which were also universities, including Nalanda, Vikramashila and Takshila. They contained thousands and thousands of monastic scholars who were studying all the schools of Buddhist philosophy. Within that complex, there were many masters who were also practicing these Vajrayana teachings. But they did it quietly. It is said that although outwardly these masters looked like monks, inwardly they were yogis. They didn't talk about it, and it did not become widespread and open, with public initiations and so forth, until it became the state religion of Tibet. I don't think the Vajrayana was ever intended to be a state religion. It was intended to be quiet and secret, just between the master and a few disciples. Before you can practice the Vajrayana, you need to receive an initiation. If you look at the early records in India, they show that a disciple was usually initiated only after years and years of testing by the guru, and then it was a one-on-one, mind-to-mind transmission. Nowadays, His Holiness the Dalai Lama gives the Kalachakra initiation to a hundred thousand people at a time.

As I mentioned earlier, the practice of Vajrayana relies heavily on the use of creative imagination. I will give an example for those who have never done anything like this before. Suppose we take the example of Guru Padmsambhava, whom the Tibetans call Guru Rinpoche. Guru Padmasambhava is very appropriate to this topic, because he was the master who came from India and established tantric Buddhism in Tibet during the eighth century. He has become a focus for popular devotion. Suppose we were to do a practice centering on Padmasambhava. Whatever we do, it is extraordinarily important to proceed with the correct motivation, which is the wish to break through to the unconditioned reality and, having gained access to our innate wisdom and compassion, benefit others. No other motivation is valid. First we would take refuge in the Buddha, his doctrine, and the community of realized practitioners. Next, we raise the aspiration to attain enlightenment for the benefit of others. At this point, we begin the meditation.

If we were doing the Padmasambhava meditation, we would visualize ourselves sitting. Then our body would dissolve into space. In the space, at the heart center, a syllable would appear. In this case it would be a *PAM*, standing for Padma. This is called a seed syllable. That *PAM* would then emanate light in all directions, purifying the entire universe. Then the whole universe and everything in it would become a realm of absolute immaculate purity, and all the beings there would be purified of their defilements and become like gods and goddesses. Then the lights would come back into the *PAM*, and in an instant one would appear as Padmasambhava. One must then see oneself as Padmasambhava, who embodies the wisdom and compassion of all the Buddhas.

When we are doing these meditations, it is very important for us to believe them. None of this is made up—everything is exact and precise. One of the problems Westerners face is that we are simply not accustomed to such detailed imagery. Many of us find it very difficult, at least in the beginning, although people who are visually oriented may find it easier. But even more important than the very detailed visualization is the belief that this is real. It doesn't work if you don't believe in it. Normally when people do these meditations, they are really thinking, "Here am I, Pat, pretending to be Padmasambhava. The reality is that I'm Pat. The fantasy is that I am now supposed to be Padmasambhava." But the truth is that we are Padmasambhava, who represents our primordial wisdom and compassionate mind. We are Padmasambhava pretending to be Pat. You see, these forms, which might seem quite alien to you, are actually emanations of our wisdom mind. They are emanations of our inherent Buddha-nature, as they have appeared to realized masters throughout the ages. They arose in minds which had access to their wisdom nature. Therefore, they are an extremely skillful conduit back to very profound realms of our psyche which we cannot access by means of logical, linear thinking.

There are very subtle levels of our psychological makeup which we can access only through enlightened imagery. These meditations, if we really become one with them, open up profound levels of the mind very quickly. They have quite an extraordinary effect. The amount of effort we expend is tiny compared with the enormous benefits to be attained. People are often startled because there is a part of us which doesn't really believe it, which thinks that we are just playing games. To gain the benefits, we must become absorbed in the practice and cease this duality of "I" doing the practice. Just become the practice. As soon as we get rid of that subject-object dichotomy and become the meditation, the results come quickly. This is why Tibetan Buddhism has remained so popular, despite that fact that it initially seems so alien to many Westerners.

Now we are seeing ourselves as Padmasambhava, and we have the certainty of being Padmasambhava. At this point, if our original wisdom nature could take form, it would take form as Padmasambhava. This is the glow of our Buddha-nature. It is like a rainbow. This visualization is not solid; Padmasambhava does not possess a liver, guts and a heart. He is made up of rainbow light. Every feature has a meaning. The two arms are wisdom and compassion. He is a conglomeration of the elements of the Buddhist path distilled into a single form. That is who we really are. This is the important thing to know. This is what I really am, not the transient identity I usually think of as "me." Then we sit and see ourselves as Guru Rinpoche (Padmasambhava), trying very hard to visualize as clearly as possible all the details, going through the visualization part by part, getting a flash of the whole thing together. Padmasambhava is sitting there, radiating light. At the heart center is a lotus, and upon that, a moon disc. On the moon disc is the syllable PAM and around that, the letters of the mantra, standing upright. Light radiates from Padmasambhava's mantra. These radiating lights go out and purify the entire cosmos. All the beings within it will naturally be purified because now we are Buddha.

This is what I was describing before as "taking the fruit as the path." Now we are Buddha, and the Buddha has the capacity to purify beings. In our minds we are doing this activity which a Buddha would do, that is, to radiate light in all directions, completely purifying everything and all beings everywhere within it. By "beings," we are not referring simply to human beings. "Beings" includes animals, insects, fish, spirits, those in the heavens and hells and everywhere. All beings throughout the incredibly vast universe are liberated. They become conscious of their wisdom and compassionate nature, and they turn into Padmasambhava. The whole world has become an immaculate pure land. Then the lights come back and again go out and make offerings to all the Buddhas and bodhisattvas in the universe and also to all the sentient beings who are now themselves Buddhas. The entire universe is now an immaculate pure land full of Buddhas. While we visualize this, we say the mantra. Then, at the end, this vast universe, now completely filled with Buddhas and bodhisattvas, melts into light. That light melts into us. We melt down into the center. The lotus and the moon melt into the mantra. The mantra melts into the seed syllable *PAM*. The seed syllable melts upwards into the tiny circle called the *nada* which then also melts. We watch this very precisely as it melts, stage by stage, until there is nothing left. Then the mind remains in its natural, immaculate state. It rests in this state which is beyond thought and beyond concept for as long as possible. When thinking starts, we again instantly appear as Padmasambhava and dedicate the merit attained by doing this practice.

Subsequently, as we are going about our business during the day, we see ourselves as Padmasambhava. We see all beings we meet as emanations of Padmasambhava. Immediately upon meeting someone, we recognize their inherent Buddha-nature. All sounds we hear are the sounds of the mantra. Nice sounds, harsh sounds, all are just the mantra. All thoughts—good thoughts, bad thoughts, intelligent thoughts and stupid thoughts—are just the play of Guru Padmasambhava's wisdom mind. We try to maintain the awareness throughout the day that all the beings we encounter are just pretending to be ordinary, but are really Guru Rinpoche in disguise. All sounds that we hear are the wonderful echo of OM AH HUM VAJRA GURU PADMA SIDDHI HUM (Padmasambhava's mantra). All the thoughts we have are just the essential nature of the empty play of wisdom. Nothing to worry about. If we can maintain that throughout the day, we will learn what it is to develop pure perception.

This is the way the Vajrayana works. I have given a very simplified illustration, but it is basically the way it works. Sometimes when people come to the Vajrayana, they are intimidated by its seemingly endless complexity. There are so many deities, so many levels, so many different practices and approaches, where does one begin? It can become quite mind-boggling. But the essential focus of the practice is actually very simple. The problem is that, as with any other practice, we have to do it. It's not enough to just do it for ten minutes a day. We need to incorporate our practice into our daily life. We have to transform our minds. It's not about playing with nice ideas. It is about transforming the very core of our being. It doesn't work unless we really take the practice and eat it, digest it, and use it to nourish ourselves, not just nibble at it from time to time. Some people do these practices a little bit every day, and then they forget them. Then they wonder why nothing is happening. But the texts are very clear that this is not just something you do when you are sitting on your mat. You have to take the visualization with you into your everyday life. This is what the early masters did. They transformed their vision into pure perception because they were using it all the time, in all their encounters.

There is another aspect of the Vajrayana which builds on this. It involves manipulating the inner energies. This is done once our visualization has become stable and we have performed the requisite number of mantras. The mantra is considered to be the essence of the nature of the deity. Every Buddha and bodhisattva has his own special mantra which is the way to connect with and experience that deity. When we say the mantra with perfect concentration and visualization, we actualize the qualities the deity represents. They are locked inside the mantra, which is like a code. We decode it and access that energy through our meditation and visualization and by saying the mantra. If we say it with perfect concentration, really focusing on the visualization and becoming one-pointed in the practice, the results come very quickly. If we harbor doubt in our minds, nothing will happen even after aeons of practice. The texts are very specific in pointing this out.

There is so much one can say, but I hesitate to say too much, because many of you may never have taken Vajrayana initiations. However, I will touch on something which often confuses people. Non-Vajrayana people are often puzzled when they enter a Vajrayana temple and find themselves surrounded by all the representations of these beings on the walls. They often ask, "What's this got to do with Buddhism?" Many of the images are naked. Many of them appear to be wrathful and look like demons. Some are even shown copulating. But this iconography is not as bizarre or as complex as it first appears. The images of the deities represent one or another of three basic levels of mood. The first mood is peaceful, represented by figures such as Avalokiteshvara, the Bodhisattva of Compassion; Manjushri, the Bodhisattva of Wisdom; and Tara, the Savioress. They are shown as quiet, peaceful, and gently smiling. People don't usually have any problems with them, although they sometimes have problems with the fact that Tara is green or somebody else is blue. But basically there is no problem, because they look nice and friendly, as if they were on our side.

Then you get the second level, which is called *shi ma tro* in Tibetan. This means "neither peaceful nor angry." These are the heroic deities, known as the *heruka* and *dakini* forms. They represent the thrust of energy towards enlightenment. Their particular quality is passion. Now, in the earlier forms of Buddhism, desire was seen as the major obstacle to liberation. But in the Mahayana, and especially in the Vajrayana, it was understood that emotions such as passion and anger, when traced to their source, consist of vast amounts of energy. At some stage this energy has become perverted into a negative force. But nevertheless, this energy is in itself very clear and wise. In other words, the flip side of what looks to us like negative energy is an innate wisdom. This was a tremendous *volte face* in the attitude towards negative emotions. Instead of having to uproot emotions such as anger, pride, jealousy, and passion, we could take that energy and use it as the fuel for attaining enlightenment. These emotions were no longer enemies to be vanquished. They had become our main helpers on the path. This is an underlying motif throughout Vajrayana. When we understand this, we will understand the iconography of Vajrayana.

The Tibetan texts tell us that the greater the negative emotion, the greater the wisdom. The corollary to this is that without negative emotions, there is no wisdom. Does this mean that we are encouraged to run rampant, giving full rein to our greed, passion, hatred and desire in the name of spiritual practice? Some people think it does, but this is a misconception. These negative qualities, if left in their uncontrolled and unmitigated state, are indeed the cause of samsara. But if we control and transform them, we can use them as the fuel to propel us beyond samsara. The example that always comes to my mind is that of a rocket. You need enormous amounts of fuel to launch the rocket beyond the earth's gravitational pull, but once it's out in space, you no longer need much power. It becomes virtually self-propelling. So also with the spiritual path. The gravitational pull of our ordinary nature, of our ordinary, ignorant, ego-based mind is extremely strong. It is incredibly difficult to make that first thrust into the unconditioned, because our conditioned mind is so powerful. Even if we are doing ordinary calming and insight meditations, it is difficult to make that thrust through. We need everything we can possibly muster for the initial push.

Vajrayana takes everything we have, even the garbage, and uses the whole lot as fuel to power the breakthrough to the unconditioned nature of the mind. That's why it can seem so threatening, and that's why it can be very dangerous and why we need the guidance of a teacher. The need for a perfect teacher is continually emphasized in the Vajrayana texts. Otherwise, it can be a very dangerous path. It is said that we won't get into much trouble driving an ox-cart along the road, but when we get behind the wheel of a sports car, we have to be very careful. You really need a good teacher before you take the wheel. This is because the Vajrayana uses the energies, especially the sexual energy, which in earlier Buddhism was sublimated or transformed in much more genteel ways. In the Vajrayana, that energy is transformed into a means to open up all the inner wisdom centers.

It is a misconception to imagine that Vajrayana gives you a license for uninhibited sexuality, to be as angry as you want, to get drunk, or to abuse the senses in any way whatsoever. On the contrary, it is the most disciplined and the most controlled practice there is. There are many, many Vajrayana vows which deal with the mind. It is not at all a path of license. But it is a path which takes everything we have. It requires great dedication and very clear guidance.

The third level of deity, which comes after the heroic level, is the *tro wa*, which means fierce. You can tell the difference between the heroic and the fierce representations by looking at the flames around them. The peaceful forms have auras surrounding them. In the heroic forms, they have a very neat frame of flames. In the fierce form they are surrounded by wild flames. The heroic deities are based on lust. The fierce deities are based on anger. They deal with all these emotions we have inside us, from mild irritation to total fury. Although they look very angry, at their heart there is total love, wisdom, and compassion. They are not really angry at all. They just manifest in that form. It is the transformed anger which has such tremendous energy. I don't know any lamas who are angry, but many of them manifest very wrathful deities in their meditation. The deities in union with their consorts represent a number of things. We are within these opposites, but these opposites are always joined in a higher unity. They represent the unity of wisdom and compassion, of bliss and emptiness, and so on. But the idea is always that we are taking two qualities of mind which become united into one. This is shown in a very graphic way through the unity of the male and female. It doesn't mean they have wild orgies in tantric monasteries.

Tibetan Buddhism places a lot of emphasis on the guru. The guru is a very difficult subject to deal with because, as I said earlier on, in the early days in both India and Tibet, the relationship between the guru and the disciple was a very personal one. The teacher had just a small circle of intimate disciples. He knew them all very well, and they knew him. There was mutual trust. The practices were very individual. When I was with my teacher in India, apart from his monastery and the Tibetan lay people, he had a very small number of Western disciples. Usually when Westerners came to him, he would send them away to other lamas. But occasionally he would select a few whom he would allow to stay. And although we all started doing the same things, within a very short time we were doing widely divergent practices. I never received teachings together with anyone else. There was also an American nun, a Dutch nun, and a Swiss nun, who came some years after I had become a nun. We were Dharma sisters. Sometimes one of us would ask for an initiation, and my Lama would say, "Let's wait until the three or four of you are together, and I will give it to all of you." So we would get the initiation and the oral transmission together, but we didn't get the teachings together.

For instance, Khamtrul Rinpoche would ask me to do a particular practice, and I would think, "Fantastic, that is just the practice I would want to do." And I would tell my Dharma sisters, and they would say, "Oh, I hope he doesn't tell us to do that." And I would say, "If that's your reaction, he wouldn't." And he didn't. I knew that my Lama knew me better than I knew myself. He would tell me to do things which had never occurred to me, but which were so completely right. That kind of confidence is very important, and you get it when you know you have a teacher who completely understands you. How could you not have trust and confidence in someone like that?

A problem has arisen now because Vajrayana has become so popular in the West and in the East, and many lamas are constantly jet-setting around the world. Say they come here. They are here for a few days, maybe they give an initiation and some teachings, and then they are off. Maybe they won't come again for another five years. First of all, how are you going to make contact with that teacher, and secondly, if you do make contact, how are you going to meet him again? And how are they going to remember who you are? It's a big problem. In the Vajrayana texts, it says that you must examine your teacher, or rather your potential teacher, for up to twelve years before accepting him.

A genuine guru is not just for this lifetime. He is for all our lifetimes. We must trust that he can take us to enlightenment, because he himself has that level of realization and can bestow it on us. Also, the genuine guru is the one who shows you the the original and inherent wisdom, awareness, and clarity of your mind. This is the unconditioned state, beyond thought, beyond concepts. The guru who shows you this mind so that you see it for an instant is the true guru. It's difficult to make that connection, but it's not impossible. In the meantime, however, we can manage quite well for quite a long time without having such an intense relationship. We can manage by receiving occasional teachings and instructions from the hands of visiting lamas who are qualified and who inspire confidence. It is not necessary for them to be our lama for our lifetime. We have devotion towards them and that will suffice in the meantime. It is necessary to have devotion towards a lama because when we do Vajrayana practice, there is always a lama at the center. We can't pretend to have devotion. Either we have devotion or we don't.

Personally, I don't think Vajrayana is for everybody. I also think that if you are going to follow the Vajrayana path, unless you are prepared to give up everything and go off to do extensive retreats, it is important to keep the practice simple. Several lamas have remarked to me how difficult it is for them. As lineage holders they have to study many different practices, but they never really get the time to observe and digest any one practice fully. They all agree that the real way to success is to concentrate on and keep at one simple practice which is meaningful to you.

One of the advantages of Tibetan Buddhism is that it's like a big spiritual supermarket. If we go into Zen meditation, we are told, "This is the way we meditate." If you don't go along with that, you have to go somewhere else. If you go to a vipashyana center, you will be told, "This is how we do vipashyana meditation." If you don't like it, it's your bad luck. But in Vajrayana, there are so many practices. There is vipashyana, there is Zen-like meditation, there is study, there is the whole panoply of technicolor Vajrayana visualizations with Buddhas and bodhisattvas in every possible color combination. There is something for everybody—peaceful, angry, sort of peaceful, and sort of angry. Male, female, green, red, blue, white, lots of arms and legs, two arms and legs, one head, standing up, sitting down, lying down; any way you want. There is lots of variety and everybody can find something to practice. When you find something you like and really identify with, then you can stay with that.

Every lama who comes to town will tell you that his particular practice is the most special, the most secret, ultimate, highest, unrevealed treasury that's ever been heard of. And you'll think, "Oh, I've got to have that." Then next week somebody else will come along with another one, and you'll finish up completely confused, completely frustrated, and worst of all, completely unrealized! The important thing is not to be too ambitious. We must go back to the foundations. First of all, the motivation. Why are we doing this anyway, what is it all for? Cultivate a compassionate heart, bodhichitta, the aspiration for enlightenment for the sake of other beings. Really get your ethical life together. Deal with non-harming, not lying, refraining from sexual misconduct. We must be realistic. If we are serious about following a spiritual path, we have to get our life together on a very fundamental basis. We must be responsible for our actions and understand what is virtuous and what is non-virtuous.

First, we have to get our fundamental Dharma life together. Then we should do a practice which is simple, accessible to us, and which we can incorporate into our daily life. Then it can work, and it can be very fulfilling. Then we can really feel things transforming. But we must avoid the pitfall of becoming too ambitious. I know people who go all around the world, taking very high initiations, then end up with all these commitments. When you take higher initiations, you often have commitments. This means that you have to do this practice every day. It might take one or two hours. If you have many such practice commitments, you end up with a meditation program of maybe three or four hours. On top of that you have your work, your family, your social life, and this terror that if you don't honor your practice commitments you'll go to hell. What is intended to be a transformation of your life into real meaningfulness and joy then becomes just a heavy burden. I know one lama who told me he had a daily commitment of three hours. If he got up early enough and did it first thing in the morning, he felt great relief. If he didn't, then for the rest of the day he felt he had this heavy burden on him because he knew that at night, when he was exhausted, he would have to do these three hours of practice. Now that is not very helpful, especially for lay people. My Lama always said to me, "Don't undertake big commitments. Keep your practice very small and simple, but do it." This is very good advice. I have always been very clear with lamas when it comes to initiations. Sorry, I am not keeping this commitment. I say this before taking the initiation, then they can decide whether or not it's okay for me to take it. Usually, they say it's okay.

It is easy to get sucked into undertaking all these commitments. It's another kind of Dharma greed. You don't want to miss anything. The point is that in Vajrayana it is important to know your teacher and your path. We should keep it as simple as possible, but do it. It should be enough to challenge us, but not so much that it overwhelms us. We must be able to continue it and integrate it more and more into our lives, our relationships, and our work, until there is no separation between practice time and everyday life.

QUESTIONS

Q: Aren't these practices and commitments just putting oneself in another kind of cage?
TP: Yes, of course, but if one is serious about this practice, it is very powerful. It can have strong psychic and psychological repercussions, and one should be very careful. It's not wrong to remind people of this, otherwise some may take it all too lightly, under the mistaken impression that it doesn't matter. But actually, it has been shown through the ages that it does matter. That's not putting ourselves in a cage, it's just being realistic. If you take the wrong dose of medicine, or neglect to take it or take something else, it can harm you. Here one is dealing with the mind, the internal energies and the various energy centers of the body. So one has to be careful. We have to know what we are doing. We have to be committed. We need to have a teacher who really understands. You have to understand your own capacity, and you shouldn't take on something which is not appropriate for your situation. These are just warnings because sometimes people take these things too casually. They may mess themselves up, then blame the practice or the teacher or themselves.

Q: How do you visualize these seed syllables?
TP: First of all, you have to have the space where you are going to put the seed syllable. But before that, you dissolve everything. You and the whole

environment become a great space. Within that space, you begin to create this alternate reality. But you have to clear everything away first. It's quite simple. You just think everything has dissolved into empty space, and then start to rebuild it all.

Is this the same as emptiness meditation, or is it different?

TP: This is a different kind of emptiness. In emptiness meditation, when we say "all dharmas are empty," it doesn't mean that they disappear. It just means that they are lacking any inherent, solid identity. But in Vajrayana meditation, when we say that everything becomes the nature of emptiness, it is taken very literally and it means that everything dissolves into this space-like emptiness.

Normally, we are so fixated on things being solid. It's what we said about impure perception, about seeing all this as real. But even physics tells us that matter consists mostly of space. The actual solidity here is minute and maybe that isn't really solid, either. But we think that the way we perceive things is the way they really are.

There are many layers of perception. Each one of us believes that our way of perceiving is the only way. But that's not so. Vajrayana deals with transforming, purifying, and opening up our perception. Dilgo Khyentse Rinpoche said that he first started doing this meditation when he was eight years old. He saw the walls and all the furniture begin to quiver and become transparent. He was a Rinpoche. But the fact is that that kind of perception, seeing things as if they were made of wisdom light, is actually more akin to reality than our normal ways of seeing things as solid. This is why when we see that things are transparent, we are able walk through walls. It is only because we have the impure perception which says, "Things are like this, and they couldn't be like anything else," that we cannot do such things. That's our ignorant mind. Vajrayana is trying to align us with the way things really are. It's not inventing anything false. It's trying to align us with a much deeper reality. Do you understand that? When we create around us this celestial mansion and this pure land, we tend to think, "Now I'm going to pretend this is like this and this and this, it's not of course, but I'll pretend." But actually, the visualization is much closer to the inherent nature of things than our usual perceptions, which is why it can affect us very deeply. This is because, at a very profound level, we recognize it. We know that it is true.

⌒ 14
Visualizing the Deity

VISUALIZATION TECHNIQUES are crucial to Tibetan Buddhist practice. Within Buddhism, deity visualization is unique to the Vajrayana path, so it's important for us to understand the rationale behind this form of practice. Unless we understand what we are doing, while we may be able to get our minds into all kinds of convolutions, we can miss the point completely. Many of us might even associate these visualizations with day-dreams and fantasies and think that imagining we are Buddhas and bodhi-sattvas is just another way of entertaining the mind. It can even seem like a waste of time. So let's look under the surface to see what this is really about!

First of all, it's important to appreciate the power of creative imagination. It is in itself a very powerful tool because the mind has many levels, and only the surface levels can be reached through verbal logic. The deeper and more primitive levels respond to images rather than to words. They don't understand meaning in the sense of verbal meaning, but they are nonetheless very receptive to images. These images percolate down and produce transformation at a much deeper mental level than mere surface concepts could ever do. We can use as an example thinking compassionate thoughts, such as taking on the sufferings of others or wishing that all beings might be happy. That is a good practice which motivates us on one level, but it doesn't percolate down through all the layers of the mind. Our very primitive mind is not in the least bit interested in all this. Such thoughts remain up in the head, at the level of the intellect. To transform the mind completely, we need a method which can reach much deeper layers. We can do this through using images. That's why so much use is made of images in Jungian psychology for example. However, the images used in the Tibetan tradition are not arbitrary. Sometimes people say, "These Buddhas and bodhisattvas we have to visualize are alien to us, they are not part of our culture, they do not form part of our Western consciousness. We should visualize images which have meaning for us."

At one level they have a point. But these images are not arbitrary. Somebody didn't just sit down and think them up. They arose from the realizations of an enlightened mind. Because of this, they can open us up to extremely deep levels of consciousness. Otherwise, we could all sit down and visualize something we feel comfortable with, such as Mickey Mouse. Why not? He's part of our culture. This might be a lot easier than visualizing Chenrezig. Mickey Mouse has only two arms, for a start. But then we would need to ask ourselves the question, "From what mind state did the image of Mickey Mouse arise? Was he conceived by an enlightened mind? Were Walt Disney and his artists enlightened? What qualities does Mickey Mouse embody?" If we meditate on an image, we will receive what it represents. Therefore we need to be careful what image we choose. If we wish to achieve enlightened qualities, we must meditate on an image conceived by an enlightened mind. So, until we have fully enlightened Westerners who can come up with appropriate enlightened images, we should be grateful to use these Tibetan ones. This is assuming that Western minds are somehow fundamentally different from Eastern minds, which is debatable. These sacred images are known to be the products of very profound states. By using them, we too can attain these profound states, regardless of our cultural context.

Once I took up this very question with my Lama, Khamtrul Rinpoche. I said, "Now I am visualizing Tara, and I have great devotion to her, but I am convinced that she is blond, so I always visualize her as a blond. If I get a true vision of Tara, what color will her hair be?" And he said, "Black." In other words, he was telling me that the appearance of the Buddhas and bodhisattvas is not dependent on our own preconceptions and state of mind, that there is a higher reality which corresponds to our inner realizations, but is also independent of them. There are many levels of Buddhas and bodhisattvas. In the East they have the problem of seeing the Buddhas and bodhisattvas as basically outside themselves, like gods and goddesses who will grant favors if you have faith and pray to them. The problem in the West is we go to the other extreme and see them as purely mental concepts. Chenrezig represents compassion. Manjushri represents wisdom. And they're all basically just fabrications of our mind, just ways for us to relate to the idea of compassion and wisdom. So we could see them a completely different way, and they would still not have any reality outside of our mind. On the one hand, of course, that is true. But then, nothing has reality outside our mind. We think that this table is solid and real, but it is also on many levels just a fabrication of our minds. The actual nature of the table is not at all as it exists to our senses and our mental interpretation. But we think the table is real, whereas Chenrezig is not really real.

We should ask ourselves whether the truth could be the other way around. Perhaps Chenrezig is the reality and all this is just our mental fabrication, because Chenrezig is the Sambhogakaya and the nature of the Dharmakaya. Of course he can appear in infinite forms, just as the Virgin Mary appears in various forms, and everybody who has faith in her tends to see her in similar ways. Likewise, for those who are meditating on compassion, Chenrezig tends to appear in a certain way. This is not a simple matter, because Chenrezig is not really a person. I'm not suggesting that there is somebody in some Sambhogakaya pure land who is called Chenrezig. But on the other hand, while Chenrezig isn't a person, are people really people? We think of ourselves as nice, individual, self-sufficient people, but we should know that this is only a delusion. And it seems to me that Chenrezig has far more reality than that because he is a genuine expression of the Dharmakaya.

We must learn to hold both of these truths in our minds simultaneously. Chenrezig is an expression of the compassionate nature of the mind, and at the same time there is this force or expression outside ourselves because outside and inside are non-dual. It's only in our deluded state of mind that we see some problem here. The apparent split is entirely due to our ignorance. So, because Chenrezig is simultaneously outside and inside, he is much more an expression of reality than our normal ideas about people, chairs, tables, and an individual ego.

It is very important when we visualize ourselves as the deity not to think, "This is me sitting pretending to be Chenrezig. I am the reality and Chenrezig is just make-believe." The reality is that we are Chenrezig, pretending to be this person here. We all possess Buddha-nature. We are all inherently pure and perfect. Our problem is that we have lost contact with what we really are. Our true nature is Chenrezig. It's not my Chenrezig, her Chenrezig, his Chenrezig, lots of Chenrezigs, but just Chenrezig as Dharmakaya. It's what both separates us and what brings us all together. The nature of the mind, the

Buddha-nature, is not my Buddha-nature or her Buddha-nature. It's just Buddha-nature. It's like the sky. It's infinite and all-encompassing. It's what we all are in our true nature. We are not separate.

Therefore, when we do these meditations, the most important thing is to have the conviction that "I am Chenrezig." This is even more important than having clear, precise visualizations. We must develop the inner conviction that "Now I am who I truly am," instead of this temporary personification we walk around with. If we do visualizations with this understanding and conviction, we will very quickly transform ourselves. If we treat this as just some kind of mind game, we can go on doing these visualizations forever and we may develop our powers of concentration, but there will be no transformation. Similarly, when we visualize Chenrezig outside of ourselves, it is good mental practice to try to see as much detail as we can. But more important is the conviction that he really is there, present at that moment. Because if we have the conviction that we are doing all of these things in the presence of Chenrezig himself, who at this point we cannot see because of our obscurations, everything takes on meaning, and all the methods for gaining positive qualities will work. But if we treat this as some kind of mental game, it won't work.

Whatever practice we do, it is important to be totally sincere. It doesn't matter if we don't visualize very well. It doesn't even matter too much if we get distracted and have to keep bringing our mind back. The important thing is to be absolutely sincere about what we are doing, otherwise the practice will not work. We must have a firm belief in the method. In order to believe in the method, we also have to believe in ourselves. It doesn't matter that we're not Tibetans. It doesn't matter that we don't speak Tibetan. It doesn't matter that we're doing it in English or in any other language. The important thing is to know that we essentially have all the qualities needed for this practice, which is bringing us back to our true nature. We don't have to do complicated practices and esoteric yogas or any of that. The simplest practice done from the heart with true understanding will work.

Visualization is a very profound tool, even on a physical level. For example, there is a practice known as *phowa*. It is used for transferring the consciousness at the time of death into a pure land of the Buddhas, so that the consciousness doesn't go down into the lower realms. Now, in order to do this, we see ourselves as a certain deity with a channel going up through the center of our body. At the heart lies a pearl-like seed. We say a certain syllable and visualize the seed jumping through this tube and out the top of the head, into the guru who is sitting above our head in the form of a Buddha. So there we are, making funny noises and visualizing this seed going up and down the central channel. On the one hand, it is an exercise in futility. Here we are imagining ourselves as some deity with a tube going up through our head and this little pearl going up, down, up, down. This is not an advanced yogic practice. Even my mother did it. Very ordinary people who have never meditated in their lives do this practice. But by the end of one day of several sessions of twenty-one rounds each, the top of the head begins to feel painful or itchy or hot or cold, and within three days, the top of the head opens and blood and lymph emerge. It's open to the extent that you can put a thick stalk of *kusha* grass into the head itself. And you will see all these ordinary practitioners wandering around with little grass stalks sticking out of the tops of their heads! Now these are not advanced yogis, as I said. These are ordinary people like you and me. Yet the tops of their heads have opened purely through the power of their visualization. What does that tell us about the power of visualization? The mind is the most powerful force imaginable. We do not always appreciate how powerful our minds are. A mind which is skillfully directed can accomplish just about anything. It can even accomplish Buddhahood. Be aware that these practices are skillfully designed to take us to profound levels of consciousness. We should not underestimate the practices, nor should we underestimate our own powers of accomplishment. Anyone who does these practices regularly and with sincerity can achieve results.

They need to be done regularly. They need to be done with our entire attention. We need to become completely absorbed in what we are doing. If we practice this way, we will have results beyond even the amount of effort we put in. This is because not only are these practices skillfully designed, but they also come with the blessings of the lineage. This means that from the time they were first created by an enlightened mind, they have been passed down to us through generations, from one enlightened mind to another. The transmission is still there. It's still warm, as they say. It's not that the masters died out and we've found the book and we're trying to revive the practices they did. They have never died out. The practices have been passed from master to disciple, master to disciple all the way down to you. We know that these practices worked in the past because if they didn't work, they wouldn't bother to pass them on. We should have respect for the fact that these practices have been passed down in a precious lineage all this time. They carry with them the thoughts, blessings, and power of those who have practiced them over the centuries. They are not empty. They are very precious, and as we practice, we should be conscious of the great privilege we have been given.

We also need to understand what we are doing. In the Tibetan tradition it's known as "recollecting the purities," which means that these figures, such as Chenrezig, are not arbitrary. This means that every single part of the visualization is steeped in meaning. For example, Chenrezig is sitting on a lotus. This symbolizes that although he is within samsara, he is not polluted by it. He sits in samsara in the same way as the lotus sits in mud. A lotus needs to have mud in order to grow roots. It needs the mud and the rotting greenery of the pond to grow beyond them and develop into its immaculate self. A bodhisattva likewise requires samsara, the mud of everyday existence. The muddier and dirtier it is, the more glorious the blossom. Similarly, if our lives are always peaceful, pure, and uncontaminated, our blossom will be weak. We need the problems, conflicts and difficulties of samsara so that we can purify ourselves and cultivate the virtues. We need our difficulties and conflicts. We need the people who trouble us and offend us because they are our practice objects. This is how we learn, this is how we find out who we really are.

While we're in retreat and everything is going well and we're feeling peaceful, it's easy to be full of love, generosity, good thoughts, and compassion. If the only thing disturbing us is the howling of a few wolves outside somewhere, there's no problem. But when we come out into the "real" world (which is not really any more real, but just a different world) we have to deal with opposition, difficulties, and problems of all kinds. That's when we find out where we're really at. The way we respond to these pressures and resolve them will indicate whether we really have Dharma in our hearts, or if our Dharma is just up in our heads. That's why when we are doing a Chenrezig practice, for example, it is not much use merely to practice while we are sitting on our cushions and then forget Chenrezig for the rest of the day. If we really want to transform our lives, it is essential for us to carry the practice into our everyday lives.

There are two ways of doing this. We can see ourselves as Chenrezig, two arms or a thousand arms, realizing this is our genuine nature, and at the same time see all other beings as Chenrezig. Some people like to see all females as

Tara and all males as Chenrezig. If we really did this, imagine how our perceptions would change! Imagine how our attitude would be transformed! It doesn't mean that you have to fall down and put your head to the feet of everyone you meet, because after all you are also Chenrezig. It's Chenrezig meeting Chenrezig. Seeing ourselves and all others as the deity brings the mind immediately to the present and gives a profound meaning to everything we do. Everything we eat is an offering to the deity; everything we speak is the sound of the mantra; every thought is the play of the Dharmakaya wisdom. We initiate this towards the end of the practice session. After we have absorbed everything back into primordial emptiness, we appear again as the deity. All sound is mantra. All thought is the play of primordial wisdom. We carry into our daily life this understanding that our "normal" perception is due to delusion. It is not reality. It is impure perception. The whole point of the tantric path is to purify our perception and see things as they really are.

The second way of practicing suggested in the texts is to bring Chenrezig into the heart. If we bring Chenrezig or the Lama, or even better, the Lama as Chenrezig into our heart, we have to make our heart ready to receive him. After all, if we invited a high Lama or the Buddha into our home, we would prepare our house by cleaning it thoroughly and decorating it with beautiful cloths and flowers. We wouldn't want anything unpleasant or disturbing to intrude on the atmosphere. In the same way, when we invite the Buddhas to reside in our hearts, we have to be careful to keep our minds pure and worthy of making a home for them. Therefore, during the day we must be conscious of what we are thinking. We must be able to identify unhelpful thoughts and emotions as they arise, and let them go. We don't suppress them. We see them, we recognize them, we accept them. But we don't hold onto them. We let them go. When skillful, helpful, and positive thoughts arise, we recognize those too. We accept them and encourage them.

This is another skillful way of learning how to live in the present and purify our perception. Not only do we have Chenrezig in our heart, but everyone else does, too. Under our habitual way of seeing, our perception is clouded over. But although we cannot see the sky today because it's hidden by mist, the sky is there. Whether we can see through to it or not, the sky is always there. However black the clouds may be, the sky is always blue. However white the clouds, the sky is always blue. Similarly, however dark and negative we may be feeling, the nature of the mind is always immaculate and unstained. However exalted our thoughts may be, the nature of the mind is always the same. It doesn't get better when we think good thoughts. It doesn't get worse when we think bad thoughts. Visualizing the Lama or Chenrezig in the heart during our everyday life is our great protection.

When I was about eighteen years old, I was in England and I had just "discovered" Tibetan Buddhism. I'd heard about the mantra, OM MA NI PAD ME HUM. I assumed that we were supposed to say OM MA NI PAD ME HUM all the time. I was working in a library, and I started saying, OM MA NI PAD ME HUM continuously. Of course I couldn't say it aloud because there were people around. But I started saying it in my heart. Within a very short time, my mind split and there was this quiet, calm, spacious mind with the OM MA NI PAD ME HUM reverberating within it, then there was this peripheral mind with all its thoughts and emotions. The two minds were detached from each other. Therefore I was able to carry on my everyday life more efficiently than before, because I was in the present all the time, yet with this detachment, this space in the mind. Whatever happened on the periphery was indeed peripheral. This gave great poise to my mind and the ability to exercise far more choice over my thoughts and feelings because I was no longer immersed in them. It was a great breakthrough for me.

In a similar way, the practice of seeing the Buddha in the heart creates an opportunity for us to develop inner space. Having this inner space enables us to view our thoughts and emotions at a distance, which means we do not immediately identify with them as they arise. Normally we identify so strongly with our thoughts and emotions. Because we identify with them, we make them opaque, solid, heavy, and real. The Vajrayana offers many skillful means to avoid this. One is to learn to identify ourselves with the mind of Chenrezig instead of the mind of a deluded sentient being. And through practicing and seeing either the mantra or the deity or both in the heart, we create space and a sense of detachment that helps us to recognize who we are and what our true nature is. This makes our everyday life much more pleasant because we have a quiet, calm center in which to take refuge. Although the practice itself is quite simple and anyone can do it, it can have an amazingly transformative effect on us if we do it conscientiously. The method itself is not difficult. The only problem is that we are lazy and just don't do it. I myself have had so many opportunities, so how come I'm not a Buddha yet? It's because of my laziness. There's no other excuse.

Somebody once asked a very lovely Lama named Jamgon Kongtrul for advice on their practice. He said, "Do it." These practices are not really complicated. We can all do them. It's up to us. Nobody can force us. Nobody can stop us. If we do them wholeheartedly as often as we can, we will have amazing benefits. If we do them half-heartedly, stumbling along, not really knowing what we're doing, not really believing it's going to work, it's very unlikely to have any effect. And then we will blame the method or ourselves. We should be grateful that the Buddha's compassion has brought us these methods. There are some which we can use anywhere and nobody will even know we are meditating.

If we don't use our daily life as a practice, nothing is ever going to change. It's not enough to just go to Dharma centers, or even to just do a daily practice. It's not even a matter of how much intellectual knowledge we absorb or how cleverly we understand concepts and ideas. The question is whether something inside is really changing. Is our mind being illuminated by these practices? Is our heart really opening? Are we kinder people? Are we more considerate? Are we feeling real compassion from the heart? If the answer to these questions is "No," we are merely indulging in intellectual play.

When I was in Nepal in 1994, I received a letter from an Australian who had been a monk for about fifteen or twenty years. It was about eleven pages long. He had read something that I had written about how many Westerners have been practicing the Dharma for many years, but effectually nothing had changed in their lives. I had mentioned that when you meet them years later, the same old problems are still there, and asked why this was so. He agreed with this observation of mine. He wrote that he had been in retreat doing Chenrezig practice when he realized that he was just doing it by rote. The practice was not transforming his mind at all. The visualizations were remaining up in his head. So he went to His Holiness the Dalai Lama and asked if he would be allowed to work for Mother Teresa for a while. His Holiness replied, "Yes, that's fine. You don't need to wear robes. Just go and work there."

The letter was mostly about his time in Calcutta, working for Mother Teresa and dealing with compassion. It was a beautiful letter and I wish now that I had kept it. As he said, compassion is about washing and caring for somebody who is filthy and covered with excrement and sores, who could not care less about being washed and cared for by you. Some of the patients are very aggressive. They don't want to be cared for. They're certainly not grateful. They despise your compassion. So what is your compassion under those circumstances? Where is it? He said that according to Mother Teresa's method, when the nuns take care of the sick and the dying, they see them as Jesus. In other words, they are not just generating pity, "Oh you poor person. Here am I, the great bodhisattva, about to care for you." They do it with profound respect and love and with pure perception. They are grateful for the privilege of being able to serve Jesus. They care for their charges with great joy and a sense of privilege, not condescending pity. That quality of mind is what sustains them. In addition, of course, they spend more than half their day in prayer and contemplation. They're not always running around the streets of Calcutta. I think this is an important point for all of us Buddhists to think about. It is absolutely essential to do a formal practice and to have the understanding and experience gained from our formal practice. But that is not enough. That understanding has to be translated into our daily actions and our interactions with others. If it isn't, there's something very wrong. It's very easy to sit on a cushion, think about compassion, and convince ourselves we are nice, caring people.

Let us now visualize Arya Chenrezig at the center of our heart, about the size of a thumb. He is either two-armed or four-armed, seated on a lotus on top of a moon-disk. He is the essence of all the Buddhas' wisdom and compassion. He is our true nature, the essence of our mind. At his heart is a moon-disk and around the circumference of the moon-disk is the mantra OM MA NI PAD ME HUM. In the center of the moon-disk is the white syllable HRIH. Light radiates from the syllable HRIH, filling our bodies and purifying all our ignorance and our negative emotions. Then it streams out and pervades the whole universe. It goes everywhere. Not just to humans and animals, but also to all the spirit realms, the heaven realms, the hell realms. It spreads out to all the realms throughout the entire cosmos. And as it touches all beings, they are also transformed into Chenrezig.

Now bring the light back into Chenrezig at the center of your chest. From now on, whatever you think or feel is the display of Chenrezig's wisdom.

Glossary of Technical Terms

Skt. after a word signifies that the word is Sanskrit; Tib. that it is Tibetan.

Akshobhya (Skt.) *mi bskyod pa* (Tib.) Buddha of the eastern direction, representing the perfected state of the faculty of consciousness and the mirror-like wisdom. *See also* **Five Enlightened Families.**

Amitabha (Skt.) *'od dpag med* (Tib.) Buddha of the western direction, representing the perfected state of perception and the wisdom of discrimination. *See also* **Five Enlightened Families.**

anatman (Skt.) Non-self. A fundamental belief of Buddhism that there is no abiding core of selfhood or an unchanging eternal soul.

arhat (Skt.) *dgra bcom pa* (Tib.) Literally "foe destroyer." One who has eliminated karmic tendencies and afflictive emotions. Arhatship is the goal of the Hinayana vehicle of Buddhism.

arhati (Skt.) Female arhat. *See* **arhat.**

arya (Skt.) *'phags pa* (Tib.) One who has attained direct realization of the true nature of reality. Also used to mean "sublime," "superior," or "noble."

ashram (Skt.) Indian place of religious retreat or hermitage.

ashuras (Skt.) *lha ma yin* (Tib.) Desire Realm gods who are consumed by jealousy, particularly regarding the gods who exist in a higher realm.

atman (Skt.) A permanent self which reincarnates. Buddhists do not accept the concept of a permanent, unchanging self. In some schools it is maintained that it is the mindstream which is subject to rebirth, and that this mindstream is subject to change and development.

Avalokiteshvara (Skt.) *see* **Chenrezig**

Bodhi tree The pipal tree under which Shakyamuni Buddha attained enlightenment.

bodhichitta (Skt.) *byang chub kyi sems* (Tib.) On the relative level, this is the aspiration to attain enlightenment in order to liberate all sentient beings. On the absolute level, bodhichitta is direct insight into the empty nature of phenomena.

bodhisattva (Skt.) *byang chub sems dpa'* (Tib.) One who has embarked on the path to full enlightenment, having taken the vow to liberate all sentient beings from the endless cycle of birth and death (samsara).

Brahmin (Skt.) *bram ze* (Tib.) Member of the priestly caste, one of the four main castes of Hindu society.

Buddha (Skt.) *sangs rgyas* (Tib.) One who has attained complete enlightenment. References to "the Buddha" usually mean Shakyamuni Buddha, who attained enlightenment under the Bodhi tree approximately 2,500 years ago

Buddhadharma (Skt.) *sangs rgyas kyi chos* (Tib.) The teachings of Buddha Shakyamuni.

calm abiding *see* **shamatha**

chakra (Skt.) *'khor lo* (Tib.) This literally means a wheel, or circle. It is used to refer to special energy centers in the body which are utilized during various tantric practices.

Chakrasamvara (Skt.) *'khor lo sdom pa* (Tib.) Meditational deity popular in Tibetan Buddhism. Known also as Heruka.

chang (Tib.) Kind of Tibetan beer.

Chenrezig (Tib.) Avalokiteshvara (Skt.) Meditational deity who embodies the compassion of all the Buddhas.

chi (also ki, Chinese origin) *srog 'dzin* (Tib.) *see* **prana**

chitta (Skt.) *sems* (Tib.) Mind, thought process, cognition, etc. This term is used more broadly than the Western concept of mind. At the mundane level, it embraces feelings and intuition.

completion stage *sampannakrama* (Skt.) *rdzogs rim* (Tib.) In Vajrayana practices, this follows the generation stage, in which the visualization of the deity has been completed. The completion stage involves manipulating psychic energies (*prana*) and fluids within the body to draw the energies into the central channel.

dakini (Skt.) *mkha' 'gro ma* (Tib.) A yogini who has achieved a high level of realization. Dakinis may be human beings with these special qualities or they may be manifestations of an enlightened mind. They are female entities who have vowed to aid practitioners by removing obstacles and creating auspicious circumstances.

Desire Realm *kamadhatu* (Skt.) *'dod khams* (Tib.) According to Buddhist cosmology, there are three realms, or spheres, within cyclic existence: the Desire Realm, the Form Realm, and the Formless Realm. The latter two are deva realms of increasing subtlety. The Desire Realm consists of six subdivisions: hells, hungry spirits (*preta*), humans, demi-gods (*ashura*), and gods (*deva*).

deva (Skt.) *lha* (Tib.) Gods, or celestial beings, of which there are twenty-six levels of increasing subtlety, ranging from the lower gods, who live in great luxury for vast periods of time, to formless beings of infinite consciousness. All these levels are within samsara and must come to an end eventually.

Dharma (Skt.) *chos* (Tib.) Used in this work to mean the teachings of the Lord Buddha, or Buddhadharma, the universal truth. Sometimes it is used to mean phenomena in general, in which case it is written as *dharmas*.

Dharmadhatu (Skt.) *chos dbyings* (Tib.) The emptiness of phenomena. All phenomena, although they exist on the relative level, are devoid of inherent existence. They exist only in dependence on causes and conditions.

Dharmakaya (Skt.) *chos sku* (Tib.) Ultimate nature of the fully enlightened mind.

Drukpa Kagyu '*Brug pa bKa' brgyud* (Tib.) Branch of the Kagyu lineage, which is one of the four principal lineages of Tibetan Buddhism. Founded by Drogon Tsangpa Gyaré in the twelfth century.

duhkha (Skt.) *sdug bsgnal* (Tib.) Suffering. The Truth of Suffering was the first of the Four Noble Truths taught by the Lord Buddha. Some writers translate *duhkha* as the "unsatisfactory nature of existence." It embraces all the experiences of dissatisfaction and dis-ease. *See also* **Four Noble Truths**.

dutsi *bdud rtsi* (Tib.) *amrit* (Skt.) Nectar. Sometimes this term refers to special pills prepared by great masters to provide benefits to those who use them.

Dzogchen *rdzogs chen* (Tib.) The Great Perfection. This is a state in which both the generation and completion stages are present effortlessly. It is a meditational system particular to the Nyingmapa school. *See also* **generation stage, completion stage**.

emptiness *see* **shunyata**

Five Enlightened Families The mandala of the Five Enlightened, or Buddha, families are the perfected states of our five elements, aggregates, sense organs, and sense perceptions. Each family is headed by a male Buddha, who represents one of the five purified aggregates, and a female consort representing one of the five purified elements. The five aggregates are: form, feeling, perception, mental formations, and consciousness. The Five Buddhas are: white Vairocana (Buddha family), yellow Ratnasambhava (Jewel family), red Amitabha (Lotus family), green Amoghasiddhi (Action family), and blue Akshobya (Vajra family).

Four Noble Truths *catvari aryasatyani* (Skt.) '*phags pa'i bden pa bzhi* (Tib.) The teachings on the Four Noble Truths belong to the First Turning of the Wheel of Dharma. They are basic to Buddhism. They are: the Truth of Suffering, the Truth of the Cause of Suffering, the Truth of the Cessation of Suffering, and the Truth of the Path to the Cessation of Suffering. *See also* **duhkha**.

Geluk (Tib.) One of the four main traditions of Tibetan Buddhism. The others are Nyingma, Sakya, and Kagyu.

generation stage *utpattikrama* (Skt.) *bskyed rim* (Tib.) In Vajrayana practice, this is the stage which involves meditating on forms, sounds, and appearances as the body, voice, and mind of the deity. This stage is a preparation for the completion stage. *See also* **completion stage**.

guru (Skt.) *see* **lama**

Guru Rinpoche The master from Oddiyana who formally introduced Buddhism to Tibet during the eighth century of the common era. Also known as Padmasambhava.

Heruka (Skt.) *khrag 'thung dpa' bo* (Tib.) Literally, "blood drinker." Term to describe a wrathful meditational deity.

Hinayana (Skt.) The "lesser vehicle," which emphasizes individual liberation from samsara. Used in contrast to Mahayana.

hungry ghosts *preta* (Skt.) *yi dwags* (Tib.) Spirits tormented by intense hunger and thirst.

interdependent origination *rten 'brel* (Tib.) This principle asserts that everything which exists does so because of the aggregation of causes and conditions—nothing exists independently, in and of its own right. This doctrine is one of the fundamental tenets of Buddhism and is closely related to the law of karma. The teachings describe twelve links of interdependent origination that keep beings bound within cyclic existence, or samsara.

Kagyu (Tib.) One of the four principal schools of Tibetan Buddhism.

Kalachakra (Skt.) *dus kyi 'khor lo* (Tib.) Meditational deity associated with the mythical kingdom of Shambhala.

kalyanamitra (Skt.) Spiritual friend. A teacher or other person who helps us to make progress on the path.

karma (Skt.) *las* (Tib.) The law of cause and effect, which teaches that every intentional action of body, voice, or mind has a corresponding result.

Karmapa The name given to the succession of great reincarnate Lamas who head the Karma Kagyupa sub-sect of Tibetan Buddhism.

Khampa (Tib.) A native of Kham, one of the three provinces of Old Tibet (Tibet prior to occupation by China). Kham is located in the southeastern portion of Tibet.

khata (Tib.) Scarf offered to lamas and high teachers. It is usually white, but may be cream or gold-colored. *Khatas* are also used as greeting scarves amongst Tibetans.

lama *bla ma* (Tib.) *guru* (Skt.) Spiritual teacher. The master who shows one the nature of one's mind. Any teacher who imparts instruction on the Dharma.

lung *rlung* (Tib.) *vayu* (Skt.) The breath and subtle energies of the body. In this context, *lung* problems refer to an imbalance in the subtle airs of meditators often resulting from over-intense exertion during meditation retreats. In traditional Tibetan medicine, *lung* refers to one of the three humors which must be in balance for good health. In the context of Vajrayana practices, the "winds" are the subtle energies of karma which carry consciousnesses, that, when refined, may be absorbed into the central channel of the psychic body.

Madhyamaka (Skt.) *dbu ma* (Tib.) This is the Buddhist philosophy of the "middle way" between nihilism (which propounds total non-existence of self and phenomena) and eternalism (which propounds the independent existence of self and phenomena). It is one of the four major philosophical schools of Indian Buddhism.

Mahakala (Skt.) *nag po chen* (Tib.) Dharma protector. The wrathful form of Avalokiteshvara, or Chenrezig, the Bodhisattva of Compassion.

mahamudra (Skt.) *phyag rgya chen po* (Tib.) Literally, "the great seal." This is the state of Buddhahood wherein the three *kayas* are accomplished. A system of meditation particular to the Kagyupa lineage. *See also* **three kayas**.

Mahaparinirvana (Skt.) Passing away of the physical body of a Buddha.

mahasiddhas (Skt.) *grub thob chen po* (Tib.) Those who have attained great accomplishments. This term is often reserved for the Eighty-four Mahasiddhas, who were great Buddhist tantric adepts during the medieval period of Buddhism in India.

Mahayana (Skt.) *theg pa chen po* (Tib.) This literally means "great vehicle." One of the two principal vehicles of Buddhism, the other being the Hinayana, or "lesser vehicle." The Mahayana is based on the great motivation to attain complete Buddhahood in order to liberate all sentient beings from samsara.

mandala (Skt.) *dkyil 'khor* (Tib.) Literally means "circle," "wheel," or "circumference." In Tibetan Buddhism, it often refers to a diagrammatic representation of the celestial mansion wherein the deity and its retinue reside. It is also used metaphorically to convey the idea of a center with its surroundings. Mandala offering practices are formal Buddhist practices to accumulate merit.

Manjushri (Skt.) *'jam dpal dbyangs* (Tib.) Meditational deity. The Bodhisattva of Wisdom.

mantra (Skt.) *sngags* (Tib.) Mind protection. A collection of specially significant syllables which, when uttered in sequence, represent the enlightened speech of the deity.

Mind *sems* (Tib.) *chitta* (Skt.) Mind This is defined as awareness of objects or events rather than "mental factors," which contain the content of thoughts, etc.

momos (Tib.) Tibetan meat dumplings.

mudra (Skt.) *phyag rgya* (Tib.) In this context, refers to the ritual hand gestures that accompany chanting.

nadi (Skt.) *rtsa* (Tib.) The channels in the body through which the subtle life-sustaining energies (*rlung*) flow. These channels also produce habitual mental conceptions which may be transformed through certain tantric practices.

nirvana (Skt.) *myang 'das* (Tib.) Liberation from the sufferings of cyclic existence. The total extinction of all suffering and afflictive emotions.

Nyingma (Tib.) The earliest of the four principal traditions of Tibetan Buddhism.

Padmasambhava (Skt.) *see* **Guru Rinpoche**

pandita (Skt.) Learned person. Traditionally, one who has mastered the five Indian sciences: art, medicine, grammar, logic, and epistemology.

paramita (Skt.) *phar phyin* (Tib.) Perfections. The sutric path is largely founded on the practice of six or ten paramitas. Attainment of Buddhahood depends upon mastery of all these qualities. The six paramitas are: giving, ethics, patience, effort, meditation, and wisdom.

phowa (Tib.) Tantric practice of transferring consciousness at death in order to attain a favorable rebirth.

pointing out instructions Special (unwritten) instructions which the Guru imparts to the ripened student to point out the nature of mind.

Prajnaparamita (Skt.) *shes rab kyi phar phyin* (Tib.) The perfection of wisdom. This is one of the six perfections. There are various philosophical definitions of this term. Prajnaparamita is also the title of a series of Mahayana sutras. Prajnaparamita is personified as a female meditational deity.

prana (Skt.) *srog 'dzin* (Tib.) *Prana* is the life-bearing energy within the body which is of great significance in certain tantric practices. This "energy force" is also important in certain Indian yogic and Chinese Taoist practices.

Prasangika Madhyamaka (Skt.) *thal 'gyur ba* (Tib.) One of the two sub-schools of the Madhyamaka that arose from a dispute between Bhavaviveka and Chandrakirti over the interpretation of aspects of Nagarjuna's philosophical reasoning. Prasangika denies any inherent existence of either external phenomena or subjective consciousness.

preta (Skt.) *yi dwags* (Tib.) *see* **hungry ghosts**

puja (Skt.) This word literally means "offering." It is used more broadly both by adherents of Hinduism and Tibetan Buddhism to describe certain types of religious rituals.

Quan Yin Chinese male or female deity who is the Bodhisattva of Compassion. Also known as Avalokiteshvara or Chenrezig.

Ratnasambhava (Skt.) *rin chen 'byung gnas* (Tib.) Buddha of the southern direction representing the perfected state of our faculty of feeling and the wisdom of equality. *See also* **Five Enlightened Families**.

Rinpoche (Tib.) Literally means "precious,"or "like a jewel." Also used as a title and form of address for incarnate lamas and some other teachers of great reputation.

rishi (Skt.) Hindu adept who has reached extremely high levels of meditative absorption.

sadhana (Skt.) *sgrub thabs* (Tib.) Literally, "means of accomplishment." In the context of Tibetan Buddhism, these are ritual meditations which are usually performed individually rather than communally. Their purpose is to help the initiated practitioner speed up progress on the path to enlightenment.

sadhu (Skt.) Indian holy man or renunciate.

Sakya (Tib.) One of the four principal traditions of Tibetan Buddhism.

Sakya Trizin His Holiness Sakya Trizin is the leader of the Sakya tradition of Tibetan Buddhism.

samadhi (Skt.) *ting nge 'dzin* (Tib.) Attainment of single-pointed meditative absorption.

Sambhogakaya (Skt.) *longs sku* (Tib.) Literally, "enjoyment body." This is the light body of a Buddha which appears only to beings who have attained a high level of realization. *See also* **three kayas**.

samsara (Skt.) *'khor ba* (Tib.) The state of cyclic existence wherein the circumstances of beings are determined by their past actions and habitual mental patterns.

Sangha (Skt.) *dge 'dun* (Tib.) Traditionally, this term is used for the community of monks and nuns. Nowadays, especially in Western Dharma centers, the term is used loosely to comprise the members thereof. In the context of the Three Refuges, it refers specifically to the Arya Sangha, those who have directly realized emptiness.

seed syllable *bija* (Skt.) *yig 'bru* (Tib.) During tantric practices, each deity emerges from emptiness in the form of its own particular seed syllable.

shamatha (Skt.) *zhi gnas* (Tib.) Technique of "calm abiding" meditation in which the meditator places the mind on a single object, whether internal or external.

Shariputra (Skt.) One of Shakyamuni's ten foremost disciples. He was noted for his intellectual brilliance.

shunyata (Skt.) *stong pa nyid* (Tib.) Emptiness, that is, the ultimate nature of reality. The lack of inherent existence of a subjective self and objective phenomena.

Six Perfections *see* **paramitas**

sutra (Skt.) *mdo* (Tib.) The original discourses of Buddha Shakyamuni which he taught publicly for forty-five years.

Sutrayana (Skt.) One of the two divisions of the Mahayana school. This is the system based on the "causal method" following the sutras, which stresses gradual purification and practice. *See also* **Vajrayana.**

tantra (Skt.) *rgyud* (Tib.) The continuum from ignorance to enlightenment. This term is also used to describe certain currents existing in both Hinduism and Buddhism which developed for the purpose of speeding progress along the path to enlightenment. Tantrayana is part of the Mahayana, whose philosophy it shares. It varies from the Sutrayana (non-tantric Mahayana) in its use of special skillful means. The term is also used to refer to the body of texts known as the tantras. *See also* **Vajrayana.**

tantrika (Skt.) One who practices tantra. *See also* **tantra.**

thangka (Tib.) Tibetan religious scroll painting.

Theravada (Pali) *gnas brtan pa sde* (Tib.) The "tradition of the elders." used in reference to the Buddhist traditions of South and Southeast Asia.

Thirty-five Buddhas of Confession. *ltung bshags kyi lha so lnga* (Tib.) In the Mahayana tradition, there is a special practice whereby the practitioner pays homage to each of the Thirty-five Buddhas in turn, in order to purify negative deeds.

three kayas Classical literature describes three (and sometimes as many as five) aspects of the Buddha-body. The emanation body, or *nirmanakaya*, is visible to beings. Shakyamuni Buddha is an example of a *nirmanakaya*. The enjoyment body, or *sambhogakaya*, is the pure light form of the Buddha-body. The *sambhogakaya* form is visible only to beings who have an extremely high level of realization. These two are known as form bodies, or *rupakaya*. The third is known as the *dharmakaya*, which is the ultimate nature of the fully enlightened mind.

togden *rtogs ldan* (Tib.) Advanced yogic practitioner of the Kagyu lineage who lived in caves in Tibet before the Chinese occupation. The lineage continues in India.

togdenma *rtogs ldan ma* (Tib.) Female *togden*. There were many *togdenma* dwelling in caves in Tibet prior to the Chinese invasion.

tonglen *gtong len* (Tib.) Giving and taking. Meditation which involves giving all of one's health, wealth, and positive karma to all sentient beings and in return taking on the pain, suffering, and misfortunes of all sentient beings. This practice trains one's mind to develop bodhichitta.

tsampa (Tib.) Roasted barely flour, a staple of the Tibetan diet.

tsog *tshogs* (Tib.) A religious feast offering practiced by Tibetan Buddhists.

tulku *sprul sku* (Tib.) *nirmanakaya* (Skt.) Emanation body of a Buddha. This term is also used to describe an incarnate lama.

tummo *gtum mo* (Tib.) *chandali* (Skt.) This literally means "the fierce one." It is commonly employed to describe the practice of generating inner heat, which burns away all impediments to cognizing bliss and emptiness.

vajra (Skt.) *rdo rje* (Tib.) Diamond. Indestructible. Often used to describe the attributes of a Buddha. Also a ritual scepter.

Vajra Hell Excruciatingly painful hell realm said to be reserved for tantric practitioners who have transgressed their vows.

vajra song This is a special kind of song sometimes performed during tantric *tsog* offerings.

Vajrasattva (Skt.) *rdo rje sems dpa'* (Tib.) The meditation on Vajrasattva and the recitation of the Hundred Syllable Mantra is used as a purification practice, especially to purify past negative karma and breakages of tantric commitments.

Vajrayana (Skt.) *rdo rje theg pa* (Tib.) Literally, "the diamond vehicle." Also known as Tantrayana or Mantrayana, a branch of the Mahayana which utilizes special skillful means to speed the trainee's passage to enlightenment. Vajrayana is known as the "resultant method," since it utilizes visualization, mantra, and other techniques which enable the practitioner to take the actual Buddha state (the result) as the path itself. *See also* **Sutrayana.**

Vajrayogini (Skt.) *rdo rje rnal 'byor ma* (Tib.) Female meditational deity. Consort of Chakrasamvara and the queen of the dakinis.

view *lta wa* (Tib.) *drishti* (Skt.) Cultivating the correct philosophical view is regarded as a necessary first step for anyone embarking on the Buddhist path.

vihara (Skt.) Literally means "secluded place." It was used to describe retreat centers extant in India during the time of Shakyamuni Buddha, where he held rainy season retreats. Also a Buddhist monastery in Theravada countries.

Vinaya (Skt.) *'dul ba* (Tib.) The books of discipline containing the ethical precepts set out by the Buddha to guide the conduct of monastics and laypeople.

vipashyana (Skt.) *vipassana* (Pali) *lhag mthong* (Tib.) Special insight meditation. This is an analytical meditation which penetrates the nature of its selected object.

Yama (Skt.) *gshin rje* (Tib.) Lord of Death.

Yogachara (Skt.) "Consciousness only" philosophical school of ancient India, which follows the tradition of Maitreya and Asanga.

yogi *yogin* (Skt.) *rnal 'byor pa* (Tib.) One who practices intense meditation techniques (i.e., yoga), which may include either physical or mental disciplines.

yogini (Skt.) Female yogi.

The Dongyu Gatsal Ling
Nunnery Project

Dongyu Gatsal Ling Nunnery was founded in 1999 at the request of His Eminence Khamtrul Rinpoche, head lama of the Khampagar Monastery, in order to provide an environment where young women from Tibet and the Himalayan border regions could come together to study and practice in accordance with the Drukpa Kargyu tradition of Tibetan Buddhism.

Here these young women are given the opportunity to develop their intellectual and spiritual potential through a balanced training of study, meditation and service. At present their program includes philosophical study, ritual, Tibetan language and writing, English language and handicrafts. The nuns also gather for daily ceremonies and meditation.

The special aim of the Dongyu Gatsal Ling Nunnery is to re-establish a precious lineage of yogic practice particularly emphasized in the Drukpa Kargyu lineage. Although there are still a few monk exemplars of this yogic tradition presently residing at the Khampagar Monastery, it seems that the female line was annihilated during the Cultural Revolution. As it is an oral tradition, handed down from master to disciple, it is essential that this rare and precious practice is passed on while there are still living masters. The yogins of Khampagar Monastery have agreed to train the nuns who show the necessary qualities and potential, once they have completed their studies and preliminary meditation practices.

If you would like to help support the Dongyu Gatsal Ling Nunnery, please contact them through the e-mail address given on their website—www. tenzinpalmo.com, or write to Dongyu Gatsal Ling Nunnery, Tashi Jong, P.O. Taragarh, Distt. Kangra, H.P. 176081 India